P9-CRR-346

"There is much in Steed's powerful book to break hearts...an intelligent and compelling read — the kind of thing one would expect of Steed, a four-time National Newspaper Award-winning journalist.... It reaches, with startling insight, right into the heads of abusers, and the hearts and souls of victims."
The Ottawa Citizen

"A journey into the complex, incredibly disturbing world of child sexual abuse. For teachers, parents, law enforcement officials, social workers, and anyone concerned about the welfare of children, this is a must read."
The Whig-Standard

"*Our Little Secret* is, by virtue of the magnitude and range of the issues it addresses...most important."
The Globe and Mail

"It's necessary and important to have a book like Judy Steed's *Our Little Secret*...this is the right primer at the right time."
Now

"Carefully researched.... The crime, the perpetrator, and, especially, the victim are all presented here in frightening and distressing detail. All parents, teachers, doctors, and therapists should read it."
Quill & Quire

"An important contribution.... Steed has told us the children's stories and she has done it well. We enter their world, we hear their voices and see how the abuse damaged them. We also see how many of them found hope."
Kitchener-Waterloo Record

"It will certainly become a classic of its kind...the stories are simply too important, too powerful, too true to be ignored.... Read this very important book."
The Evening Telegram

"A surprising accessible, hard-to-put-down book about child sexual abuse in Canada...Must read for parents."
The Winnipeg Sun

"Steed's haunting book is a must read...paints a disturbing picture of how pedophiles prey on children...gripping...compelling."
Winnipeg Free Press

"A horrifying telling of the lives of children who survive sexual abuse.... For survivors, the path to healing is enraging and emotionally draining. Steed painstakingly clears a way, treading lightly on the fragile emotions of the children."
The Financial Post

OUR
LITTLE
SECRET

Confronting Child Sexual Abuse in Canada

Judy Steed

Vintage Canada
A Division of Random House of Canada

First Vintage Edition, 1995
Copyright © 1994, 1995 by Judy Steed

All rights reserved under International and Pan-American Copyright Conventions. Published in Canada by Vintage Canada, a division of Random House of Canada Limited, Toronto. Originally published in Canada in hardcover by Random House of Canada Limited, Toronto.

Canadian Cataloguing in Publication Data

Steed, Judy
Our little secret: confronting child sexual abuse in Canada

Includes index.
ISBN 0-394-22443-4

1. Child sexual abuse - Canada   I. Title

HV6626.54.C3S74 1995   364.1'5554'0971   C95-930223-9

Cover design by Kevin Connolly
Cover photo © Jeffrey Cadgel, The Image Bank of Canada
Printed and bound in Canada

1 3 5 7 9 10 8 6 4 2

For the children

Contents

Foreword

Child sexual abuse is our problem; it is not little and it should not be a secret.

Although we say our children are our future, sexual abuse of children is a good example of the human race's proclivity for living in the present. For personal, societal and political reasons, it has always been more expedient for us to deny this problem, letting our children conceal their shame and suffer in silence while we adults indulge our ignorance and get on with our lives.

The price the children pay is everyone's expense. Society has sacrificed these healthy, joyful young people filled with hope and has increased their risk of becoming damaged, despairing adults filled with anger or emptiness. We have lost our full complement of competent parents and caring adults, and have produced some people with crippled psyches, some of whom become dangerous offenders.

This book demonstrates quite clearly how children are lured into the web of the offender, how parents are neutralized as their children's protectors and become enablers of the abuse, and how society cares more about its pecking order than about any of them. For those who are new to the problem of child sexual abuse, this book will serve as a shocking eye-opener. For those experienced with the problem, it will provide patterns, examples and personal stories that will impart new understanding and add yet further layers of knowledge derived from a variety of perspectives.

This book is a testament to the resilience of children. We are not surprised that so many of them do have problems after the abuse they have endured; we are inspired by their courage in enduring and surviving their abuse, in preserving themselves and their vitality as well as they do.

The parents and professionals who deal with this problem on a daily basis, who follow the children into their emotional turmoil and assist them to deal with it and overcome it, without distorting the reality of the event for them, are all crucial guides along their road to discovery. They are uncovering the secret.

The legal system must constantly be challenged to recognize the special needs of children who have been sexually abused, not to violate the rights of the accused or the family, but to stop the continued violation of children. Much still needs to be learned about children's response to trauma, their ability to recollect and to recount that trauma. The courts and their officers must learn more about this if they are to help reveal the secret.

At a time when many have come to believe that the sexual abuse of children is a big hoax that must be dismissed, this book reminds us that it is a major, deep-seated societal ill that must be addressed. It requires the contribution of all good and caring persons, regardless of the capacity in which they deal with children, to recognize this evil, to identify its victims and to help them move beyond their secret into the light of truth.

MARCELLINA MIAN, M.D., FRCPC
Pediatrician and Director
Suspected Child Abuse and Neglect (SCAN) Program
The Hospital for Sick Children, Toronto

Introduction

Most of us react to allegations of child sexual abuse with disbelief. The thought of an adult sexually violating a child is so abhorrent that we cannot bear to believe it happens. Yet our horror of the act leads us to abandon children and protect perpetrators.

Child sexual abuse is such an explosive topic that I have selected cases typifying situations prevalent across North America, in which the accused have pleaded guilty or been convicted, where the facts are not in dispute. The offenders in these cases are people who live and work among us, our friends, family and colleagues. I have taken great care to focus on only the most respected professionals, who at every step of the investigative, diagnostic and therapeutic process insist on a careful, neutral approach. No one benefits when false charges are laid. Children must be heard, but they must not be told what to say. They must feel free to confide whatever they want, without expectation or blame.

This book is not a collection of horror stories, though much of the material is horrific; yes, it was difficult to write, but the emphasis is on the progress being made in stopping the sexual exploitation of children.

The vast majority of abused children are preyed upon by parents, relatives or trusted friends within "affinity systems," writes Ann Burgess in *Child Pornography and Sex Rings*. This is a crime, she adds, that generally goes unreported, undetected and undisclosed. Of those that are reported, less than one-third of alleged offenders are charged. "Of these, the number that actually get convicted may represent another third," says David Finkelhor, co-director of the Family Violence Lab at the University of New Hampshire. "Of those that get convicted, only a minority actually end up incarcerated or in a treatment program. If you are an upstanding citizen who has a good job, friends and money, it is very likely that your denial will be believed. Even if you do get convicted, the chances you will be sent to jail are very low." As we shall see, however, this dismal prognosis is changing.

In 1896, Sigmund Freud delivered a paper titled "The Aetiology of Hysteria," in which he described how he'd traced "hysterical symptoms" and other neuroses back to childhood trauma involving sexual violation. Though he knew he was likely to meet with "contradiction and disbelief," he put forward the thesis that "at the bottom of every case of hysteria there are one or more occurrences of premature sexual experience." He later, notoriously, changed his mind. In *The Assault on Truth: Freud's Suppression of the Seduction Theory*, psychoanalyst Jeffrey Moussaieff Masson characterized Freud's repudiation of his own insight as "a personal failure of courage" caused by his fear of ostracism from Viennese society and professional peers whose Victorian-era prudery prohibited open discussion of sexual matters. Henceforward, psychoanalysts were trained to treat memories of child sexual abuse as pure fantasy.

Almost a hundred years later, we know a great deal more about the sexual exploitation of children, but still we cling to turn-of-the-century denial. A 1992 random survey designed by the Institute for Social Research at York University found that 43 per cent of female respondents reported a sexual-abuse experience in childhood; 17 per cent were incest survivors. A decade earlier, American sociologist Diana Russell found that one in three women had been sexually abused in childhood; 16 per cent were victims of incest. The Canadian government's 1984 Badgley Report, based on a four-year task force that documented 10,000 cases of child sexual abuse, concluded that one in four girls and one in seven boys experience unwanted sexual acts. These figures, now a decade old, are regarded as conservative estimates; the shift in reporting trends is toward males. Many more boys are coming forward and experts are beginning to think boys may be as vulnerable to sexual exploitation as girls. Certainly that is what I found.

Professor Nico Trocmé of the University of Toronto School of Social Work estimates that *every year* in Canada, 42,000 children under the age of fifteen are sexually abused by an adult. This figure may be the tip of the iceberg. John Gallienne was convicted of sexually abusing thirteen boys, but the police estimate that he probably molested 200 to 300 victims — a range that is common for a pedophile of his type.

Adult prevalence surveys show that most victims, as children, tried to tell someone, were not believed, and consequently did not go to the police. Even so, Statistics Canada revealed in 1992 that 40 per cent of all reported sexual assaults were committed against children aged eleven and under. Dr. Roland Summit, a pre-eminent American psychiatrist and authority in the field, states that the sexual violation of children is so prevalent as to be "a normative experience." It has been a devastating scourge in Canada's aboriginal community. During a period of almost one hundred years, three or four generations of native children were forcibly removed from their homes and placed in residential schools where many of them were terrorized by Catholic priests and teachers. "The exposure of native children to sexual abuse at the hands of their so-called caregivers is a phenomenon unparalleled in Canadian history," says Vancouver author Suzanne Fournier, who is writing a book on the issue.

What is child sexual abuse? I take my definition from Rix Rogers' 1990 *Report of the Special Advisor to the Minister of National Health and Welfare on Child Sexual Abuse in Canada.* It is "the misuse of power by someone who is in authority over a child for the purposes of exploiting a child for sexual gratification. It includes incest, sexual molestation, sexual assault and the exploitation of the child for pornography or prostitution." In Canada, the age of consent is fourteen; children under fourteen cannot give informed consent to sex. Many victims are seduced into sexual involvement with adults, not knowing what sex is; they cannot be held responsible for the long-term damage done to them.

Police forces are overwhelmed by three kinds of cases: adult survivors reporting childhood abuse; current incest violations; and children abused in pedophilic sex rings, which may include sports teams and choirs. The use of pornography tends to be a factor in all three categories. Strictly speaking, pedophiles select only prepubescent children, but you will meet perpetrators in this book who do not fit any known definition. There are no stereotypes, says Dr. Bill Marshall, former co-director of the Kingston Sexual Behaviour Clinic. Offenders can be male or female and belong to all socio-economic spheres. Some present themselves as macho womanizers, the kind of men who, in the words of an acquaintance of one such fellow, "would have sex with a fire hydrant." Others play the role of saintly priests or selfless teachers. They can be extroverted, charismatic types or quiet, passive individuals who "wouldn't hurt a fly." Some build their lives around access to children and abuse large numbers in highly organized schemes; others work as executives, firefighters, police officers, physicians, secretaries or salespeople, sexually abusing children "on the side," as it were. Some focus on their own children, while others roam more widely, exploiting kids in the neighbourhood or in the extended family.

What they all have in common is a sexual addiction that masks a power dysfunction. They feel inadequate with their peers; the only way they can feel powerful is by sexually dominating children. Most have strict "age preferences" but some will chose victims of either sex, ranging from infants to teenagers. Most perpetrators are heterosexual males, but many more female offenders are being identified than earlier research showed. And despite the pioneering work done in this field in the past ten years, there is no known "cure" for child abusers.

The destruction of childhoods and wreckage of adult lives, in the wake of child sexual abuse, is monumental. In the ever-expanding networks of Alcoholics Anonymous, Al-Anon, Overeaters Anonymous, Narcotics Anonymous and various twelve-step, self-help programs, child sexual abuse has emerged as a major underlying cause of adult despair, dysfunction, addiction and criminal behaviour. Males are conditioned to act out their pain and hurt others, females to internalize and hurt themselves. The risk of rape, sexual harassment or battering "is doubled for survivors of childhood sexual abuse," Dr. Judith Herman states in *Trauma and Recovery*.

Abusive men, battered women: they are pieces of the same puzzle, variations on a theme — but victims respond so differently, depending on other aspects of their lives, that broad generalizations predicting behaviour cannot be made. If the only form of intimacy you know involves abuse, you may find yourself drawn to danger, fantasizing about rape, seeking out sado-masochistic sex games. The impact of child sexual abuse on adult sexual practices is profound and little understood. An addiction to pornography or masturbation can be a symptom of child sexual abuse; many men and women have discovered that what they regarded as bizarre sexual fantasies were memories in disguise.

But survivors cannot be stereotyped. Some become powerful adults driven by childhood pain to confront injustice wherever they find it; others become bullies, prostitutes or seemingly ordinary people haunted by psychic "black holes," plagued by bouts of depression and nameless fear. Sharon Carstairs, the former leader of the Manitoba Liberal Party, was sexually abused as a child by a trusted family friend. At the age of fifty-one, she is still afflicted by flashbacks. The long-term effects, she wrote in her autobiography *Not One of the Boys*, are multifarious, and isolated her from people: "Since I had this great secret deep within me I couldn't get close to anyone — otherwise I might blurt it out, and I knew this was something I must not do."

In most cases, recovery is possible — if the secret can be told and the survivor supported. The therapeutic process is about opening to the truth, understanding the imprint of childhood trauma and going through the pain. At the heart of the abuse is silence: in case after case, we learn about children being violated while in the next room a mother cooks spaghetti, a father reads the paper, a dinner party goes on. From survivors, we learn that they tried to tell, by acting out their anguish. From non-offending adults, we hear confessions of guilt, wisdom derived from hindsight: *Yes, I see it now, looking back, my child was in pain but I didn't listen....* The good news is that victims can be identified by their distress signals and perpetrators can be detected by their behaviour patterns, if we know what to look for.

But don't expect abusers to acknowledge their crime. "In the vast majority of cases, the identified adult [offender] claimed total innocence or admitted only to trivial, well-meaning attempts at 'sex education,' wrestling or affectionate closeness," Dr. Roland Summit wrote. "After a time in treatment, the men almost invariably conceded that the child had told the truth. Of the children who were found to have misrepresented their complaints, most had sought to understate the frequency or duration of sexual experiences. Very few children, no more than two or three per thousand, have ever been found to exaggerate or to invent claims of sexual molestation."

You are about to meet some wonderfully heroic people; the pioneers who have led the way in the past two decades, and the survivors who have dared to speak out and have battled enormous fury released in defence of offenders. But when we grapple with raging debates about false allegations and repressed memories, we discover one undeniable fact on which all sides agree: there is such a crime as child sexual abuse, and that's what this book is about.

Because victims are silenced, I've tried to communicate their perspective as directly as possible; we have so much to learn from them. In order to protect their privacy, I have not been able to describe them in as much detail as I might have liked. To all who shared your personal stories and insights with me, I thank you for your wisdom and inspiration. I have attempted to retain the clarity of your voices and the power of your experiences without blurring your message.

JUDY STEED
Toronto, 1994

1

Kingston:
Corruption in the Cathedral

I never could speak about what Gallienne did; we were all silent for so long, I guess we felt we were implicated, we were somehow to blame, we must have asked for it, we let him do it. Yeah, I thought of killing myself. People don't understand what it does: you're a little kid, you don't know anything about sex and all of a sudden your body is invaded by someone you trusted, and everything changes, for ever. He killed something in us.

— Alastair Crawford, one of thirteen
young men who made statements
to the police about John Gallienne

KINGSTON, ONTARIO, population 60,000, is a 300-year-old university town on the north shore of Lake Ontario at its juncture with the St. Lawrence River. Once a French fort, conquered by the British in 1758, Kingston was briefly the capital of Upper and Lower Canada. Beginning in the 1840s, its pre-eminent politician was John A. Macdonald, a local lawyer who went on to become a father of Confederation and Canada's first prime minister. Nowadays, there's a sense that the city's distinguished past has conferred a superior presence on its intellectual inheritors. From the ivy-covered campus of Queen's University to the grand marching promenades at Royal Military College to the forbidding fortress of Kingston Penitentiary, the Anglo-Canadian establishment rules the roost. This is Canada as it used to be, as it still is in certain quarters — smug, white, a little self-righteous. This is a culture that concealed a deadly secret.

To walk the streets of Kingston, from the historic city hall overlooking a harbour bobbing with sailboats, past the austere grandeur of the dome of St. George's Cathedral, along leafy avenues lined with magnificent mansions and greystone homes, is to experience the charm of another age. Dominating the scene, socially and spiritually — until recently — was St. George's, the oldest Anglican church in Ontario, gutted by fire in 1899, rebuilt with its great dome modelled on St. Paul's Cathedral in London, England. St. George's was notable for its exceptional architecture, exquisite stained-glass windows, distinguished parishioners — and the music program. Oh, the music! "You see, we were all so attached to that place, to the music – it was sublime, it was the centre of our lives," says James Burton,*[1] a professor at Queen's University. "It was one of the great things to do in Kingston, to put your boys in St. George's choir. It was almost like a cult of boy soprano voices. It's hard to explain — I question it now — but it really was like a cult."

Climb the stone steps of the cathedral, pass between tall Roman columns, through enormous doors that open heavily into the echoing hush, the spiritual stillness that restores the soul. This dim, grand cavern was the stage for John Gallienne's command performances. The choirboys, costumed in burgundy cassocks and ruffled collars, gazed up at the choirmaster who towered above them. They were sweet-faced children; he was larger than life, "an awesome figure," says Bob Burton,* James' son. "John Gallienne was like God." Sweating and straining, he conducted his choir of angels through Mozart's Requiem mass; the music soared into the dome, sweeping the congregation into heights of ecstasy. Who could have imagined that this majestic man had transformed the choir into a child sex ring, and operated with impunity for sixteen years?

1. An asterisk appears at the first mention of pseudonyms for survivors and family members who wish to protect their privacy.

John Gallienne was only twenty-nine when he was selected for the plum post of organist and choirmaster at St. George's. He arrived in 1974 and took the cathedral by storm. Tall and well built, bearded and bespectacled, he wasn't a handsome man, but he had a commanding presence and an attractive wife eager to play hostess at an endless round of elegant dinner parties. Gallienne was stimulating, unpredictable, volatile; nor was his a superficial show of artistic temperament. He knew his music, and for this crowd of music lovers, it was like having their very own maestro to entertain them. Phillip Rogers, a longtime chorister at St. George's and a professor of medieval literature at Queen's, wrote about Gallienne's "boundless energy," his "devotion to English church music," his "extensive repertoire [which] included most of the major work of Bach as well as a large amount of the work of the late-19th and 20th-century French composers."

St. George's upwardly mobile congregation, consisting largely of professors and professionals, adored their new choirmaster's upper-crust eccentricities, though he came from humble origins. Born on October 12, 1944, in Guernsey, one of the Channel Islands off the French coast, John Gallienne was the son of a fisherman. Trained at the Guildhall School of Music in London, England, he immigrated to Canada in 1964 and worked as a choirmaster at St. Mark's in Ottawa, Ontario, and St. John the Divine in Victoria, British Columbia, before coming to St. George's, where he replaced George Maybee. A native of Madoc, Ontario, Maybee died in 1973, having run the choir to extravagant praise for more than thirty years; his claim to fame was that in 1954 the cathedral choir had become the first Commonwealth choir to sing services at Westminster Abbey.

For many of his Anglophile parishioners, Gallienne quickly eclipsed Maybee. He worked hard, directing three choirs totalling one hundred and fifty singers at St. George's, and taught student organists at Queen's University and younger pupils at Lord Strathcona Elementary School. What's more, Gallienne established his dominance at the cathedral, playing favourites, picking intimates, eliminating anyone who didn't succumb to his seductive spell. Those who were "chosen" — adults and children alike — entered the labyrinth as courtiers, never suspecting they were being groomed as victims. He kept everyone — adults and children alike — off balance with his

3

mercurial manner, intensifying their sense of inadequacy, flattering their pretensions, buying their loyalty with special treats and privileges. Young boys saw their parents caught up in the clamour of loquacious evenings, while Gallienne poured the drinks, settled the adults down and slipped away on his secret prowl, molesting the sons of his hosts between courses at dinner parties.

His ability to lead a double life in such close quarters was stunning. In hindsight, one wonders how parents could have been so blind to his treachery; at the time, they were entranced by his charm. If someone questioned his behaviour, Gallienne's coterie — comprising the (unknowing) parents of his victims — closed ranks: "That's the way John is," they'd say. John the Genius. John the *Artiste*. The rules governing human conduct didn't apply to Gallienne. If he upset people with his temper tantrums, Lannie, his wife, was always there to smooth ruffled feathers, reminding everyone how much John sacrificed for the choir, for the cathedral, for the boys. Lannie drew the choir mothers around her in a discreetly alcoholic haze. They gathered at the Galliennes' house during Tuesday afternoon choir practice, for sherry and gossip. They called themselves the Women's Convivial Tuesday Union, or WCTU, a play on the Women's Christian Temperance Union; they weren't at all temperate, and they bonded in ever tighter knots around the man who dominated their lives.

In September 1976, two years after Gallienne arrived at St. George's, Henrik Helmers, fourteen, quit the choir. His parents, Queen's business professor Hank Helmers and his wife, Joan, noticed that Henrik seemed uncharacteristically morose; he was the youngest of three children, they were experienced and loving parents, and they tried to find out what was wrong. Henrik finally blurted out the truth: he'd been molested by Gallienne, he said, but he'd promised not to tell, and he insisted that his parents not do anything about it. Faced with Henrik's refusal to speak further, the Helmers felt powerless. They did not realize that an apparently minor molestation can cause major psychic damage. They knew nothing about sexual abuse and had no inkling that children who've been violated can feel suicidal.

On January 20, 1977, the day before Henrik's fifteenth birthday, Professor Helmers rose at 7:00 a.m. and went to Henrik's room to wake the boy for school; he was not in bed, so his father began to search for him. Hank discovered his son in the basement workshop, hanging from an exposed beam with a length of electrical extension cord wrapped around his neck. Henrik's body was already cold.

His parents were devastated, and in March they confronted the church. At a meeting with Reverend David Sinclair and John Gallienne, Professor and Mrs. Helmers said they held Gallienne responsible for the sexual molestation and "therefore he was a major contributor to Henrik's death." Gallienne did not seem particularly distressed by the charge, which he neither confirmed nor denied. "He merely stated that he was very fond of Henrik and never intended to hurt him," Helmers says.

Stunned by the church's apparent indifference, Professor Helmers sought the counsel of Stuart Ryan, Chancellor of the Anglican Archdiocese of Ontario, a member of the congregation of St. George's and a lawyer known for his progressive stance on human rights issues. In Ryan's opinion, there wasn't much of a case against Gallienne since the only witness couldn't testify; Henrik was dead. However, Professor Helmers was assured that St. George's would take steps to monitor Gallienne's behaviour. Helmers made the mistake of trusting the church.

In May 1977, the parents of another choirboy informed Reverend Sinclair that their son said he had been molested by Gallienne, who, when confronted by Sinclair, admitted that he had touched the boy. Sinclair ordered Gallienne not to be alone with boys, and if he was, to leave the door open. During the same period, Ned Franks, a Queen's political science professor and a St. George's warden, heard rumours about Gallienne's predilections. Franks queried church officials and was told that preventive measures were in place and not to worry.

For a man addicted to sex with children, Gallienne was perfectly positioned. Being a choirboy, Alastair Crawford observes, "was like a job." Bob Burton agrees: "We spent more time with him than we did with our parents." Most boys joined the choir at the age of eight or nine and stayed with it until their voices changed at about thirteen. They practised three days a week: after school on Tuesdays from 4:00 to 6:00 p.m., on Friday evenings from 6:00 to 9:00 p.m., and on Saturday mornings from 9:00 to 11:00 a.m. On Sundays they arrived at the cathedral by 8:00 a.m. to sing at 9:15 and 11:00 a.m. services and came back for Evensong from 7:00 until 8:30 p.m. In addition, there were special performances, concerts, weddings, funerals and a vast array of "private lessons" and "organ-tuning" sessions, and ten-dollar payments for secret activities — a lot of money to a boy in the mid-seventies.

"He was like God," Bob Burton says, and God had an office. Turn right in the cathedral, go along a nondescript hall lined with notices of upcoming events and see the choirmaster in his private room, behind his desk. Close the door. The choirmaster is supposed to be giving private singing lessons in the choir room across the hall, but he has brought the boy into his office and there is no singing to be heard. "He'd sit in his chair and he'd say, 'Come and sit on my lap,' and you had to go." Alastair Crawford was a timid ten-year-old. Gallienne's infamous chair — a tatty upholstered easychair — was positioned between two windows, "so people couldn't see what he was doing from outside," Alastair says. "He figured everything out in advance. I was very shy, physically, and I didn't like it that he could make me sit on his lap and undo my pants any time he wanted, but he was John Gallienne and I was just a little kid. You feel helpless. You think this person likes you and then wham! he starts doing these things to you and all of a sudden it's like you don't exist. I could have been asleep or dead for all he cared, when he was doing it. You go numb, you feel like you're nothing, you just give up. I lost my motivation, I couldn't do anything in school, I fell by the wayside, I felt like I had nothing in my life after he finished with me."

For Alastair, the abuse continued for two years, in the choirmaster's office and at summer choir camp. "I learned how to throw up walls like you wouldn't believe, to keep the secret." He couldn't tell his parents and became ever more alienated from family and friends. "Finally one day I wouldn't do it any more but the secret was literally locked inside me. I couldn't talk to anyone because I was afraid it would come out."

It was the perfect crime: the victims, unable to identify the criminal, believed they were guilty. They trusted their abuser; he molested them. "You have to remember how little the boys were," says Peter Franks, once a head chorister at St. George's. "We were very small and he was a very large, physical, demanding person, like a Messiah with his beard and his authority." If the practice wasn't going well, Gallienne would slam books, stomp about and frighten the boys. Afterward he romped with them and tickled them. "I didn't like it,"

Peter says. "It felt like a loss of control and I wouldn't let him do it to me, so he left me alone. But we were trained to follow him like sheep and it wouldn't have taken much for him to abuse his power; it would have been easy, so easy."

It was easy. Apart from the choir activities, there were so many opportunities: special outings with special boys, sailing trips, family dinner parties, and of course the summer choir camp where "a special boy" would be selected to share Gallienne's cabin and the other boys would peek in the window to see "who was getting it next." Depending on how much of a favourite they became, the victims were on call for Gallienne's pleasure. It was part of the job. "This is my way of showing how special you are," he'd whisper in their ears. What could they do? He was the dominant authority in their lives; they were dependent on him; their parents adored him. "He was like a father figure," says Andrew Swainson. As a child, Andrew perceived his relationship with Gallienne "like a marriage." The distortion is a bizarre one — a nine-year-old boy "sexually married" to a pedophile — but it's at the heart of the abuser's hold over children: the illusion of the special bond. "I thought we had a monogamous relationship," says Bob Burton.

Like most child victims, Bob is unable to specify exactly when the molestations began: "I don't remember the first time, it was so gradual. I just remember the pressure to be in the choir, not wanting to be left out — my parents worshipped the music. I joined when I was nine. I took private organ and singing lessons, and it just evolved. I trusted him. When he touched me, I didn't know what he was doing or why. I didn't know what orgasms were. I had no idea what he felt when he ejaculated, or that that was the whole point of it, for him." The molestations occurred during Bob's tenth and eleventh years. He knew nothing about sexuality. All Bob knew was that he had been selected for special attention: when Gallienne played the organ at a recital, he let Bob turn the pages — that was a really big privilege — and then on the way home in the car, Gallienne would molest him, achieving his own orgasm, using the child as an erotic tool. Thus Gallienne taught his victims that they had to "pay" for his approval. But his messages were contradictory: he paid too. "He'd take me to the Dairy Queen, after, and I could get anything I wanted," Bob says. Gallienne proved that he could do anything he wanted to children under his control, that he could prostitute them while holding their loyalty — which is the cruel art of the pimp.

Then there were children who didn't belong to the choir, who were subjected to sudden molestations during innocuous social events. Sam,* the ten-year-old son of a lawyer, was tucked in bed during a family dinner party when Gallienne wandered off after the main course — his disappearing act was a well-known quirk — and climbed two flights of stairs to Sam's attic bedroom. Gallienne sat down on Sam's bed and the little boy lay as still as a mouse while Gallienne groped under his pyjamas. Sam was unable to squeak a syllable of protest, and didn't tell, not until he made a statement to the police in 1990.

Why didn't Sam get out of bed or call for help? "I couldn't, it felt like I was pinned down, the way he sat on the covers, they were pulled tight over my chest." At the age of twenty-one, Sam hasn't forgotten his fear, "up on the third floor in my little room, all the adults far away." The Galliennes were old family friends, he'd known them since he was little, he played with their children, but he'd never liked John Gallienne. "That night, he talked to me as if nothing unusual was happening, trying to persuade me to join the choir while he molested me. It was like I was paralysed. After, I think I tried to tell my parents in subtle ways, but they didn't get it."

Sam's strongest statement came that Christmas: his parents always spent Christmas Eve with the Galliennes, who held an annual party that was *the* place to be on that sacred night. Sam refused to go. His mother says she "respected Sam's decision" and left him at home. It didn't occur to Sam's parents to ask the questions they could have asked: *Is there a reason you don't want to go to Mr. Gallienne's house? Has Mr. Gallienne ever done anything to make you feel uncomfortable?*

In the summer of 1977, Kate Burton,* with two sons in the choir, was delegated "to tell John to lay off, just a little. He was always roughhousing and tickling the boys," Kate says, "and some people thought it might be misinterpreted." Preparing for the delicate task of speaking to him, Kate was thrilled to receive an invitation to the Galliennes' cottage on Muskrat Lake near Cobden. "We were the first choir family to be invited," she says. "It was quite a privilege, to be chosen." The Burtons took their son Bob and they had a lovely time, or so Kate thought. Toward the end of the weekend she got up her courage: "I sat on the beach and felt terribly awkward because I was afraid of hurting his feelings, but I told him, I said, 'John, please don't take this the wrong way, I know it's just your fatherly affection for the boys and I don't intend in any way to insult you because we are so grateful for the time you spend with our boys, but perhaps you could not get so close to them, *physically*.' He assured me he understood and he said not to worry." Kate coughs and a stray nerve under her eye darts like lightning across her cheek. "We found out later that Gallienne sexually abused Bob that very weekend. You have no idea how many times I've thought about that scene, me on the beach with John, not wanting to hurt his feelings, and him taking Bob out sailing and molesting him." Another weekend, the Burtons went out of town and the Galliennes offered to let the Burtons' other son, Billy, stay with them. "Billy was abused that weekend, in the Galliennes' home."

And so it went: every boy a potential victim. By the late seventies, Gallienne's child sex ring was operating in high gear. With access to a steady stream of new recruits, he constantly initiated eight- and nine-year-olds via masturbation, "grooming" them, going as far with each one as he could, escalating his activities to oral sex, anal penetration and group sex. He seems to have taken a particular delight in pursuing the children of his "best friends" — the adults most under his control. Did he experience sadistic pleasure in their distress as their sons grew into disturbed adolescents? Eleanor Swainson was just one of the choir mothers who teetered on the brink of a nervous breakdown over her son's increasingly hostile behaviour; when she turned to Gallienne for emotional support, he promised to deal with Andrew, whom he'd been sexually abusing for at least five years, and whom he continued to abuse as he pretended to help the Swainsons sort out their problems.

Donald and Eleanor Swainson were among the most assiduously courted, the most profoundly betrayed. Donald, a large, balding professor, has a Ph.D. in Canadian history and has been teaching at Queen's University since 1963. Eleanor, trained as a social worker, is the daughter of a former premier of Manitoba. In 1970 they adopted two brothers, Eirik, born in 1967, and Andrew, a year younger; the boys were beautiful fair-haired cherubs and it wasn't long before they came to Gallienne's attention.

"We weren't members of St. George's," Donald says, "but Andrew

9

was quite musical. He played the violin and he wanted to carry a candle in the choir." The Swainsons followed Andrew to the cathedral and fell under Gallienne's spell. He had spotted them as a vulnerable family: perfect prey. Donald and Eleanor were demanding parents; the boys felt pressured to perform, and lost their bearings amid the alcohol-fuelled soirées with the Gallienne crowd who invaded the Swainson home. It was at one of those gatherings that Gallienne first molested Andrew, a nine-year-old tucked upstairs in bed. Hands on the boy's genitals, big Mr. Gallienne whispered in little Andrew's ear how special he was; the child was trapped. There was no way out.

Even so, Andrew didn't give up without a fight. He tried to withdraw from the choir and refused to go to choir practice, but his father dragged him there, kicking and screaming. "I thought he was just being rebellious," Donald Swainson says. " 'You undertook it, you've got to see it through, you don't just quit, that's not the way you do things' — that's what we said. Our confidence in Gallienne was so high, we could never have conceived of… Now we know that Andrew was trying to show his distress, and we didn't read it. If a child says, 'I don't want to go there,' you should ask questions, you should take it seriously, you should listen to your child. I wish I had."

In 1978, Tim Franks, fourteen, suddenly quit the choir and fell ill with oral herpes and mononucleosis. His father, Ned Franks, remembered the 1977 incident "and the thought actually went through my mind that Gallienne might have abused Tim." Weeping unabashedly as he tells his story, Ned says he didn't want to intrude on his youngest child's privacy and didn't ask questions. Ned and Daphne Franks had three children; Tim was the baby of the family, a sweet-natured boy with great natural ability and appeal. His sudden illness distressed his parents, but like the Helmers, the Franks didn't know what to do. Tim wouldn't talk and Ned believed the church had instituted procedures to keep Gallienne in check. And there was another factor: Ned had himself been sexually abused as a boy, and couldn't bear to think about anything like that ever again. However, he raised his suspicions indirectly that September with the Vestry Council, a group of about twenty people who are supposed to represent the concerns of the congregation to the church hierarchy. Franks asked for an investigation into the "low morale" of the choir. Dr. Christopher Padfield, head of the child protection team at Hôtel-Dieu hospital, leaped to Gallienne's defence and said morale was excellent, and indeed a report in October 1978 indicated no problems. But in Ned Franks, Gallienne had crossed the man who would ultimately bring him down, though it would take another eleven years, and Tim Franks' suicide, to expose the choirmaster's secret life.

In the meantime, Gallienne played his hand with aplomb, eliminating all challengers. The most persistent was James Burton, whose fate demonstrates the choirmaster's ruthlessness. In 1978, in the lead-up to the choir's much-anticipated 1979 trip to England to sing at Windsor Castle, among other ancient venues, Professor Burton became aware "there was a manipulation going on [with the choir] that I didn't understand, that made me profoundly uneasy." Burton had respected Gallienne for his musicianship, but gradually realized something was very wrong: "I couldn't pinpoint it, other than that there was no accountability, no control over Gallienne."

In the previous year, Burton had noticed that his son Bob received a lot of attention from Gallienne; on choir trips, Bob sat with Gallienne in his car, while the rest of the boys were in the bus. Bob thought his parents knew what was going on. "Mr. Gallienne's set-ups to get us alone together seemed so obvious to me, that I couldn't believe my parents and his [Gallienne's] wife didn't know," Bob wrote later in his victim-impact statement. "I believed that my parents accepted his actions, even to the point of helping get us together, and I hated them for it. I didn't trust them throughout my youth and I ignored them as role models. I grew very suspicious of any advice they, or anyone of authority, gave to me.... I became depressive and antisocial (both are still problems I have to deal with) affecting my schoolwork and my ambition. I have entertained thoughts of suicide many times, just to escape a life which at times seems totally worthless."

At the time, the Burtons knew Bob was becoming withdrawn but they didn't suspect sexual abuse. "We wouldn't have believed that a young choirmaster with a family and a brilliant future ahead of him would have jeopardized his career," James says. "There were stories about the previous choirmaster [Maybee] and Gallienne's appointment was supposed to get us away from all that." Alastair Crawford, whose years in the choir overlapped Maybee's reign and Gallienne's ascension, remembers that "Maybee made advances to boys, he came on to a friend of mine [in the choir], but he was interested in older boys, around the ages of fourteen or fifteen, not the little ones." Maybee's sexual proclivities were no secret to many St. George's parishioners, who understood, as James Burton did, that Gallienne's appointment was supposed to be "a fresh start."

Being a rational man, Burton did the rational thing: he tried to establish a choir association that would have input into the way Gallienne ran the show. There were whiffs of tales about nine- and ten-year-old boys being given liquor on choir trips (the stories were true) but that wasn't why Burton insisted changes be made. It was gut instinct; he'd caught the scent of the predator, without knowing quite what it was.

Gallienne recognized the danger presented by Burton's proposal for democratic reforms and wasted no time getting rid of his enemy. He flew into a high operatic rant that would have been laughable if he weren't so deadly. Supported by his cathedral coterie, Gallienne drove Burton out of the church. Mocked and maligned, sidelined from his own family by Gallienne, Burton grappled to confront the formless threat he felt but couldn't name; he almost had a nervous breakdown — testimony, it turned out, to his good instincts. In 1990, he found out that Gallienne had sexually abused Bob in 1976 and 1977.

In the late seventies, the Burtons' marriage practically disintegrated. Kate remained attached to the cathedral and loyal to Gallienne. "It was a mesmerizing place, and superb musical training for the boys," she says. Finally, James delivered an ultimatum: Kate had to choose between the church and their marriage. She chose wisely. How does she feel about Gallienne now? "He nearly destroyed me," she says. She takes a deep breath, at a loss for words. Her husband speaks sardonically: "Gallienne gave the congregation what it wanted: world-class recognition."

A portrait of the choir taken at King's College, Cambridge, on the 1979 trip to England, only two years after the suicide of Henrik Helmers and a year after the abuse that would torment Tim Franks until his death, shows dozens of boys in burgundy cassocks arrayed in rows, their faces emerging like worried flowers from ruffled collars — the faces of little hostages, trapped in the grip of Gallienne's addiction. There is Andrew Swainson, bottom left, tiny and fair-haired, only ten, already victimized and beginning to act out his anguish. There is Alastair Crawford, inducted into the routine of "private singing lessons," silenced by the price he paid to sing in the choir. There are Bob and Billy, two brothers, abused — and on it goes, at least half the boys abused, according to other victims who pick out the ones they know about.

Standing upright at the left, back row, is the guardian of the flock, Dr. Christopher Padfield, pediatrician, chief organizer of the England trip and a close friend of Gallienne's. Trained to identify the characteristics of sexually abused children, he would later say he had noticed nothing.

In the middle, seated, is the choirmaster, hands folded on his lap, smiling sweetly. "The worst single story, the one that hit me in the gut during the court proceedings," says a choir mother, "was the boy who was molested during the 1979 England trip. He was a little tyke, only nine, and he'd propped a shoe against the door to keep the door open, because he was sleeping in a strange place and he was afraid of the dark. John Gallienne came into his room and shut the door and the little fellow was trapped in the dark. That story broke my heart."

By the mid-eighties Gallienne was getting careless. His voracious appetite for sexual gratification with prepubescent boys seemed unquenchable, and as with any addict who's managed to feed his addiction without getting caught, his "success" made him feel invincible. But he had close calls: when Andrew Swainson was nine or ten years old, the senior minister, Dean Grahame Baker, walked into the choirmaster's office unannounced to find Gallienne and Andrew with their pants undone; Baker backed out and later said he'd noticed nothing. One day during Alastair's private singing lesson, Bob's mother walked in on them, and Alastair had to pull up his pants very quickly. At choir camp, the boys saw Gallienne lie down at night, after lights-out, with various campers. At church, a choir mother twice saw Gallienne coming out of his office with a boy and thought, *Something's the matter with that boy; he's very pale.* Then she did a double-take: Gallienne looked like someone who'd just had sex, but she figured she had "a dirty mind" and dismissed it.

If the secret of Gallienne's success was the extraordinary control he exerted over the parents of his victims, his wife, Lannie, was his ideal helpmate. As he tightened the clamps on the clique, she devoted herself entirely to his needs, organizing a whirlwind of festivities that revolved around John. "Lannie is like your perfect person, the hostess with the mostest," says Holly Mitchell, Lannie's younger sister.

The sisters grew up in Montreal, where their father, Gifford Mitchell, was the charismatic music director at St. James United Church. In the summer of 1969, Lannie was managing a choir camp in Quebec, where Gallienne was teaching. Lannie got pregnant, and married Gallienne on March 21, 1970, at St. Mark's Anglican church in Ottawa, where he was the choirmaster. He was twenty-five, his bride twenty-two. Holly, at thirteen, was the maid-of-honour; that Christmas, when the Galliennes' first child was baptized, Holly was named godmother.

In 1975, a year after the Galliennes settled in Kingston, Holly enrolled in political science at Queen's University; she was thrilled to be living in the same city as Lannie, but horrified to discover that her brother-in-law was emotionally abusive to his wife. "John treated Lannie like a dog. He dominated her; she was like his slave," Holly says. But she remained loyal to her sister and by 1983 she and her husband, Jon Barna, were regulars in the Gallienne crowd. The partying was constant. "Holly and I had our biggest fights about the control the Galliennes exerted over us," Jon says. "It seemed as if our lives revolved around accommodating John. I had a bad feeling about it. I actually had the thought, one day, that Holly was married to them, not me. She'd get hysterical at how badly John treated Lannie, but Holly enjoyed the social life, and it *was* exciting: beautiful music, great parties, a lot of fine food and drink, interesting talk " — all orchestrated by Gallienne, the maestro, with Lannie working as the selfless backstage caretaker. Her friends called her a saint. "She was so warm, so kind, always thinking about everyone else," Holly says.

How could Lannie be so cheery in such difficult circumstances? Was she out of touch with reality? A psychologically battered wife? Happy to have a husband who wasn't interested in her sexually? (Gallienne would later be diagnosed as a homosexual pedophile who had an aversion to sexual contact with women. Indeed, he told a friend that he could not stand the smell of women.)

Then came 1985, the beginning of the end. At summer choir camp that year, Gallienne molested ten-year-old Clark Rowan.* It was a routine encounter for the choirmaster, but the outcome was not: in a rare act for a victim of sexual abuse, Clark told a camp counsellor, a young woman who did not belong to the cathedral crowd. She, in turn, did what no one else involved with Gallienne had had the courage to do. She called the Ontario Provincial Police, who came to the camp and questioned Gallienne. At once, the great actor switched personae, from Zeus-like flamboyance to meek, remorseful martyrdom. *It was just an accident, a one-time thing, a slip of the hand, he was over-tired, over-worked, the boy over-reacted, it would never happen again.* The police questioned other campers; not one boy would admit to having been molested, though many were victims. Clark, isolated by his peers, having broken the code of silence, was propelled into an emotional chaos that few adults, let alone a ten-year-old boy, could have handled.

Marv and Laura Rowan* were summoned to pick up their son. On their arrival at camp, they were shocked to find Clark hysterical — about Gallienne's fate. Terrified that Gallienne would be sent to jail and that he, Clark, would be held responsible, the boy faced the cataclysmic prospect that typically confronts abused children: by telling the truth, they tear their world apart.

But Clark had nothing to fear on Gallienne's behalf. Once again, the system protected the choirmaster. "The performance of remorse — I have never seen such an act in my life," Marv Rowan says. Gallienne mollified them all: the Children's Aid Society, the police, the church. (Ironically, that summer the Anglican Church published a pamphlet on child sexual abuse, stating that pedophiles lie, cover their tracks and always have more than one victim.)

Gallienne agreed to get treatment; he told Marv Rowan he'd been in touch with Dr. Padfield and would be referred for therapy. He eventually saw Dr. Rebecca Young, a junior psychiatrist who subsequently concluded, with the support of her supervisor, Dr. David Surridge, that "Gallienne was very much at the benign end of the spectrum of this disorder [homosexual pedophilia]." Gallienne was listed on the Child Abuse Register maintained by the Ministry of Community and Social Services, a relatively useless procedure since almost no one is allowed access to it apart from the Children's Aid Society — not even school boards, which have a legitimate need to screen employees. At the cathedral, Gallienne portrayed the Rowans as supporters because they didn't insist on charges being laid, "but the police advised us not to," Laura says. "The police said we wouldn't get anywhere with just one incident, just one victim."

Laura Rowan is a sensitive woman; she was not part of Gallienne's group, and she had a close relationship with her son. In the aftermath of the abuse, she saw Clark sink into a deep depression — a classic case of post-traumatic stress disorder, as manifested by Henrik Helmers and Tim Franks. The Rowan parents, too, responded normally: they felt powerless. "I can't describe the pain of what we went through," Laura says, weeping as she tells her story. For three days after the Rowans brought Clark home, he did not utter a word. He was a different boy. "I sensed he'd died," Laura says. "I felt as if I'd lost my son. I thought I was going crazy." Then he asked her, "Is it wrong for someone to kill himself?" He started acting out suicidal obsessions, playing with matches, climbing up onto the roof of the house, behaving in ways that were totally out of character. Laura watched her son like a hawk. One day, looking out the kitchen window, she saw him get off the school bus and walk down the lawn toward the river, which was barely frozen. He ran out onto thin ice and she went after him, dragging him back. The next day he was out there again and fell through; again she rescued him. Then he let slip more information: Gallienne had abused him on another occasion. This was typical of victims, who tend to leak details of abuse in a manner that professionals term "incremental disclosure."

The cathedral elite responded to Gallienne's molestation of Clark Rowan with apparent calm. Dean Grahame Baker assured Marv and Laura it was "just a one-time thing," although Baker had heard similar allegations before. He told them to go home and have a nice cup of tea. Fran Harkness, a choir mother, informed Dean Baker about another alleged victim, Jason Bond,* who'd told Fran's son that he'd been abused by Gallienne. Baker did nothing, and when Harkness, with great trepidation, warned Janet Bond* that her son was at risk, Janet was angry at Fran. Janet, a successful executive, was active in the choir guild and very close to Gallienne.

"I was part of the group that surrounded John and protected him." Janet Bond speaks slowly and carefully. "I refused to believe the rumours; I thought people were jealous of him." Gallienne persuaded her that certain people were out to destroy him, that he was being attacked because he was a genius. All the while, he was sexually abusing Janet's two sons.

Convinced of his omnipotence, Gallienne did not anticipate that his victims would return to haunt him. In 1987, Tim Franks, then in his early twenties, made a secret visit to the Kingston Police and gave a formal statement about having been abused by Gallienne in 1978. This was a momentous step for Tim, but he didn't want his parents to know and insisted his information could be used only if another victim came forward. He was not, apparently, informed that another victim had already done so: Clark Rowan in 1985.

The same year, 1987, Sandra Rowland,* a distraught choir mother, went to the Children's Aid Society (CAS), seeking help with her teenage son. For the past few years, she'd been tormented by changes in Mike.* "At Evensong, I would look at Mike [in the choir] and cry," she says. "All I knew at the time was that Mike was more Gallienne's son than mine." Gallienne undercut parental discipline, calling Mike at all hours of the day or night; Mike would always go, no matter what his mother said. Sandra came to feel that Gallienne enjoyed exerting control over her son and humiliating her, "making me fight for my own son. I couldn't win." Her voice is shaking. "I just gave up and let Mike go." By the time he was fifteen, Mike was depressed and dangerous. He punched holes in walls, threatened his parents, had trouble in school, used liquor and drugs in excessive quantities. The day he grabbed his mother around the neck and rammed her against the wall was the day she called the Children's Aid Society. "I wanted Mike out of the house, he was so uncontrollable," she says. This was a painful admission for a woman raised in a fundamentalist church, a highly educated woman who'd sacrificed her career for the sake of her family.

When she spoke to the CAS worker, Sandra mentioned that Mike had been in the choir and was informed that Gallienne was listed in the Child Abuse Register. Sandra was horrified. As close as she was to the church hierarchy, she had never heard about the 1985 incident. But the CAS worker insisted that "precautions were being taken and Gallienne was getting therapy." Still, Sandra felt she should do something. She went to the cathedral and collapsed in the office of a church official. "John Gallienne is on the Child Abuse Register," Sandra sobbed. The official promised to talk to Dean Baker.

Mike's destructive behaviour escalated. He was caught stealing; he tried to torch the house. Sandra thought he was suicidal, if not homicidal. Finally Mike's father sent the boy to stay with the Galliennes, against Sandra's wishes; Mike's father insisted that Gallienne knew how to handle troubled boys, and insisted on Gallienne being made Mike's godfather.

"I felt like I was going crazy," Sandra says. No wonder: the CAS knew about Gallienne, the church knew, the police knew and nobody would do anything. Sandra gave up. Even so, her "negative attitude" toward Gallienne was noticed and she was "blackballed," she says, by John's inner circle, which was what happened to anyone who began to suspect him. (Her worst fears were later confirmed: Gallienne had abused both her sons, but Mike was the worst damaged, having been sexually violated for more than three years, through grades six, seven and eight.)

Then came a seismic shift in national consciousness. It began quietly on April 18, 1989, when Judge Samuel Hughes, seventy-five, having retired six months earlier from the Supreme Court of Ontario, flew to St. John's, Newfoundland, to initiate a royal commission into allegations of physical and sexual abuse of children at Mount Cashel orphanage. The Hughes Inquiry crashed through our collective denial: public hearings began on September 11, 1989, and ran for 150 days, broadcast across Canada, showing the heartbreaking testimony of grown men as they described being sexually abused as children by Christian Brothers, a Roman Catholic lay order. The trick, for the perpetrators, had been in keeping the victims quiet, maintaining their shame and thus their silence. For the first time in Canadian history, a group of adult victims of child sexual abuse were publicly identified as they told their story on television — real faces, real names, men in sweaters and trousers leaning into the microphone, sobbing.

Listening intently was Judge Hughes, an elderly man peering over his glasses. He felt, he said later, "that all of a sudden, there was almost a national crisis." He was not personally shocked by the evidence: after thirty years on the bench, "You get used to human depravity. But nobody can be unmoved by a destroyed childhood, and that's what happened to these children. I was staggered by the extent of the abuse. People don't want to believe, still cannot believe, what adults will do to children." The crisis, he thought, was caused partly by dawning awareness of the levels of abuse tolerated by an institution that was supposedly dedicated to the spiritual care and nurturing of its flock. "So overwhelming was the prestige and authority of the Catholic Church in Newfoundland, and of the Christian Brothers in particular, that the government didn't dare interfere with their activities, no matter what terrible rumours they heard," he said. The outcome of the hearings was a weighty two-volume report that runs to 1,000 pages: *The Royal Commission of Inquiry into the Response of the Newfoundland Criminal Justice System to Complaints: Report of the Commissioner*. Judge Hughes' personal summation, delivered in the summer of 1993 from the living room of his Toronto home, was that Mount Cashel reinforced a conclusion he had come to over the years: "I believe in the existence of evil. Only humans are guilty, it seems to me, of torturing their young."

Mount Cashel impinged on the consciousness of Bob Burton in an unexpected way. He'd dropped out of university and was leading a transient life, travelling, working at odd jobs, briefly distracted by new places and faces before he came to despise everyone around him. Then he'd pack his bags and move on. He scared himself with some of the things he did. Like many of Gallienne's victims, he was confused about his sexual orientation. (Some later identified themselves as homosexual. "I knew I was gay before Gallienne abused me," says one ex-choirboy, "and that made it worse; I thought he could tell, and that it was my fault, because there was something wrong with me.") Bob hadn't had a girlfriend in a long time, he was obsessed with masturbation and he dropped in to gay bars. He couldn't communicate with anyone and sank into despair without knowing why. He thought about suicide constantly.

Then one day in the fall of 1989 he turned on the TV: "I saw all these people at a big inquiry, talking about sexual abuse. They were treating it like it was really serious and I thought, *They're lucky, because it happens to a lot more people who don't get any attention.* But I wasn't jealous, because I saw this guy breaking down [on TV], and I thought what happened to me must have been insignificant compared to what happened at Mount Cashel."

Tim Franks would not live to know about Mount Cashel. In the summer of 1989, he was on a meteoric rise, finishing a year of scholarship studies at L'Ecole Normale Supérieure, an elite institution in Paris, and heading back to Harvard to complete his Ph.D. in history. He was twenty-five years old, and tormented by thoughts of suicide.

"Tim got in states, usually at exam times," says his brother Peter. "He wouldn't eat, he couldn't sleep, and we just thought it was the way Tim did things. Now I connect it to the abuse, but I didn't then." Tim had told Peter, years earlier, that he'd been sexually abused by Gallienne, but Peter hadn't known what he meant or how to react, so he hadn't said anything — an omission that still, so many years later, haunts him. "Now, when I read about sexual abuse, I want to throw up," he says. "I blame myself; I was his brother and I didn't do anything to support him."

At the end of the summer of 1989, en route from Paris to Cambridge, Massachusetts, and then to his girlfriend's family cottage in Maine, Tim dropped in on his parents at their country home in Caledon East, near Toronto. Daphne Franks sensed that Tim was going through a difficult time, but she didn't want to be an overly protective mother, so she didn't pry. She figured that Tim was a grown-up; he would get sustenance from his fiancée, and that was the way it was supposed to be at this stage of his life.

Telling this part of their story, Ned Franks can't stop crying; Daphne is pale and still, barely able to breathe. They loved their son and they will never get over the loss of him. "We were originally supposed to help Tim get settled at Harvard, but our plans changed at the last minute," Ned says. He and Daphne, accompanied by Peter, went directly to Maine, to Tim's girlfriend's cottage, planning to meet him there. That's where they were when the call came from Harvard, that Tim's body had been found; he'd committed suicide and he'd died the same way Henrik Helmers had, by hanging. "It is the most awful thing, to think that if we had known what was going through his mind," Peter says, "we could have linked things, we could have acknowledged what had happened to him, it would have been so simple, and now it's so tragic, it's the worst embodiment of evil you can imagine, that Gallienne did this to my brother and to so many boys."

Tim Franks' memorial service was held in September at St. George's Cathedral. John Gallienne conducted the choir. The church was packed with four hundred mourners, including Tim's fiancée, Laura,* who was filled with fury at the sight of Gallienne. More than anyone else, she understood the impact of the abuse on Tim; he had told her that he thought about it every day, and couldn't escape it. After the service, Gallienne came through the reception line and shook Laura's hand. She thought to herself, *This is the man who killed Tim*, and decided she had to tell Tim's parents what had happened to their son. She informed Caroline, Tim's sister, who took the message to the Franks' country home.

After Tim's ashes were buried, the critical moment arrived. Gallienne might never have been brought to justice if Caroline hadn't said to her parents: "Tim was molested as a boy." Her words hit Ned Franks with a terrible jolt. His mind flashed back eleven years, to Tim's mononucleosis and his decision to quit the choir, to Ned's own suspicions at the time. "It was John Gallienne," he said. Daphne was immobilized with shock and then blurted out, "I wonder if that's what happened to Henrik Helmers?" It became a tragic game of connect-the-dots: Ned added two other "incidents," one from 1977, another from 1985, and they saw the outlines of the monster taking shape.

The Queen's reunion weekend in early October brought the Reverend Canon David Sinclair to town. He visited the Franks to extend his condolences. He'd been a minister at the cathedral when Henrik Helmers committed suicide in 1977, and he confirmed that he'd confronted Gallienne on two separate occasions that year about allegations of abuse. In a state of shock, the Franks called their family doctor, David Hemmings, who was chairman of St. George's School, a new private school being organized with Gallienne as music director and star attraction. Hemmings, a close friend of Gallienne's, minimized the Franks' concerns and refused to take action. The Franks were stunned. "It was as if the victims didn't matter," Daphne says. "That's what haunted me: the children were invisible. Everybody wanted to protect Gallienne."

The Franks' immediate goal was to remove Gallienne from the cathedral, by any means necessary. In October, they tried again to get help. Ned went to see his lawyer, Bob Little, whom he'd known for decades and whose moral support provided the first beacon of hope. Little helped them write a letter to the cathedral that pointed out the legal ramifications of St. George's employing a man known to have sexually abused four boys over a twelve-year period. This time, the church responded, partly because the letter had serious financial implications in relation to its insurance policy, and partly because the letter got into the hands of another doctor, Richard MacLachlan, a warden who did not belong to the Gallienne crowd and who, unlike Hemmings, took the Franks' charges seriously. On November 3, 1989, Dr. MacLachlan and another warden met with Gallienne to discuss the allegations; the choirmaster assured them he'd done nothing to harm the boys mentioned in the Franks' letter. But four days later, MacLachlan met with the Children's Aid Society, which called the Kingston Police.

Detective Rick Carter and Staff Sergeant Paul Lorenz of the Criminal Investigation Division (CID), Kingston Police, were assigned to the Gallienne case. Both in their mid-forties, Carter and Lorenz had walked the beat together for more than twenty years, and in the past seven they had learned more than they ever wanted to know about the sexual exploitation of children. "We're better at it now than we were in the beginning," Carter says. "Now we know how pedophiles operate, how clever they are, how they set traps for their victims. They believe in what they do, they have no guilt or remorse — at least I've never met one that did." Pedophiles are very careful, they don't push, they're in no rush; they break down children's defences gradually, violate personal boundaries imperceptibly. "It's conditioning, pure and simple," Lorenz says. "The big thing you learn, as a police officer, the number-one thing you try to communicate to victims, is that it's not their fault."

The major lesson they have learned prosecuting pedophiles is "power in numbers." Generally speaking, it is difficult to convict on the allegations of a single child victim testifying against an upstanding member of the community. Offenders are usually vehement in their denials — until the numbers of victims start to add up. That's when aggrieved accused — like Gallienne — who've loudly proclaimed their innocence suddenly switch gears and plead guilty: they don't want the details coming out. But no police force in the world has the capacity to track down all the victims of a single pedophile: Carter and Lorenz cite estimates from various studies that for every victim who comes forward there may be 25 to 40 who remain hidden. Multiplying from the conservative end of the spectrum, that would mean Gallienne could have left behind 325 victims. "With Gallienne," Carter says, "we only saw the tip of the iceberg. We'll never know the full story."

When the Gallienne investigation began in the autumn of 1989, St. George's closed ranks. The cathedral was like a medieval fortress surrounded by a moat, with the drawbridge pulled up, the gates locked, the windows shuttered. "The people at St. George's were very tight," Lorenz says, with wry understatement. "You have to realize these were very influential people who didn't take kindly to outsiders messing about in their private affairs."

The investigation was emotionally exhausting. The problem was not that the police couldn't find victims — they were inundated with them — but that none would make an official statement. Carter, who did most of the legwork, interviewed many ex-choirboys three or four times; he explained that under Canadian law, victims of sexual assault cannot be publicly identified; but Gallienne's victims were terrified of being branded as "a fag who was fucked by the choirmaster," in the words of one young man. Homophobia was a major problem. A boy who's grown up in a family that constantly denigrates homosexuals is not going to say to his parents, "Guess what happened to me?"

After four months, Carter, Lorenz and the Children's Aid Society had interviewed about a hundred possible victims and had no evidence, not a shred of a statement on which charges could be laid. "The kids would tell us not to tell their parents," Carter says. "They said they wouldn't go to court, that we couldn't use their information." For the police, this was the worst-case scenario: they'd identified criminal activity on a horrific scale, and they couldn't touch the criminal.

Gallienne's inner circle, meanwhile, rallied round their leader and declared that a witchhunt was being led by crazed parents — the

Franks — who couldn't come to terms with their son's suicide. At parties during that period, there was an outpouring of sympathy for "poor John," who played the martyr role to the hilt, while the Franks were attacked for blaming their son's death on the choirmaster.

In January 1990, Tim's former fiancée arrived for a visit with the Franks. Ned was on the board of the public library and took her out to show her the new library building, where they ran into the Gallienne crowd, including David Hemmings and Donald Swainson, all dressed up for a fancy reception for St. George's School, scheduled to open that fall. Franks was stunned to see their continued adoration of Gallienne, who they knew was under investigation by the police. A week later a posh brochure was mailed out with an invitation to enroll children at St. George's.

The brochure, dated January 20, 1990, arrived at Bob Little's home and his wife expressed interest in sending their son to the new private school. Little recoiled, and realized he had to do something to protect other children. He discussed the Franks' knowledge of Gallienne's pedophilia with his law partner Dave Bonham; they approached Peter Swan, another partner in the firm, who represented the cathedral school. Swan acted decisively. He confronted Dr. Hemmings, met with the board of the cathedral school and explained the legal implications of hiring a man known to have sexually abused children. Swan laid it on the line — so effectively that, after an intense battle with Gallienne's supporters in a series of top-secret negotiations, the scope of the choirmaster's operations was severely curtailed for the first time. Gallienne was furious and his friends were enraged, but within weeks he was forced to withdraw from St. George's school and, in rapid succession, removed from teaching in the public school system. (Having spent almost $100,000, the proposed private school collapsed in the wake of criminal charges against Gallienne.)

The Franks kept up the pressure and Gallienne felt the heat; he left town for long stretches, looking for a new job, making preparations to move away. On January 23, the Kingston Police sent a formal letter to the cathedral stating that the case had been put aside, due to lack of evidence. On March 4, the choirmaster's resignation was published in the church bulletin; he'd negotiated a secret resettlement package from St. George's. On March 7, a photo of a smiling John Gallienne appeared in the Kingston *Whig-Standard,* accompanied by a brief story that quoted Galliene's announcement in the church bulletin: " 'It is with very mixed emotions I have to inform you that I have handed my resignation to the Dean and Wardens of St. George's. We have loved you all dearly, and have been overwhelmed with your generosity. Although we will be leaving Kingston, your kindness to all the members of our family will remain forever with us.' "

It took an insider who was an outsider to break the stalemate. Dr. Richard MacLachlan was a family physician who'd moved to Kingston in 1986 and three years later had been appointed a warden at St. George's, where his son sang in the choir. Now the medical director of a 700-bed hospital in Halifax, he regards the Gallienne affair as "the worst experience of my life, bar none." Once he began to realize how many boys had been abused — "it was many more than the thirteen who made statements to the police" — and what Gallienne had done to them, he was "revulsed, appalled, terrified."

In the first few months of the police investigation, he had watched from the sidelines, not wanting to interfere. But when Detective Carter was forced to abandon the investigation because he wasn't able to obtain statements from any of the victims, MacLachlan jumped in. He personally contacted dozens of ex-choristers, assuaged their fears of exposure, spoke of the Helmers and Franks suicides and encouraged them to speak out for the sake of other children. Eventually his persistence paid off. "He notified us that he'd spoken to a few boys who were willing to come forward," Carter says. "That's how we got our foot in the door. Without his assistance, I can't be one-hundred-per-cent sure we would have successfully completed the investigation."

Bob Burton was living in Vancouver — "no, make that drifting," Bob says — when his parents called and told him about the allegations against Gallienne. There was an awkward pause on the long-distance line and then they asked if he'd been affected. Bob took a deep breath and said, "Yes." He agreed to speak to MacLachlan the following evening and to make a statement to Detective Carter.

The next move came from the Kingston *Whig-Standard.* After it ran the innocuous item about Gallienne's departure, the newspaper received a couple of anonymous phone calls about Gallienne's pedophilia, and a reporter recalled rumours about Henrik Helmers' suicide. Publisher Michael Davies, scion of an old-money family that had owned the *Whig-Standard* for sixty years, tracked Hank Helmers to California and was shocked to find out that Helmers had filed an affidavit about his son's suicide with his Kingston law firm, which, it turned out, was the same firm that represented Ned and Daphne Franks. Davies, an old friend of the Helmers and the Franks, became directly involved. He went to see Ned: "It was a tragic situation," Davies says emotionally. "Ned was a basket case, but he agreed to go public. Tim was a great kid, he worked for us all through high school — I'm sorry, it's hard. These boys were the sons of my friends, and they died. You can't say Gallienne caused those suicides, and you can't say he didn't. You forget what it's like for young people, how vulnerable they are at that stage."

On Saturday, March 10, 1990, the *Whig-Standard* broke the silence with the story of Henrik's 1977 molestation and suicide, and printed a statement from Hank Helmers: "In light of the latest revelations of a number of alleged overt sexual acts or child molestations committed by Mr. Gallienne...during the period 1976 through 1989, we, the Helmers family, can only conclude that [the church has shown] religious, social and criminal irresponsibility and neglect." Kingston Police Chief Gerald Rice made a plea for victims to come forward.

The Helmers story, followed by the Franks story, sent shock waves through Kingston. CHOIRMASTER CONNECTED TO A SECOND SUICIDE read the March 12 headline. BRILLIANT STUDENT SECRETLY REPORTED SEXUAL ABUSE TO CITY POLICE IN 1987. Two days later, the *Whig-Standard* reported an emergency meeting at St. George's at which "parents' faces turned white and their voices broke" when they heard the allegations. The Gallienne loyalists rushed to attack the paper's coverage in letters to the editor: "In my opinion the reports in the *Whig-Standard* have been written for maximum shock value," wrote Godfrey Spragge, a former warden at St. George's. Mary Ev Wyatt condemned the newspaper for "its rush to apply the boots to the fallen figure of John Gallienne, forgetting the very substantial contribution that he has made over the years to the Kingston musical scene."

The Gallienne affair struck very deep in the community; this wasn't a scandal on the wrong side of the tracks, it was happening at St. George's, among the best and the brightest. "There was a lot of pressure to stop writing about the case," says Neil Reynolds, then the *Whig-Standard's* editor-in-chief. And as the *Whig-Standard* followed the story, even those people who gave the paper information at the beginning became part of the problem; they hadn't acted when they should have, or they belonged to other institutions, such as the CAS, which should have done something long before they did. Michael Davies and Neil Reynolds were personally subjected to vehement attempts by rich and powerful friends to make them drop the story; their achievement was that they stuck with it. "What we did," says Davies, "was make the victims out there, who thought they were living their own isolated horror stories, realize they were not alone."

On John Gallienne's twentieth wedding anniversary, March 21, 1990, he was a passenger in his van, in downtown Kingston, when the police pulled him over and arrested him on four counts of sexually abusing children from 1975 to 1987. When Detective Carter laid the first group of charges, he had three victims; the following day, two more came forward; by mid-April thirteen young men had made statements to the police. Andrew Swainson was not among them; the police tried to talk to him, suspecting he was the most damaged of victims, but he couldn't speak — not yet. He did, however, go to see Deborah Hoffman, the therapist hired by the cathedral in April to run a therapy program for victims, their parents and other parishioners. The service was used mostly by parents; their sons couldn't bear to talk about the abuse, and only a few were willing to see Hoffman.

In the autumn of 1990, in a stunning anticlimax in a half-empty Kingston courtroom, after vehement denials, after waging an offensive war against anyone who suspected him, Gallienne pleaded guilty to twenty counts of sexually abusing thirteen boys during his sixteen years at St. George's Cathedral. The charges ranged from molestation to fellatio and sodomy. By pleading guilty, he ensured the victims' silence; they wouldn't get to testify, and the press wouldn't get to hear their personal accounts of childhood betrayal. (The Crown prosecutor read the victim-impact statements to the court but they didn't convey the extent of the damage done.)

Gallienne was supported in court by his wife and by an Anglican clergyman; no one from the church sat with the victims, a few of whom came to the proceedings along with a handful of parents. Gallienne looked grave that day, though the night before he'd enjoyed an evening at the home of his in-laws, laughing as he read aloud from the victim-impact statements, cheered on by his wife and her parents.

Dozens of members of the cathedral hierarchy had supplied the judge with glowing character references for their dear maestro. They seemed to regard the victims as criminals and the criminal as a victim; as strange as this may seem, it's typical of adults who've been manipulated and co-opted by a dominant abuser. Jean Baxter, head of Christian education at St. George's, praised Gallienne's "superb professionalism at all times." Ron Fairley, a senior official at Correctional Services of Canada and head of the cathedral's subcommittee on youth and children's issues, applauded Gallienne's "desire to do good and contribute to society." His wife, Tanis, a teacher, wrote that "nothing in the world can ever damage the admiration and respect I will always have for you...." On United Church letterhead, Fred Kimball Graham identified himself as the godfather of one of Gallienne's daughters and a consultant on congregational worship; he wrote that Gallienne was "imbued" with "Christian principles." It is odd reading these letters, overflowing with sympathy for a man who had destroyed the childhood of so many boys; few of Gallienne's admirers even hinted that he might have done something wrong.

On October 2, 1990, in his reasons for sentence, Judge Richard G. Byers stated: "This accused was given a most precious trust. It was to teach music to children. Instead he broke that trust and he violated those children. He did that over and over again. Make no mistake about it, these children are innocent victims and they have been badly wounded. The scars from those wounds may well last a lifetime and so there is an account to be settled for that. Please stand up, sir. On each and every count you will be sentenced to four years and six months in the penitentiary, each count to run concurrent."

Gallienne was taken to Warkworth Penitentiary, a medium-security institution not far from Kingston, where his wife would go to see him for conjugal visits, bringing lobster and white wine. Bill Marshall, then co-director of the Kingston Sexual Behaviour Clinic, stated in his assessment of Gallienne: "He has declared himself to be sexually attracted to boys [and] not at all attracted to adult males." (Pedophilia, an apparently irreversible orientation in which adults are sexually attracted to children, has nothing to do with homosexuality.) "Related to his difficulty in adult heterosexual relationships, Mr. Gallienne has trouble achieving intimacy with adults," Marshall observed.

The prognosis for sex offenders is uncertain. In one study, Bill Marshall found that the recidivism rate for 126 child molesters was 43 per cent; in many cases of re-offending, "the men were not prosecuted," Marshall wrote, sometimes because they were "judged to be of such good character that charges were deemed unnecessary." Treatment reduces recidivism but is not a guarantee against it. In the sexual offenders program at Warkworth, Dr. Howard Barbaree finds that half the group initially deny having done anything wrong, and the rest blame their victims, alcohol or the "disease" of pedophilia. But it's not a disease, according to Marshall; the disease model implies no individual control, "and these guys obviously have control over their behaviour." They're very careful about where, when and whom they abuse; they manipulate adults and children alike, they establish trust relationships, they threaten and intimidate children, and generally display a mastery that in Marshall's eyes has nothing to do with disease.

Gallienne, the master manipulator, would be eligible for day parole after serving one-sixth of his sentence and full parole after serving one-third, which meant he could anticipate spending about eighteen months in jail. But his plans would go awry. Unbeknownst to Gallienne, Andrew Swainson was waiting in the wings, a wounded phantom bearing a tale that had to be told.

A year later: a fire glowed in the Swainsons' fireplace, casting flickering shadows on the early Canadian antiques and the well-dressed, articulate crowd — a party scene, except for the topic of conversation and the reddened eyes, the tears, the anguish. "When Gallienne went to jail we thought it would be over," said Donald Swainson, Andrew's father. "Nothing's over." These people were supposed to be the lucky ones, white middle-class Canadians with education and access to power. Yet they were like scavengers picking through the ruins of a bombed-out city, in mourning for their lost boys. "It destroys a whole chapter of your life," said Eleanor Swainson, a small, sophisticated woman with sad eyes. "Andrew took out his choir photos and burned them."

When the revelations about Gallienne first hit, each affected family suffered alone, afflicted by the peculiar guilt that victims feel. In group therapy with Deborah Hoffman the parents' sense of isolation was replaced by horror at the predatory march of Gallienne's addiction. They saw that they'd been pawns, manipulated in a massive hoax, and their feeling of helpless victimization gave way to collective rage. They formed the St. George's Association for Action against Child Abuse and demanded systemic change within the church — as well as an apology. They got neither — and they were very angry.

It was the autumn of 1991, Gallienne had been in jail for a year and the cathedral had entered a dangerous phase. It had just fired Deborah Hoffman, who for eighteen months had stood alone in the eye of the hurricane, grappling with the torrent of emotions released in Gallienne's wake. In October 1990, she told the *Whig-Standard*, "There certainly is an indication that the problem is greater than what we've seen [in terms of criminal charges]." In her characteristically understated way, she indicated that many parents still didn't know their children had been abused, and didn't want to know. "As parents they can't bear to hear it, and they give out that signal to their child. You can ask the question and not want to hear the answer, and kids are sensitive to that."

By all accounts, Deborah Hoffman had done a phenomenal job; Bob Burton and Andrew Swainson credited her with saving their lives. They couldn't quite say how she'd done it, but they felt she had provided a lifeline that allowed their blocked feelings to start flowing. "It's very scary to approach the pain when you've tried to push it away and cut it off," Bob says. "You're afraid it's going to overwhelm you. You have to go through it, to recover, but you need help."

Hoffman had been terminated just as her clients were finding their voices. The church had spent $60,000 on therapy fees over eighteen months and now wanted the victims and their families to find medicare-covered psychiatrists, but the few professionals in Kingston with expertise in dealing with sexual abuse had long waiting lists. In any event, Hoffman's clients wanted to continue with her. The parents needed an enormous amount of support in order to confront Gallienne's crimes and their own limitations; not only had they failed to protect their children, they had embraced the viper. "It's tough facing the fact you've worshipped false gods," Hoffman says.

It was also hard to believe that *these* people had been so thoroughly conned. They were an impressive group in terms of education, erudition and professional expertise: scientists, lawyers, academics, artists, executives and entrepreneurs; half the women had their own careers, the rest were stay-at-home mothers who did volunteer work on the side. Most of the marriages had one thing in common: a traditional alignment of domestic duties, with the women primarily responsible for child care. Their children, it must be underlined, had not been neglected in any conventional sense.

Pedophiles are always scanning for vulnerability, searching for children hungry for recognition, connection, intimacy. Intimacy is not about sex, Hoffman emphasizes; it's about children's need for relationships with available adults — which is why boys with emotionally distant fathers are so vulnerable to coaches, Boy Scout leaders, teachers and choirmasters. Children yearn for male attention; they need it. This is not to blame fathers. No parents are perfect; all families go through difficult times when adult preoccupations may result in children feeling neglected. Gallienne's victims were boys who wanted to feel special in the eyes of a man — especially a man whom their parents revered. Winning Gallienne's approval was a way to win their parents' love.

"We're absolutely mortified and devastated and so upset, to think this could have happened in a church," said St. George's warden Janice Deakin, the official spokesperson for the cathedral, in the fall of 1991. "You're supposed to be safe in a church; evil is supposed to be outside, good inside. We had a serious pedophile who was incredibly skilled at covering his tracks." Deakin, a physical education professor at Queen's, felt she'd been the target of unwarranted attacks from afflicted families because she was the person who had announced the cancellation of Hoffman's therapy program. The church was experiencing severe financial constraints, she said: with seven hundred families on its books and sharply declining attendance following the revelations of the Gallienne affair, St. George's was running an unprecedented operating deficit of $120,000.

Why didn't the church keep records about Gallienne's behaviour? "We had a problem with keeping records," Deakin admitted. "No consistent records were kept. One can't expect ministers to transmit information from one set of wardens to another." Why not? "We're a volunteer organization, we had a problem with communication, no doubt about it, and we're changing our procedures." But she was not prepared to acknowledge that church officials bore any responsibility for allowing the tragedy to occur. "John Gallienne abused the boys at St. George's."

Asked why the church would not apologize — a deed fervently longed for by victims and parents — she said sternly: "John Gallienne is responsible for what he did to the children." But St. George's, as his employer, had information about Gallienne's pedophilia dating back to 1977; the church had the deaths of two boys on its conscience, and it continued to entrust children to the care of a predator. Again, she repeated: "John Gallienne is responsible. There are legal ramifications associated with an apology." This was the crux of the matter: the church had consulted lawyers, who advised that an apology could be construed as an admission of guilt. "The parents' support group has said it wants redress and financial remuneration....There's a consideration in terms of civil litigation." Indeed there was. It wouldn't be long before the therapy fees looked minuscule next to the cathedral's legal bills.

But not all parents of victims supported the St. George's Association for Action against Child Abuse. "I wish they would shut up and go away," said Sandra Rowland. She thought they were "harassing" the cathedral unfairly. "This isn't Mount Cashel. The boys weren't locked up. We all have to share the blame. We sent our boys to that choir."

Sandra's two sons, both abused, had refused therapy — like most of Gallienne's victims. They roamed the streets with their friends, getting stoned, getting into trouble. Mike was arrested one night for drunk and disorderly behaviour outside Gallienne's home. (The former choirmaster was still in prison.) Sandra's husband was still a defender of the cathedral. Sandra admitted defeat: "My marriage was on the rocks, fighting over Gallienne. I gave in, to save my marriage." The marriage, not the children's safety, came first. "It's all so twisted," she said.

In public, the cathedral remained aloof from — and sometimes hostile to — the mounting anguish. A former church official screamed and swore at Sandra Rowland for telling a reporter that she, Sandra, had informed the official about Gallienne's pedophilia in 1987. This attitude exemplified the church's public posture: don't talk about it, period. The St. George's Association for Action against Child Abuse received no positive response to its demands for systemic change and was advised to "forgive and forget," says association president Holly Mitchell. "The victims have been silenced; now it's our turn to get lost. The church's only concern is protecting the hierarchy." The personal price she paid for supporting Gallienne's victims was ostracism by her parents, Gifford and Phyllis Mitchell, and by her sister, Lannie. "It broke Holly's heart to lose Lannie," says one of Holly's friends. "She loved Lannie; she wanted to save Lannie."

Like many wives of offenders, Lannie remained bound to her husband. Shortly after Gallienne was arrested, she wrote a letter to a few of her old chums from the Women's Convivial Tuesday Union and said how hurt she was that half the group, having discovered that their sons had been abused by the choirmaster, now shunned him. "Does their hatred of John affect how I feel about them? Of course! The fact that they can only see his flaw — and forget all his good parts, or even try to accept him as a person whom they used to love — is hard for me to accept." Lannie was incapable of grasping what he had done. She saw the world only through his eyes. "Despite everything, I still love him," she wrote — even though he had been identified as a homosexual pedophile with an aversion to women. Holly now saw her sister's seamless charm in an eerie light: "Someone could drop dead on the floor in front of Lannie and she'd go on being perfect, denying what she'd seen."

Holly was surrounded by estranged relatives and toppled authority figures. One of the most prominent was Dr. Christopher Padfield, her pediatrician of many years, whom she "fired." If anyone was in a position to see what was going on at St. George's, it was Padfield, the child abuse expert and former church warden who had organized the choir's

1979 trip to England and accompanied Gallienne on the tour. Welsh-born, a graduate of Cambridge University, Padfield had been on staff at Queen's University and Hôtel-Dieu Hospital for twenty years. In the business of assessing and diagnosing children who've been abused, he is well versed in the behavioural indicators of child sexual abuse. Between 1987 and 1991, his child protection team examined 530 children and he was frequently called upon as an expert witness in court cases.

Padfield knew Gallienne well; he'd stayed with the Galliennes when his own marriage broke up and continued to socialize with Gallienne after charges were laid. Interviewed at his hospital office in the fall of 1991, he became enraged when asked about Gallienne. He reared up behind his desk and expressed the urgent desire to eject the interviewer from the hospital. Why would the head of the child protection team *not* want to talk about Gallienne? Had he ever suspected Gallienne? "I was a warden at St. George's, both my sons were in the choir, I was a great personal friend of Gallienne's," he said. "Do you think I would have had two sons in the choir if I thought they were being abused...? The *Whig-Standard* says this is a monstrous cover-up. We knew nothing. How can you spot this?"

Medical journals are full of articles about behavioural indicators — Padfield didn't need to be told; he was the expert — and Gallienne's victims had exhibited classic signs of distress, ranging from depression to hostility, withdrawal, hyperactivity, substance abuse and criminal behaviour. Some of these boys were Padfield's patients. Hadn't he ever wondered? He responded with a rhetorical question: "Can we blame everything that happened to these boys on John Gallienne?" Many of the choirboys came from "troubled families" or "broken homes," he said. "Not everyone who's abused becomes a criminal or a psychopath. John Gallienne took an extra interest in a lot of these boys; they needed help. He is not a monster. He was good to them." It was astonishing to hear a child protection expert say that a pedophile had been "good" to boys he groomed for sexual abuse. Surely what Gallienne did was a monstrous betrayal? At that point, Padfield changed his tune. His voice resumed its softer, sweeter tone. "What he did was a heinous crime," he said. "But if you say 'monster' you think he can be recognized; you cannot recognize pedophiles.... I could be a pedophile, you could be a pedophile."

Padfield turned his attention to Gifford and Phyllis Mitchell; they'd written to him "saying the Greeks and Romans and Oscar Wilde did it, so what's so wrong with sex with children?" he said. Phyllis Mitchell, reached by phone, confirmed she had indeed sent a letter defending pedophilia to Padfield. Her easy admission was startling. But perhaps she was mistaken about Oscar Wilde; he was a homosexual, not a pedophile. "I know, but we have come that far that we don't throw homosexuals in prison any more. We're still far behind in terms of our dealing with sexuality. Pedophiles shouldn't be in prison. Most pedophiles aren't violent. I think society will change in regard to sex with children." Her pro-pedophile views are not as unusual as they might seem; the unspoken assumption of many defenders of abusers is that they tolerate, without question, the acts of abusers.

Did Mrs. Mitchell admit Gallienne's victims were damaged? "Oh certainly, but it's overdone. People over-react. It's like these so-called rapes. I don't think every so-called rape is the fault of the man. It's mutual in a lot of cases.... A lot of these boys had problems at home and they turned to John for comfort. Poor John, he's not an evil man, he's a kind man, a talented man, and he tried to help the boys. I know that's what the problem is, abuse of trust. Well, he repents, he feels remorse and he's doing a lot of thinking with the support of his family. People should show more forgiveness to John."

The Gallienne case entered a painful state of limbo. For the parents of his victims, the trauma seemed only to get worse, as they struggled helplessly with the devastation of their families and their own feelings of shame and self-blame. Ned and Daphne Franks saw a psychiatrist who said they were like people coming through a minefield with a live grenade in their hands. "He was afraid this was going to destroy us," Ned says. Haunted by the thought that if only they'd known, they could have saved their son, they carried an enormous burden of guilt. But they'd made a heroic effort, out of their personal tragedy, to protect other children. Without them, Gallienne would probably not have been caught. "What have I learned from this?" Ned says. "I understand in my guts — I'm a political scientist — how Hitler got away with it." He quotes Edmund Burke: "The sole condition necessary for evil to flourish is for good men to do nothing."

Alastair Crawford moved to Toronto, went into therapy, and gained insight into the powerlessness of his ten-year-old self. "The only reason I'm talking about this is to reach other kids and encourage them to get professional help," he says. "If you don't, you just suffer and waste your life. You watch everyone else go by and you can't do anything and the rage builds. I still have a lot of impediments. I gave up on education during high school. I'm afraid I'll never be able to have a lasting relationship. I hate it when people invade my personal space. I don't like being touched. I have a horrible fear of being dominated."

In a conversational leap that at first seemed incomprehensible, Alastair began to talk about John Gacy, whom he described as "a perfect citizen, like John Gallienne, an upstanding member of the community." Gacy was a pedophile who, after being caught and jailed in Iowa, moved to Illinois and started killing his victims. In the 1970s, he seduced, raped and murdered thirty-three teenage boys, twenty-seven of whom he buried under his house in Chicago.

"What will Gallienne do when he gets out of jail?" Alastair says, eyes reddening. "Will he start killing boys?" Did Alastair really believe Gallienne was capable of murder? "He did kill something in us — he destroyed our childhood."

The most obviously damaged soul was Andrew Swainson. From a clever little boy who wanted to carry a candle in the choir, he'd been transformed into a high school dropout, petty criminal, drug abuser and inmate in a psychiatric ward. When he met Deborah Hoffman, in June 1990, he was a wild child, all frantic upheaval and incoherent rage, unable to identify the crimes committed against him. At the age of twenty-one, he was a textbook case of trauma bonding, a human being shaped by an abusive relationship that dominated his formative years.

But Andrew had put up a fight, and he was still fighting. As a child, he'd refused to go to choir practice, and his father had dragged him there; he'd thrown tantrums, threatened homicide, attempted suicide, but no one had heard him. "Andrew had been screaming his pain for years," Hoffman says. Yet during the police investigation he'd refused to talk to Detective Carter, and when Gallienne was convicted, Andrew still couldn't speak to the police. But he continued to see Hoffman, even after her therapy program was cancelled by the cathedral in the fall of 1991. Her gift to Andrew was the healing light of insight: she liked him the moment he walked in her door; beneath his rough exterior she saw the frightened child. "He felt, I think, that I saw the essence of him — and he wanted to be seen," she says. Her understanding broke the myth in which he was trapped: that he was a bad guy, so bad he was a criminal and a drug addict. Like so many victims, he'd never made the connection between what Gallienne had done to him and his adult problems. With Hoffman's help, he caught a glimmer of the helpless child he'd been, and then the miracle happened: Andrew found his voice.

In April 1992, after many approaches on my part, Andrew agreed to meet me at his Kingston home. He was thin and tense, with fair hair, wary blue eyes and a nervous grin. He wore a T-shirt and jeans and looked younger than his twenty-three years. The darkened living room was lit by the eerie glow of two enormous fish tanks swimming with sleek iridescent shark (a miniature variety, Andrew explained) and bulbous red-headed Orandas (an exotic type of Japanese goldfish). His wife, Marika, bustled about in the kitchen with their small daughter, Melissa, while the living room was occupied by Andrew's assorted pals, some of whom lived there, others who hung out on a semi-permanent basis.

Andrew was a bit of a patriarch, presiding over a home for lost boys, young men like himself who'd been damaged as kids, had dropped out of school, had nowhere to go. He worked hard to fit in with his chosen crowd. In his ungrammatical speech, studded with double negatives, swear words and monosyllabic mutterings, there was little trace of the boy who'd been a straight-A student, a violinist in the Kingston Youth Orchestra, a choirboy who wanted to be a doctor when he grew up. The transformation was quite unbelievable, but then so were the conditions of his childhood.

Andrew and I drove to his mechanic's shop, a garage he'd rented a few blocks from his house. The workspace was tidy, floor carefully swept, tools neatly arranged; a blue muscle car occupied centre stage, hood open, engine dismantled. He talked knowledgeably about cars and engines and was proud of his work. At one point, he suddenly said he'd told his story to Paulette Peirol and Michael Den Tandt, reporters at the Kingston *Whig-Standard*. They were preparing a series on the

Gallienne legacy; their article on Andrew wouldn't be published for another month, but already trouble was brewing. Against the advice of Deborah Hoffman and his parents, Andrew was insisting that his real name be used in the article. Having waited so long to speak, he seemed to want to shout from the highest mountaintop.

I asked how he was feeling. "Oh, all right, trying to take it easy, whatever." He shrugged, emitting a mirthless chuckle. "I'm fucked up, man." The grin disappeared and he looked at me with haunted eyes. He talked about Gallienne in short, muttered sentences. "When he started on me, I was so young and he was like this power figure, my parents worshipped him and I didn't know what he was doing. It was like a marriage or something weird. I couldn't stop him, I blamed myself, I hated myself."

Andrew paced the garage. Brittle with tension, he shivered in the chill April evening, burdened by an emotional pain that was palpable. "I never had a childhood," he said, hugging his arms across his skinny chest. "I'm always trying to pretend everything's okay, I try to help other kids who have nowhere to go, then I get frustrated and I want to destroy everything, including myself. It's hard for me to cry. It's easier for me to smash things or steal things — at least then I feel like I'm getting back at someone. I got so much anger, I can't do anything with the anger. I got a wall. It's hard for me to feel emotions. I don't trust nobody. I'm stuck. I work and work and basically just get by, then I get depressed and I go down, down, down. People think I'm a bum."

Andrew locked the garage and we walked outside. He kept talking about how "messed up" he was, and "stuck in a rut." I asked if he was ready to make a statement to the police, which could result in more criminal charges against Gallienne, who was supposed to be getting out of jail any day. He shrugged; he'd tried, he said — he'd made appointments to see Detective Carter, but hadn't shown up. As I got into my car to drive back to Toronto, I asked him if he wanted me to go with him to the police station in the morning. "Sure," he said. "Yeah, let's do it."

In hindsight, the rest happened very quickly. On Monday, April 27, 1992, I picked Andrew up, as agreed, at 8:30 a.m., and we drove down Princess Street to police headquarters. The moment we entered the building, he turned pale. Detective Carter appeared with another officer, whom he introduced as his new partner. Both men were burly and uncommunicative, armoured in stiff, dark suits. They showed us into a tiny, windowless interview room and shut the door.

Instead of making a compassionate overture to Andrew, Carter berated him for giving an interview to the *Whig-Standard*. Carter's anger was understandable, in one sense: Andrew was the prize witness, the victim Carter had tried so hard to get in the long, slogging months of his investigation, when no one would talk, and now Andrew had gone to the *Whig-Standard* first. However, here was the most vulnerable of victims, about to say the most difficult words of his entire life, being greeted by a verbal assault.

Finally Carter subsided, shifting into good-cop mode, and prepared to take Andrew's statement. Andrew spoke quickly, wasting no words. After twenty minutes, realizing Andrew was in for the long haul, Carter said he had an appointment he would have to cancel, and left the room with his partner in tow. Andrew turned to me, took a deep breath and heaved a sigh of relief. "I'm glad I'm here," he said. "I'm ready to do this." When Carter and his partner returned, I left, so Andrew could finish his statement in private — an ordeal that lasted more than three hours.

That afternoon, Deborah Hoffman dropped by Andrew's house, by chance. She found him staring into space, in a daze, absolutely drained; she'd never seen him like that. She held his hand and he said, "Deborah, I did it, I told the police." Deborah was amazed. "That's great, Andrew, you finally did it."

When I reached Andrew the next day, he told me he'd made up his mind: "I want to sue the cathedral." He was absolutely firm — even though he didn't know if anyone had ever sued a church — and he would never waver in the ensuing months, although the delays would drive him crazy. He asked if I could help him find a lawyer. No problem, I thought. I spoke to Bob Little, the lawyer who'd helped Ned and Daphne Franks confront the cathedral, and Little recommended three Kingston lawyers. Marika called them, but not one was prepared to sue St. George's, whose elite, after all, ruled Kingston. Andrew finally found a lawyer who said he'd do it, but he wanted $2,500 cash up front, and Andrew didn't have any money.

On May 16, 1992, the *Whig-Standard* published the first in Peirol and Den Tandt's series on the Gallienne legacy — a series that would win them a National Newspaper Award. The first instalment confirmed that the church's former dean, Grahame Baker, had heard allegations for many years that Gallienne was a child molester. The following day, a picture of young Andrew as an innocent choirboy dominated the front page; his story hit Kingston with a cataclysmic jolt, shattering the cosy denial in which the cathedral's parishioners had wrapped themselves. Although Gallienne's confession had confirmed his guilt, they'd never been forced to confront the sordid details of his activities.

"For $10, Mr. Gallienne would invite Andrew to come to the church at night to tune the organ with him, or help put that week's sheet music in individual folders," wrote Peirol and Den Tandt. "Yet more often than not, the organ was already tuned and the music was already done when he got there." Andrew's comment was that "he'd give you the money and then he'd abuse you. When I think back on it, it's like giving you candy for what he's doing to you." Afterward, Gallienne sometimes drove Andrew home and stayed for a glass of sherry with his parents. The Swainsons "routinely allowed their son to stay with the Galliennes when they were out of town. On two of those occasions, Mr. Gallienne abused not only Andrew alone but Andrew with other choirboys." According to Andrew, "Mr. Gallienne forced the boys to perform sexual acts while he himself watched."

The article detailed Andrew's increasing alienation and criminal activity. In February 1986, he was charged with two counts of break and enter; his parents felt they had to draw the line, and testified in court that he'd threatened to burn down their house and to kill them. Andrew spent seven months in Kingston Psychiatric Hospital."I was in a big, huge ward with all these other crazy people," he said. But he received no treatment that helped identify the problem. Three years later — facing more criminal charges, including possession of drugs and stolen property — he was back at Kingston Psychiatric, heavily medicated, and the secret slipped out. But he was humiliated by the response to his disclosure that he'd been sexually abused by John Gallienne: "Are you sure you're not just gay?" said the staff member. "Are you sure you didn't like it? Why did you let it go on for so long if you didn't like it?" Andrew cried that day. "They had put me on chlorpromazine because my nerves were so gone. I really freaked."

Andrew's story attracted the attention of Libby Burnham, a Toronto lawyer, who called me; she knew I was writing this book and wanted to make sure I was aware of his case. I told her Andrew was looking for a lawyer who would sue the cathedral on his behalf. Could she recommend someone? Within forty-eight hours, Dan Ferguson, a partner in her firm, Borden & Elliot, one of the biggest, most power-ful law firms in Toronto, had taken on the case.

Ferguson moved fast. He visited Kingston three times in two weeks, meeting Andrew and contacting other abused choirboys and their parents — some of whom had been picketing the church for the past few months, unable to figure out any other way to attract the cathedral's attention. They called themselves the St. George's Marching and Debating Society; they marched up and down the side-walk in front of the church before Sunday services, carrying picket signs — Mount Cashel Apologized said one — and infuriating churchgoers.

On June 23, 1992, at about the time Gallienne could have expected to be released on parole, a warrant for his arrest was served on him at Warkworth Penitentiary. He faced three new charges, covering eleven years of sexual abuse, based on Andrew's statement: indecent assault on a male, buggery and sexual assault.

Four days later, a meeting was held at James and Kate Burton's house to formalize taking legal action against the church. It was a momentous occasion, though none of them knew what a landmark case it would become. Dan Ferguson arrived from Toronto, and Andrew was there, with Bob Burton and three other survivors accom-panied by girlfriends or spouses. "It was incredible," Bob said, "to hear the guys talk about the abuse in front of their girlfriends. I mean, this was the deepest, darkest secret in the whole world, and now some of us can actually mention it in front of other people." Marv and Laura Rowan came, and so did Clark, a strapping seventeen-year-old, who was ten when he disclosed being abused at summer choir camp in 1985.

Deborah Hoffman arrived late and Ferguson motioned her to sit beside him on the couch. She was given a thank-you card signed by the group, which had agreed upon a name to be used in the lawsuit: Families and Victims in Crisis. She was astounded by how quickly Ferguson had drawn people together and mapped out a game plan. He

handed round a piece of paper that was signed by five young men —
eventually ten primary victims would take part in the suit, along with
ten parents, for a total of twenty plaintiffs — formally retaining
Ferguson to sue the cathedral, the diocese, selected clergy, former wardens and John Gallienne. "It was a big moment," Bob says. When they
signed, Andrew and Bob leaned over and whispered to each other, "If
you're in, I'm in."

James Burton was able to step back, in his professorial way, and
analyse the phases the victims and parents had evolved through: first
had come denial, then therapy, which produced insight and led to
anger when they realized the devastation Gallienne had wrought; their
next step had been to organize the St. George's Association for Action
against Child Abuse, to bring about systemic reform within the
church. Blocked at every turn, they'd moved into the picketing phase.
"Now the picketing's given way to the litigation phase," said James. It
couldn't have come at a more ominous time, for the cathedral. As
Andrew's lawsuit was gathering momentum, the Roman Catholic
Church, the Christian Brothers in Ottawa, and the Ontario government
announced a $16-million settlement for three hundred victims of St.
John's and St. Joseph's training schools, where boys had been sexually abused by Christian Brothers in the fifties and sixties. (By June
1993, fourteen Christian Brothers had been convicted of offences
ranging from buggery to assault causing bodily harm; an additional
three hundred victims had come forward and the settlement had
increased to $23 million.)

Dan Ferguson spent the month of July 1992 at his summer cottage on
Georgian Bay. At the beginning of August, he announced that he'd
been appointed a judge of the Ontario Court (General Division) and
turned over the Gallienne case to a partner at Borden & Elliot, John
Morris. Clearing out his office, Ferguson mused over the church's
refusal to acknowledge its responsibility. A fight was brewing between
the cathedral and its insurance company, which took an opening position that it didn't have to pay for Gallienne's crimes. Ferguson, who'd
acted on behalf of large insurance companies in the past, had spoken
to the cathedral's insurance representative, "and he doesn't get it. He
sees the case as a complaint about deliberate sexual abuse committed

by an individual, and the insurance doesn't cover deliberate acts. I explained: the church is being sued for *negligence*. But the church still doesn't understand why. They amaze me, with their ostrich-like stance. I've not run into this kind of intransigence before, ever. It's fascinating. They are still unwilling to look at what Gallienne was doing in that church for sixteen years, and how he did it. Why didn't someone stop him?"

On Tuesday, August 25, 1992, John Gallienne was taken in shackles from Warkworth Penitentiary to the Kingston courthouse. Shortly after 2:00 p.m., he was led into a courtroom where his ever-faithful wife, Lannie, supported on either side by two women friends, sat in the front row. Across the aisle, also in the front row, was Bob Burton, now in his late twenties. He held hands tightly with Catherine,* his girlfriend. She was hyper-alert, acutely attuned to the "surreal weirdness" of the occasion, feeling "how profoundly hurt on so many different levels people were by this man they'd adored."

Also in the front row were Laura Rowan and Marika Swainson. Andrew had intended to come — this was his day in court, after all, the day Gallienne was to be held accountable for the devastation he'd wrought on Andrew's life — but when the time came, Andrew couldn't bear to see him.

Gallienne's eyes remained fixed on the floor as the charges were read; he pleaded guilty. Jack McKenna, the Crown prosecutor, read Andrew's ten-page police statement into the court record. "I've never heard anything so horrific in my life," Laura said. Marika wept; Bob dissociated, in agony for Andrew, in fear for his younger self. Lannie Gallienne and her two friends were calm: "They looked impassive, as if they weren't affected by what they were hearing, as if it wasn't real," Catherine said.

At the end of Andrew's police statement, Gallienne whispered to his lawyer who stood up to quibble over minor details that Gallienne wanted changed in Andrew's statement. Laura was revolted, "in the face of these atrocities, that Gallienne would be concerned about trivial corrections, changing a couple of dates. That reinforced for me what a monster he really is."

McKenna said he had personally prosecuted Andrew for a variety of criminal offences and now believed Gallienne was responsible for every day Andrew had spent in jail and in psychiatric institutions. He informed the court that Andrew had turned down a request to submit a victim-impact statement. Andrew had not forgotten that the statements from the original group of thirteen complainants had been supplied to Gallienne as part of the Crown's disclosure, and that the night before he was sentenced, Gallienne had enjoyed a little send-off party at which he'd read aloud, laughing, the words of his victims.

The judge sentenced Gallienne to an additional eighteen months in jail. Asked if he had anything to say, Gallienne rose to his feet, pulled a piece of paper from his pocket, looked Bob straight in the eye for a moment and read a brief apology. Catherine worried that Bob Burton would hyperventilate or pass out. Laura's heart pounded in fury: in her eyes, Gallienne had the same pathetic look he had had on his face seven years earlier when Clark had disclosed at summer choir camp and the choirmaster had grovelled in front of the Rowans, "It's never happened before, it was just the one time, it'll never happen again, please don't tell Lannie."

As Gallienne finished his statement to the court, Laura leaped to her feet in a spontaneous burst of emotion, clenched her fist and shouted, "He's a bloody liar, that's a bloody lie!"

In October 1992, I met John Morris in his office on the forty-seventh floor of Scotia Plaza in downtown Toronto. "The church is behaving like an animal caught in the middle of the road, frozen in the glare of headlights," he said. He had just filed the first legal document, the notice of action, informing the cathedral, John Gallienne, Stuart Ryan, Grahame Baker — in all, a total of eleven former or current St. George's employees or associates — that "a legal proceeding has been commenced against you.... The plaintiffs' claims are for compensatory, aggravated and punitive damages, pre-judgment interest and costs." The ten ex-choirboys and ten parents were listed anonymously as plaintiffs.

> The plaintiffs allege that John Gallienne is liable for assault, and further, for negligence in failing to seek, receive and comply with treatment for his illness.... It is alleged that the individual defendants and other persons for whom the

44

Corporation of St. George's Cathedral and the Incorporated Synod of the Diocese of Ontario are in law responsible:

a) were negligent in hiring John Gallienne and supervising his activities;

b) failed to warn the plaintiffs of the risks presented by the past behaviour of John Gallienne;

c) breached their fiduciary duty to the plaintiffs to provide a safe, wholesome, supervised and religious environment and program for the boys entrusted to their care;

d) fraudulently concealed their misconduct and that of John Gallienne and thereby prevented the plaintiffs from discovering their cause of action and from seeking help and treatment at an earlier date;

e) failed to advise other responsible persons of their knowledge, information and belief concerning the risk presented by John Gallienne's behaviour and failed to take any reasonable steps to prevent a continuation of his behaviour.

Morris described the issue of negligence as analogous to a medical malpractice suit in which a doctor fails to disclose that something has gone wrong with the operation, and the patient discovers ten years later that a sponge left in his body is causing ongoing problems. The cathedral's position, and that of the individual defendants, is that they acted "reasonably and responsibly" once they had been informed of Gallienne's alleged and actual conduct with choirboys.

At the end of October 1992, the Supreme Court of Canada, in a unanimous 7–0 decision, upheld the claim of Karen Miersma, who as an adult sued her father for sexually assaulting her as a child. The delay in her civil lawsuit exceeded the statute of limitations but the court's support for her position became a critical precedent for the Gallienne case. Miersma challenged the statute of limitations on the grounds that she hadn't realized until she was twenty-six that her father had sexually abused her between the ages of eight and sixteen. In the decision, Mr. Justice Gerard La Forest wrote that the law failed to take into account the "unique and complex nature of incest," which causes long-lasting pyschological damage that often isn't manifest until the victim becomes an adult. As a result of the Miersma decision, the statute of limitations starts ticking only when victims become aware of the impact of the abuse and are able to act on their knowledge. Further, the court held that there is a breach of trust for which there is no statute of limitations, when the abuse is perpetrated on a child by an adult, such as a parent or schoolteacher.

On November 11, the news was out: CHOIRMASTER'S VICTIMS SEEK $9 MILLION said a *Toronto Star* headline; the primary victims were claiming damages of $750,000 per person, while their parents were seeking $100,000 per person. In fact, the claim for the young men would include an additional $200,000 for aggravated and punitive damages, for a total, per person, of $950,000. It was unlikely they would ever see that amount; Morris encouraged his clients to keep the door open to a negotiated settlement, and tried to prepare them for the reality of the system. "Most court cases end with a settlement that doesn't entirely satisfy the plaintiffs," he says. "I don't think they realize how painful this process can be. Personally, I'd love to have a trial, for my own sake; it would be a very exciting trial, but I'm not sure that's in the best interests of my clients."

Before the new year, there was a startling development in the case. Morris had delivered a routine caution to his clients, explaining that he needed to anticipate how the defence would attack them. "I'm your lawyer," he said. "Don't keep anything from me. If there's anything you haven't told me, tell me now. If, for instance, any of you were abused by someone besides Gallienne, let me know." Morris wanted to avoid a nasty surprise such as Gallienne saying, "I'm not the one who damaged X, it was really Y who assaulted X." Within a few weeks of the caution, the police opened a new investigation that led to the laying of charges of sexual assault and gross indecency against John McNevin, a member of St. George's adult choir. McNevin had been a board member of the Children's Aid Society from 1985, the year Gallienne was caught at summer choir camp, until 1988. The number of lawsuits proliferated: McNevin sued the Kingston *Whig-Standard* and John Morris, while the defendants — the cathedral *et al.* — announced that they were claiming against the Kingston Police, the Children's Aid Society and Dr. David Surridge, the psychiatrist who had advised the church that Gallienne posed no risk to children.

On the last Sunday in February 1993, Bishop Peter Mason, having occupied the senior ministerial post at St. George's for less than a year, delivered an apology that came too late for many of the victims. "It is our hope — my hope — that at some time all of you will be able to reconcile your pain and find spiritual peace," he said. "We ask you to accept our sincere expression of sorrow and regret for all that has happened." Bishop Mason repeated his message twice, once to a group of seventy-five people gathered outside the cathedral, then from the pulpit to a throng of seven hundred. Seated among the parishioners was Hank Helmers, who had travelled from his California home to Kingston for what turned out to be a disappointing event. "Sorry isn't good enough," he said afterward.

In March 1993, John Morris made his examination for discovery of Gallienne, who was again brought from Warkworth Penitentiary with shackles around his ankles and chains around his wrists. The three-day session took place in a Belleville courthouse; the chains were removed from Gallienne's wrists so he could move his hands freely when he spoke. Morris approached this encounter with trepidation. "I went there with the impression I'd be dealing with a mastermind, and I expected to be intimidated by him, but I wasn't." Instead of an evil genius, Morris saw a man who appeared to be normal, "and in a way that's even more frightening."

Gallienne's stance was the same as at summer choir camp in 1985. *Look at me,* he seemed to say, *I'm a man who loves music, who worked so hard, who gave the church and the boys so much; sometimes I got carried away, I crossed the line, I admit it, but it was out of love.* What was missing from his self-serving portrayal was reality: the reality of his dominance, his egomania, his volatile personality, the awe and fear he instilled in children and parents, his control over the cathedral community, his contempt for anyone who challenged him, his inability to love. What was missing was his power, and his capacity to abuse that power.

Three months later in June, the examination for discovery of the plaintiffs began in Kingston. The cathedral had taken out a $250,000 line of credit to pay for legal fees; one could only recall the days when church officials bemoaned the $60,000 cost of therapy. Bob and Billy Burton were first up; Andrew Swainson would speak midweek. As the victims told their stories to the assembled lawyers — seven or eight, at various times, representing the cathedral and various defendants — the examining lawyers were seen to be visibly wilting. Their questioning of the plaintiffs was relatively gentle; they had no ammunition with which to attack; there were too many victims. By Thursday, there was more bad news for the defence: a victim had come forward from Gallienne's past, from St. John the Divine, the church in Victoria, British Columbia, where Gallienne had been choirmaster from 1970 to 1974. More charges of indecent assault had been laid.

In July 1993, John Morris arranged for Dr. Harvey Armstrong, a Toronto psychiatrist, to undertake to a full round of psychological evaluations of the victims. "We've done everything that has to be done before the trial," Bob Burton said in August. He'd spent six hours with Armstrong, and was now "sitting back and waiting." There were rumours of an out-of-court settlement. "We may have to decide whether to accept a negotiated deal," Bob said, "which would entail not being able to talk about it, which would piss off my father."

In October, a year after Andrew initiated the lawsuit, John Morris was pushing for a trial date to keep the pressure on the cathedral and the other defendants. By November, St. George's was in court fighting its insurance companies, who argued that they couldn't be held responsible for Gallienne's crimes. A pretrial date was set for December, when the lawyers for all sides would sit down with a judge and offers for settlement could be made, but it was delayed until 1994. Morris, in the meantime, had become something of an expert in dealing with child sexual abuse in a legal context. The educational aspect of the lawsuit was phenomenal. Terrified by victims' claims of $950,000 per person, churches, institutions and insurance companies were scrambling to learn about child sexual abuse. Morris was able to explain the underlying reactions of victims. In regard to Henrik Helmers' suicide in 1977, many people thought the boy had killed himself over a relatively trivial molestation — but they missed the point, Morris says. Even Gallienne had acknowledged that he thought he had been instrumental in Henrik's death. "People don't understand how shattering sexual violation can be," Morris says. "It doesn't have to be penetration; it's the loss of control, especially if the molestation is committed by a powerful authority figure, that can devastate kids." Another issue that troubled his clients, Morris found, was guilt about not disclosing immediately, right after the abuse occurred; but the first time it happened, they couldn't believe it; the next time they felt they must have let it happen — and so they were trapped. "That's the awful burden victims carry," he says, "feeling responsible, wanting to tell, but thinking, *How can I speak now?* when they didn't speak before."

Andrew, having spoken, has not become a saint. His life lurches forward. He and Marika have had another baby, named Andrew; they have moved to a basement apartment; he plans to admit himself into a drug rehabilitation program. Andrew doesn't realize it, but he is a hero. He accomplished what no one else could: he held the cathedral accountable. He demonstrated a powerful truth: if individuals and institutions will not respond to evidence of abuse — as many have shown they will not — their attention is riveted by massive lawsuits. Money talks.

John Gallienne did not apply for parole after serving one-third of his sentence, as he was entitled to do. Instead, he was discharged in October, 1994, at the time of his statutory release date. He changed his last name to Mitchell and moved to the Ottawa area with his ever-faithful wife Lannie. Gallienne has reportedly "found God," as many prisoners do while incarcerated. He has also earned a psychology degree from Queen's University via correspondence courses. Lannie has taken a course in lay counselling; together, family members say, they intend to set themselves up in business as therapists.

The key to recovery, in the opinion of Laura Rowan, is finding ways to take control while going through the pain. "Talk about it, do something about it and don't give up." At our first meeting, two years earlier, she wept through our entire conversation. Now she felt powerful. "It's as if we came out of the closet: we told our story to the media and we said, 'Yes, our son was abused.' " Clark had been "transformed" by joining the lawsuit. "He's gotten over it being a dirty little secret. We have to expose these acts for what they are. To take the devotion and trust of a small child and use it to destroy the child is a crime beyond words. We're all of us vulnerable. Look at me. It happened to my son. But we're recovering. The lawsuit rolls on. Good can come out of bad."

2

Investigating the Crime: Detective Wendy Leaver

You want to know how to stop the sexual abuse of children? Stop ignoring kids. If we can educate parents to listen to children, we can stop it. Pedophiles are like sex addicts. Left to their own devices, the average pedophile abuses three hundred to four hundred children over a fifteen- to twenty-year period, before he's caught — if he's caught. Communication with children is the key.

— Detective Wendy Leaver
Metropolitan Toronto Police
Sexual Assault Squad

ALEX HAMILTON came to Wendy Leaver's attention in May 1992, via the Federal Bureau of Investigation: that spring, FBI Special Agent John McCarthy flew from Erie, Pennsylvania, to Toronto, to meet with Detective Leaver. McCarthy brought with him boxes of files, copies of letters, index cards and photographs that were part of the "collection" belonging to Mark Harvey, an Erie pedophile who was serving a four-year sentence for possession of child pornography. He'd been fined $10,000, and ordered to make a $5,000 payment to an organization opposed to child pornography and to pay for his own incarceration and treatment, a bill that could exceed $100,000. (Harvey is currently imprisoned in a federal institution in Pennsylvania.) The collection that got him in so much trouble included correspondence with Alex Hamilton, a Toronto-area high school teacher who became the focus of Detective Wendy Leaver's investigation.

The FBI was alerted to Mark Harvey's activities in 1988, when he was one of twenty-six men, including two Canadians, deported from the Philippines for prostituting children. Harvey was a businessman in his fifties, college educated, never married, twice convicted for sexually abusing children in the United States. He professed to have curbed his sexual appetites at home in order to "let loose" on holidays in Third World countries, where it is "safer" to exploit poverty-stricken children who will "do anything" for a few pesos. Favoured vacation destinations for pedophiles are Thailand and the Philippines, although in fact they aren't so safe: AIDS is spreading like wildfire, carried by girls and boys who help support their families by servicing pedophiles, mostly from Europe and North America.

Informed about Harvey's Philippines activities, the FBI obtained a search warrant on the grounds that he was likely to be in possession of child pornography, a criminal offence in the United States (though legal in Canada until August 1993). When Special Agent McCarthy executed the search warrant, he found a massive collection that included two thousand photographs of children, mostly colour shots of naked, prepubescent boys with erect penises, spread-eagled on beds, arms above their heads in identical poses, like trophies; hundreds of index cards covered with dense notations — coded records of a vast range of sexual activities; and meticulous diaries detailing holiday sex in the Philippines. Harvey "did" girls and boys, though he had a primary interest in uncircumcised boys, with a preference for eight- to eleven-year-olds, depending on their physical development. There were snapshots of Alex Hamilton and Mark Harvey in the Philippines; Alex, a white, middle-class Canadian teacher in his early forties, on a scooter; Mark with his arm around a nine-year-old Filipino boy who held a Frisbee on his lap; Mark and Alex kissing little boys on the lips; Mark dressed in a toga, being served food by a boy.

There were lists of boys, detailing their sexual characteristics and attitudes: "Arthur, 12, *supot* [uncircumcised], big titi [penis], no pubic hair, not much *leche* [semen], does not like to stay all night, a little commercial — i.e. 'finish — I go now.' Kissing OK, no O [anal intercourse]." There were pages and pages of similar data. Felix didn't go to school, was very amenable, "can be O'd but doesn't like it." Robert didn't dress well, but he "will do BJ [blow job]." Joel was very affectionate "but reluctant to kiss on the lips." Some boys became "too commercialized" and were noted to be "pests" or "hangers-on" or thieves. The comment next to Marlon's name was "money, money, money & no output." When the boys became too demanding and too corrupted — and of no further interest to the pedophiles — they would usually migrate into the "meat markets" in Manila, where many of them ended up dying of AIDS.

A box of Mark Harvey's index cards covers three out of eight years of holidays in the Philippines, and documents sexual contact with 259 children. At that rate, the FBI estimated Harvey had sex with more than seven hundred Filipino children over eight years. On the top left corner of each card, neatly printed, is the year, 1986, the boy's name, Carlo, his birthdate, 6/3/74 (thus he was twelve years old at the time), followed by a list of dated, coded activities that extended to the back of the card. The first item: "April 3, ST CUNN, NoF, P43." Translation: short time, cunnilingus, no fuck, paid forty-three pesos (about ten cents). Another entry: "O/N CUNN, Kwell, haircut, tried F nogo." Translation: overnight, cunnilingus, Kwell shampoo [tastes better for blow jobs], shaved pubic hair, tried to fuck him but couldn't. Another card, for Danny, age nine: "Massive skin lesions and crusty sores inclu on titi. Titi swollen. FOS, 2BJ." (Fuck on side, two blow jobs.) Another child, Danny L: "Short husky boy, midsize titi, large eggs, PH, cannot finish BJ, only JO." "Eggs" refers to testicles, "PH" means pubic hair, "JO" stands for jerk-off — Danny couldn't finish the blow job. And so on, ad nauseam.

Why this obsessive need to record? "They want to relive it afterward," FBI agent McCarthy says. The collection can be used to aid masturbation and to trade with other pedophiles. "This is a major addiction; this is the focus of their lives, and they have to have a constant supply." How did McCarthy feel, having to itemize Harvey's collection? "The thing that turned my stomach was when we searched his house and I opened the closet door adjacent to his bathroom; it was full of Kleenex boxes. He bought in bulk — for wiping his semen off the kids." Did Harvey — or any of the many pedophiles McCarthy had investigated — ever show any remorse? "No. None. Never. They believe they're right and we're wrong." And they're dedicated to keeping their collection, which is like having a supply of heroin around the house; the dehumanized objects of desire — little human beings — are added to the stash, to be used whenever the craving hits, though "fresh meat," or "live bait," to use their terminology, is preferable.

While the FBI agents gathered the evidence — eight big boxes of child pornography and data about children — Harvey was acquiescent; he thanked them politely for "being professional" and asked them to keep his collection in good condition. McCarthy understood Harvey's concern: "It was his life's work, and we were taking it away." Harvey had saved everything: newspaper clippings of little-league baseball tournaments where he picked up children; home-room assignments with children's names underlined. He'd done an enormous amount of research and was always hunting for more children. He'd tried to adopt; he preyed on poor families, single-parent families. Many pedophiles marry single mothers to get access to children.

When McCarthy went through Harvey's files, he spotted correspondence with a Toronto address; these letters contained more detailed descriptions of sexual activity with children. The FBI contacted the Royal Canadian Mounted Police, which passed the case to the Metropolitan Toronto Police, where Inspector Joe Wolfe, founding head of the Sexual Assault Squad, asked Detective Leaver to take a look at the material and advise him if it was worthwhile to proceed.

Wendy Leaver was forty years old, a twenty-year veteran of the force, a university graduate and a lecturer at the Canadian Police College in Ottawa, the Ontario Police College in Aylmer, and the University of Toronto. She has a long history dealing with human trauma. In 1981, she was seconded from the Metro Police to the Badgley Commission on child sexual abuse, headed by Robin Badgley, a Montreal-born sociologist with a doctorate from Yale University. Badgley taught at Yale and Columbia University and consulted for the World Health Organziation, the U.S. Public Health Service and various governments around the world before embarking on the four-year Canadian government study. Published in 1984, the *Report of the Committee on Sexual Offences against Children* is an exhaustive, two-volume, landmark work that documents ten thousand cases of child sexual abuse and demonstrates that at least one in four girls and one in seven boys experiences unwanted sexual acts at the hands of adults.

From 1981 to 1984, Leaver was on the frontlines of this massive project, responsible for the street research in the child prostitution section; she worked with thirty police forces across Canada and interviewed juvenile prostitutes who earned their living "in the front seat of a car with their heads between some guy's legs, doing blow jobs," as she puts it. When Leaver returned to regular police work, she expanded her expertise to sexual assault, child pornography and pedophilia. In 1989, the Metropolitan Toronto Police Sexual Assault Squad was formed; as one of the first of its kind in North America, its mandate was to investigate attacks by unknown offenders on adult victims, "but we became a resource for all kinds of sexual assault," Leaver says. "We don't turn cases away." What no one had understood, until the data were collected, was that the majority of sexual assault victims are children and teenagers. In the opinion of police experts, however, most assaults go unreported, and it is only many years later that some victims will come forward. "We constantly receive calls from adult victims of child sexual abuse," Leaver says. "Nobody can provide accurate numbers because we're just at the beginning of finding out how prevalent it is."

As for the profile of the "average" abuser, Leaver knows better than most investigators how rarely they fit stereotypes. Strictly speaking, pedophiles are sexually attracted to prepubescent children, but some also engage in sexual acts with teenagers or adults of both sexes. Some are also exhibitionists or peeping Toms who stalk and/or rape adults. There is a "pedophile continuum" that ranges from the mildest form of fantasizing about children to "the multiple offender whose life revolves around the sexual victimization of minors," wrote Daniel Campagna and Donald Poffenberger in *The Sexual Trafficking in Children*. Incest perpetrators may seduce and brutally exploit their own children while flaunting extramarital affairs, presenting themselves as promiscuous studs; in fact, most convicted child abusers are married men, and most have exploited many more children than their criminal record shows. At Kingston Penitentiary, it's not uncommon for offenders convicted of a few assaults to admit, during treatment, to having sexually abused hundreds of children. One of the reasons for the huge number of victims is the obsession with a specific age group — five to seven, for instance, or seven to nine; perpetrators continue to target new victims as the "old" ones mature.

The common denominator among abusers is an inability to develop intimate relationships with their peers. Often victimized in childhood, they are primarily male — fathers, uncles, cousins and brothers who target children within their "affinity groups" — but many more female abusers are being identified, just as many more male victims are coming forward. It is important not to stigmatize victims by assuming they will become abusers, since the majority do not. But some children — primarily males — grow up programmed to abuse, while others — primarily female — continue to be victimized as adults, though these roles can be reversed. People brought up to experience intimacy in the context of abuse will often struggle with sado-masochistic power dynamics in adult relationships. They may fantasize about being abused or raped, or insist on playing the dominant role, not understanding that their compulsive behaviour is linked to early exploitation.

The route to becoming a sex offender is a clearly marked highway along which thousands of people pass every year. It's not surprising that a minority of abused children, as they develop, begin to abuse others without any conscious awareness of crossing the line. Those who've been habituated to sexual activity from an early age can become fixated on sex; their social, emotional and cognitive development are profoundly altered by sexual activity they're not equipped to handle. Lacking personal boundaries, they may have no understanding of, or respect for, another individual's right to an inviolable self. Why would they? Anybody could do anything to them, and they can do anything to anybody; that's all they know.

Some of these boundaryless victims turn into threatening bullies. If they get into positions of power, they can wreak havoc in organizations and in people's lives, while blandly denying they've done anything wrong. Some structure their entire lives around access to children, while others "make passes" at whoever's vulnerable. They tend to swing between grandiosity and self-pity; they have no middle ground, in the emotional field. If they're not dominant, they often feel sad, lonely and isolated.

It is only with children that pedophiles feel they truly connect, but the connection is an illusion drawn from their need to gain control. Beneath a thin veneer of charm, they are ruthless; they may possess many psychopathic features. Defined by *The Random House Dictionary*, a psychopath is "an individual [who] manifests amoral and antisocial behaviour, lack of ability to love or establish meaningful personal relationships, extreme egocentricity, failure to learn from experience." Psychopaths are glib, superficial and manipulative; they lack an inner sense of social connectedness, and they have no empathy for others. They are so dangerous because they don't believe there's anything wrong with them.

Dr. Harvey Armstrong, an authority in the field of child sexual abuse, says that the thrill for abusers, in preying on children, is that there's no threat; the "partner" can't challenge them or hurt them because the child doesn't know what's going on. "In adult relationships, there's power-sharing and give and take. In child sexual abuse there's total dominance, and that's the kick, the opportunity to do anything they want to another human being. They get into their addictive behaviour, pull out the porn, get excited, start hunting victims, over and over." The block to treatment is their refusal to acknowledge their own victimization; in order to understand the pain they've caused children, they have to experience their own pain, and that they can't, or won't, do.

The pedophile's attitude is illuminated by "Men Loving Boys Loving Men," an article by Gerald Hannon, a Toronto journalist, published in *The Body Politic* in 1977, and included in *Flaunting It: A Decade of Gay Journalism from The Body Politic*, edited by Ed Jackson, a founder of the paper, and Stan Persky, a columnist for the *Globe and Mail*. The editors observe that the article, intended to stimulate "rational discussion of adult-child relationships," was greeted with "Anita Bryant–inspired hysteria." The anthology also contains a supposedly thoughtful "second look" at the article, describing the "oppression" faced by pedophiles, and their joyful coming together at the first North American Man Boy Love Association (NAMBLA) conference, in Boston in 1978.

"Boy-love is not child molestation," Hannon wrote in "Men Loving Boys Loving Men." "Boy-love is Simon." Simon was a thirty-three-year-old elementary schoolteacher who had sex with boys in his class, who volunteered with Big Brothers, had sex with his "little brothers," and was described in glowing terms. Simon had fun with his little "lovers." They went downtown, to the Arcade, to movies, for rides on their bikes: "We buy records and come home and listen, we bowl, we watch TV, we fuck.... I never felt any guilt about the fact that these were kids — I worried about being caught, that's all."

Hannon described Peter, forty-eight, a wealthy businessman who picked up boys in movie theatres. They tended to be disadvantaged, "not very articulate and not very well educated." Like Simon, Peter believed sex was just "another form of experience, like going to the movies...." Hannon asked Peter if he'd ever wished he weren't a boy-lover: "No, I'm crazy about lobster," said Peter, "and there never was a time when I wished I didn't like lobster. Why would one wish not to like something one likes?" Hannon concluded that Simon and Peter deserved "our praise, our admiration and our support."

"My view is still the same," Hannon said when I called him in 1992 to inquire if he'd had second thoughts, since the revelations about the sexual abuse of boys at Mount Cashel. Hannon firmly defended the article for which he'd been arrested fourteen years earlier for "use of the mails to transmit indecent, immoral or scurrilous material." (He and the paper were eventually acquitted.) He feels that pedophilic sex has been unfairly vilifed by a puritanical, hypocritical society. Had Hannon talked to the boys about the long-term impact of their sexual involvement with the men in his article? No, he had not. "Men Loving Boys Loving Men," he admitted, was written strictly from the pedophiles' perspective. I suggested there was another side to the story; Hannon did not agree.

He subsequently wrote a two-page letter to me, received on February 18, 1993, prompted by my call to Dayne Ogilvie at *Xtra* (the successor to *The Body Politic*) to confirm that *Xtra* accepts advertising from NAMBLA. (It does.) Hannon's arguments are reminiscent of the insights offered by Phyllis Mitchell, the mother-in-law of John Gallienne, with her "Greeks and Romans did it so what's so wrong with sex with children?" Pedophilia is "a fact of life," Hannon wrote.

(A spurious point: public beheadings and widow-burnings are or have been "facts of life" at various times.) It is "a sociosexual relationship between two people. I can't see how the age difference *automatically* makes the relationship reprehensible." (Adults *automatically* have power over children.) He concluded: "I can't recall whether you mentioned what your book is about, but let's not have another book on that most tiresome of creatures, the victim. Victims are never interesting — though their tormentors sometimes are. Let's not have a book that equates pedophilia with victimization...."

The majority of gay and lesbian activists are unequivocal in their condemnation of pedophilia. NAMBLA has been barred from most Gay Pride Day marches in North America. "Men Loving Boys Loving Men" outraged Toronto's mainstream homosexual community. "That article made me gag," says Myra Lefkowitz, a five-year veteran of the Metropolitan Toronto Special Committee on Child Abuse and an expert on victimization and the criminal justice system. She characterizes Hannon's article as "garbage, full of the rationalizations that pedophiles use to defend their violations of children."

Christopher Kendall, a lawyer and gay activist, agrees. "Clayton Ruby [the *Body Politic*'s defence lawyer], argued 'Men Loving Boys Loving Men' as a freedom-of-expression issue," he says, "but it has nothing to do with freedom of expression; it's just an extension of harm, harming those who can't fight back." For Kendall, the heart of the matter is that children do not have freedom of speech. "This is a debate in which children are silenced."

Pedophilia, he notes, is not about homosexuality. "Most pedophiles are heterosexual; most victims are female. But the fringe group that espouses man-boy love destroys the credibility of the gay rights movement. Pedophiles like to portray themselves as martyrs silenced in a censorship battle by puritanical people who won't allow them their democratic rights, but the reality is that NAMBLA advocates the abuse of power, masquerading as a legitimate lifestyle choice."

Like John Gallienne, Alex Hamilton had worked hard to gain a position of trust and authority over children. He graduated from the University of Toronto in 1968 with a degree in physical and health education; he has a Master's degree in school counselling from the

University of Ottawa; he taught gymnastics; coached boys' sports teams; taught English as a second language; and has a Master of Divinity from the Ontario Theological Seminary.

His daily life, as revealed in his correspondence with Mark Harvey, adhered to a simple routine. He'd come home from the Brampton high school where he taught, and go out on his rounds, strolling over to neighbourhood parks and schools, cruising for children. He targeted Asian immigrant children who couldn't speak English very well; they were the most vulnerable prey. Alex wrote to Mark about moving into a Filipino neighbourhood in Toronto's west end. He had a lot of luck hanging around a Filipino community centre, playing the role of a kindly uncle available to tutor children. His *modus operandi* was to proceed slowly, winning the trust of boys aged eight, nine or ten. He would take them out for hamburgers, meet their parents, infiltrate their families. The pattern, typical of pedophiles, amounts to "a deliberate campaign," Detective Leaver says, "painstakingly conceived and executed."

But after a time, the Filipino boys began to avoid him and Alex redirected his attention to recently arrived Vietnamese children. Traumatized by war and refugee camps, they were having the usual difficulties adapting to a foreign language and a strange culture; their parents worked long hours, often at two jobs, in order to establish themselves in their new country, and the boys were lonely. Alex also had a special advantage, as a teacher: in Vietnamese culture, teachers are revered.

"The Vietnamese kids have picked up where the Filipinos left off," Alex wrote happily to Mark. Alex wondered how he could have overlooked such an easy-to-score supply. Without much effort, he had Vietnamese children flocking to him. He hung around Queen Victoria elementary school in Parkdale, in Toronto's west end, where he met Tan.* Born in Vietnam, Tan was eight years old when his family came to Canada in 1982; they'd been here only two years when Tan met Hamilton. As Tan would later explain, "I was new to Canadian culture and ignorant about what goes on. I thought all Canadian teachers acted like that."

Alex played tag in the schoolyard with boys. He offered to help them with their homework, drove them home, exchanged phone numbers. His strategy was to make the boys emotionally dependent before initiating them into sex. With parental approval, they came to his house after school and sometimes slept over; he took them bowling, to the zoo and on camping trips. Tan quickly became a favourite; he was a naive, innocent, trusting child — characteristics appropriate for his age — and he needed adult attention. Alex Hamilton had all the time in the world for him, as long as Tan, a slight, physically immature boy, fit into Alex's age preference range. "Tan calls me every night on the telephone just to talk and often he will call two or three times in one evening," Alex wrote. "I don't know how much I told you about Tan but he is a real sweetheart." And in another letter: "I have limited myself recently to just Tan, no need for others. He is a perfect little delight. He is really dependent on me.... When I talk to him about my vacation [in the Philippines], to prepare him for my leaving, he cries. You're right. He is a ten."

There was a flurry of exchanges between Mark and Alex about their stable of Filipino boys. The two men paid the school fees of selected youngsters as a form of retainer, to keep the boys available for sexual services under certain strict conditions; one of the rules was that the boys remain uncircumcised. (In the Philippines, boys are traditionally not circumcised until puberty.) Pablito was one of their favourites: preparing for his holidays in the Philippines, Alex wrote to Mark that he wanted to hire Pablito as his houseboy "so that he would have to live with me," but Alex was concerned that Pablito's mother wouldn't allow it. "The stated reason why she would not allow him to stay with me last year was that she was worried he might become a drug addict — what? at my house?!!! that's really scraping the bottom of the barrel for an excuse.... also thanks for continuing to administer my financial matters with Pablito and Andy and Ben. When you think my account is running low and needs a refill just let me know.... I'm not surprised that Enrico has hit the big time in Manila. I can well imagine how he has turned into a real beauty and that combined with his lust for pesos makes him prime meat for the market in Ermita."

Mark wrote back from the Philippines about his efforts to "keep [Pablito] uncut." Pablito was ten, in grade four, "short, built like a boxer, hung like a horse," he noted. But Pablito's mother didn't co-operate, and Mark sent her a stern letter stating that he and Alex would no longer pay for the boy's schooling: "One of the conditions Alex made in leaving money with me for Pablito's school expenses and other needs was that he stay *supot* [uncircumcised]," Mark wrote to Pablito's mother. "I'm sorry to say that when they cut the *tuli* [foreskin], they also cut Alex's financial help."

Back in Toronto, Alex lost interest in Tan and was attracted to a new eight-year-old named Van,* but a pedophile pal seduced Van from under Alex's nose. Tan, meanwhile, was jealous. He'd bonded with Alex; he didn't understand he'd grown past Alex's age preference range. For Alex, the thrill was gone, and Tan was nothing but a pest. Alex's letters to Mark dripped with disdain for the boy, who persisted in hanging around.

Alex cheered up when school was out for the summer; he flew to Manila and travelled to Pagsanjan, where he stayed at "the Lodge" and dutifully wrote to Mark, back in Erie, about the dozens of boys he'd had sex with in just a week. "People such as us must share our good fortune and not be possessive," Alex moralized, as he took advantage of boys passed along by Mark. He visited their schools, took them to movies, referred to them as "livestock" and traded them with other pedophiles at the hotel. Sometimes the children would try to "get away with" just letting him hold them but he was firm on this point: "no fuck, no pesetas." And so it went, a litany of fucks and pesetas and school fees and appointments, dozens and dozens of boys moving on an assembly line through his life.

There was, however, a looming problem in Southeast Asian tourist regions: governments were attempting to restrict the child sex trade. Alex was informed by hotel staff that boys would be required to show letters of permission from their parents before they could visit a tourist's room. Alex raised a storm of protest and made arrangements to move to another hotel, where "there would be no problem with admitting my guests," but his hotel relented. However, holiday snapshots showed a mounting campaign by townspeople to run "foreign pedophiles" out of town. On a stone wall, SCUM PEDOPHILES SCUM was painted in angry red letters. A sign near a cathedral in Pagsanjan read:

> Pedophiles are known carriers of the highly contagious and incurable disease called AIDS and the equally dreaded disease called HERPES. SAVE YOUR CHILDREN FROM

THESE DISEASES!!!!!! SAVE PAGSANJAN FROM SHAME!!!! DRIVE THE PEDOPHILES OUT OF OUR TOWN.

Detective Leaver located Alex Hamilton's criminal record: born in Ireland, he had three previous convictions in Canada, the first in 1965, at the age of nineteen, when he was convicted of indecent assault on a six-year-old boy. His punishment was a suspended sentence and one year of parole. In 1975, at the age of twenty-nine, he was convicted of indecent assault on an eight-year-old boy; he received a suspended sentence and two years' parole. In 1986, another indecent assault conviction, this time involving a seven-year-old boy, brought him a two-month jail term (of which he probably served thirty days) and three years' probation. (Since school boards do not have access to criminal records or the Child Abuse Register, Hamilton was easily able to lie on teaching applications. To the question, "Do you have a criminal record?" he simply answered no.)

From examining the letters, Leaver figured there were at least fifty possible victims to be interviewed in the Toronto area, but she had no idea who they were or where they lived, nor did she have the financial or human resources to send out police officers accompanied by interpreters to track down fifty Asian boys identified only by first names. Yet without victims willing to make a statement, she had no case. At that time, possession of child pornography was not against the law; if it had been, she would have had grounds to get a search warrant to go into his house and find the records he was likely to have, from which she could have extracted the names and phone numbers of his victims.

Pedophiles such as Hamilton and Harvey are often linked in informal networks via computers, and share their collections of home-made pornography in the form of videos, photographs and letters. A favourite meeting ground is NAMBLA, which publishes a bulletin that runs advertisements offering sex with children on routes throughout North America. NAMBLA also holds conventions, which Hamilton and Harvey attended, where pedophiles often trade pornography.

"Child porn is an actual record of child sexual abuse," says Detective Staff Sergeant Bob Matthews, who presides over the joint forces Pornography/Hate Literature Section of the Anti-Rackets

Branch, Ontario Provincial Police and Metro Toronto Police. Formed in 1975, Matthews' team has six full-time officers; there is only one comparable unit in North America, in the Los Angeles Police Department. Matthews' presentation on child pornography to the House of Commons justice committee in 1993 was the turning point in transforming an abstract debate about censorship into a gut-wrenching session about the human rights of children. Civil libertarians, who have controlled the political ground in this debate for decades, defend the right of pornographers to express themselves, framing the issue as a freedom-of-speech matter. But not everyone has an equal ability to speak. As American law professor Catherine MacKinnon wrote, "The speech of the powerful impresses its view upon the world, concealing the truth of powerlessness under a despairing acquiescence that provides the appearance of consent and makes protest inaudible as well as rare."

Matthews showed members of Parliament samples of typical child pornography, such as a magazine for "boy lovers" featuring a photo spread titled "Billy 5 fucked in his ass," with pictures of a man shoving his erect penis into the anus of a five-year-old boy; the boy's face bore the distorted stare of a torture victim. There were pictures of little children in dog collars being urinated, defecated or ejaculated on; the children's faces were blank, eyes dead. A magazine cutline: "Young meat made the way you like it." In the NAMBLA bulletin, there were ads for child sex, bestiality, sado-masochistic and other abusive rituals. (Sexually abused children are often exposed to pornography and forced to re-create its imagery. Sherry,* a runaway who ended up in Grandview, an Ontario training school in which male staff members have been charged with sexually abusing female inmates, was "trained" by her father to mimic porn movies: as a six-year-old, on her mother's night out at church, Sherry would be made to go down to the basement, where her father and his friends got drunk and watched pornographic films; the little girl was required to sexually service the men by acting out the celluloid fantasies.)

Matthews' squad had seized thousands of videocassettes of home-made child pornography. One of the most prolific videographers, now in jail, operated much like Alex Hamilton, hanging around schoolyards and playgrounds. One of his videos began with children running around a sun-dappled Toronto park, then zoomed in on a sturdy little boy, perhaps six years old, in a striped T-shirt and blue shorts. The images were accompanied by a soundtrack of happy children's music, supplied by the video artist. The location shifted and the same little boy marched through a forest; some time later, he looked up at the camera, face scrunched unhappily, and said, "How can we go fishing if you don't have no fishing rod?" He seemed to sense he was in danger.

"That's okay, don't worry, we'll go swimming," said the videographer, voice smooth, well educated, reassuring. "Take off your clothes." The boy was reluctant; the man insisted, his voice becoming urgent. As the boy pulled his underpants down the man hissed: "Hold it there." He zoomed in on the boy's penis. "Don't move. Rub your dick a couple of times." The little boy was frozen, unable to respond. "Do what I tell you," commanded the invisible man, voice harsh; the camera remained in close-up on the boy's penis. "Rub your dick, rub it, it's okay, *I said rub it.*" The boy finally did as he was told, like a puppet. This was it, the dehumanization caused by violation — a six-year-old reduced to a traumatized cipher in a matter of minutes. Catapulted from being a child with some sense of autonomy into a powerless creature, he was now trapped in the trauma bond — a survival response to overpowering violation. If he failed to maintain his connection to the abuser, he could be abandoned, lost in the woods. An essential human instinct in the boy had been shattered. "Human beings strive to stay in control," wrote Dr. Lenore Terr in *Too Scared to Cry: Psychic Trauma in Childhood.* Young children, especially, are "mortified by loss of autonomy and personal control."

The videographer's voice was insistent: "Do you want me to come and suck it?" The little boy wrinkled his forehead and shook his head, no. "It doesn't matter," he said, eyes darting for a way out. There was no way out. The videographer positioned his camera on a tripod and walked into the frame; he was a fair-haired man in his late twenties. He sat down beside the little boy and started rubbing the boy's penis. It was an astounding moment: the man so large next to the small child, and so obsessed with the child's tiny penis, the child so utterly paralysed.

The tape continued. Much later, another scene with the same man: the front door opened and a dark-haired boy in a baseball cap bounded in. The boy was a teenage cynic, maybe thirteen, accustomed to the routine. "The purpose of this game," he said, "is to jerk off and spurt the camera with sperm." Cut to the boy naked on the bed with the man. After a round of oral sex, the man prompted the boy to talk about when he first came to visit, five or six years earlier, and how the boy learned, in his words, that "it was good for kids to know how to fuck and it was stupid people that had hang-ups about kids fucking." Then the man asked the boy a question: "The last time I bumfucked you, you said you were afraid you were going to get pregnant. You didn't really mean it, did you?" The man was amused. The boy looked worried. "It can happen," he said, bravado slipping. "It happened to some kid in South America." He dissolved into a frightened child. "I've heard about it happening," he insisted, looking as if he was going to cry. The man laughed and laughed.

Another tape, from another pedophile's home-made collection, showed a little girl about six years old with pale skin and dark, straight hair cut in bangs across her forehead. She was placed on a man's lap. She was wearing a T-shirt, but was naked from the waist down. The camera zoomed in between her legs. A man's fingers rubbed the area around her clitoris, in a frenzy of rubbing; the man pushed his fingers into her vagina, then his penis. The child shifted and the video camera strayed idly past her face. There was that awful expression again, the dead-eyed face of a child in trauma. An erect penis moved into the image from the right, then one from the left, and the little girl's head was rotated, right to left, as each penis was shoved into her mouth. There were three men assaulting her.

"This stuff is addictive to its users," Matthews says, "and it goes on day and night. In any community you want to name, there's people abusing kids like this and other people looking away." The little girl was lifted up, legs high, while one of the men penetrated her anus with his penis. Matthews pointed out that she was bleeding. The scene went on and on; it was unbearable to watch.

To get a search warrant for Alex Hamilton's house, to find information about his victims, Detective Leaver needed to show reasonable, probable grounds that an offence had been committed against children, which meant Hamilton would have to be followed. From a discussion with her boss, Staff Inspector Wolfe, the decision was made to put a surveillance team on Hamilton. Leaver then drove out to take a look at Hamilton's house, a middle-class home close to the Vietnamese/Filipino community. He'd rented his basement apartment to an Asian family with two little boys — another reason for concern.

Alex Hamilton was placed under surveillance for three days; that was all it took. He was observed leaving the high school where he taught, going to an elementary school playground and into a nearby park where he played with children. He focused on one boy, with whom he engaged in animated conversation, touching him, holding the boy's face in his hands. Leaver had to make a quick decision: with the mountain of information she had about the potential danger Hamilton posed to children between the ages of six and twelve, she was concerned about passively watching while he targeted yet another child. So the squad applied for, and received, a search warrant on the grounds of "conspiracy to commit sexual assault," backed by the evidence contained in Hamilton's correspondence with Mark Harvey.

On June 17, 1992, at 5:30 a.m., an undercover officer settled into an observation post across the street from Hamilton's house. At 8:00 a.m. Hamilton came out, hopped on his motorcycle and rode to the Brampton high school where he was teaching. Leaver and another police officer arrived at the school. Hamilton was called to the principal's office and Leaver showed him the search warrant; he asked what it was for and she said: "You are under arrest for conspiracy to commit sexual assault on children." (Hamilton was immediately suspended from teaching with pay.) She gave him a copy of the warrant and asked him to accompany her back to his house, where the police took photographs before and after their search so they couldn't be accused of damaging his property. They went through his belongings and found lists of addresses and phone numbers of children, and hundreds of computer disks.

Within a month, through intensive outreach into the Asian community, Leaver had interviewed thirty-five Vietnamese, Filipino and Vietnamese-Chinese boys. The work was time-consuming and costly. Accompanied by interpreters, she arranged to meet some parents in Buddhist temples: "It's the best place," advised a Vietnamese social worker. "They can't lie in a Buddhist temple." Leaver visited other parents at home, in the evenings, when they had finished work. The interviews were strained: some of the parents didn't speak English and they were suspicious of strangers. Like most people, the Vietnamese do not talk openly about sex. In traditional Vietnamese culture, children are not supposed to know anything about sex until they marry — a prohibition that makes them vulnerable to sexual abuse.

Detective Leaver arranged to interview Tan's parents. Her interpreter was Nguyen Van, a counsellor in victim services at Metro Police headquarters. Nguyen had had the typical Vietnamese refugee experience: escaping Vietnam in a raft that sank at sea, being rescued and dumped in a refugee camp. A former law student in Saigon, she prepared for the interview with Hamilton by reviewing his correspondence with Mark Harvey. "I read the file and I wanted to vomit," she says. "You have to understand, in Vietnam, the sexual abuse of children is the worst crime. In Vietnam, a child cannot say no to a teacher."

At 8:45 p.m. on a cool summer evening, Detective Leaver and Nguyen Van arrived at Tan's apartment in Toronto's Parkdale district, a low-rent neighbourhood overrun by drug dealers and prostitutes. Tan's parents were courteous and reserved; the mother worked in a factory, the father ran a couple of pizza outlets. Leaver tried to explain, with Nguyen translating, what Hamilton had done to many, many children. The parents, eyes downcast, said they had made Hamilton the godfather of Tan because "Mr. Hamilton is a teacher." Every time Nguyen mentioned the word "sex," the parents' eyes seemed to turn inward. Leaver tried to explain what Hamilton had done to their son, and that Tan might need their support in going to court; but when Tan finally testified, many months later, he came alone. Leaver found out that it was almost impossible to crack "the code of honour and silence," as the Vietnamese refer to their refusal to shame their community, as they see it, by revealing disgraceful secrets.

The following week, Leaver talked to Toronto-area teachers and school administrators about setting up pedophilia-prevention classes for children of immigrant families, particularly Asians. "We can't attack the problem case by case," Leaver says. "There are too many pedophiles, too many victims. We've got to reach the children directly." She spent many evenings with Chinese and Vietnamese parents' groups, speaking about pedophilia. They greeted her information with shocked disbelief. She told them they weren't much different from other Canadian parents, who also had great difficulty discussing these issues with their children; Canadian children in all communities can be trapped by pedophiles, she explained. "There's only one way to stop this from happening," she said at every stop. "Educate the children."

While Leaver continued her work in the schools, her major responsibility was building the case against Hamilton. She eventually got signed statements from three boys, including Tan. Additional sexual assault charges were laid, based on their complaints. At the same time, she combed through the material removed from Hamilton's house, which included diaries, letters and cryptic codes (now part of the public record). With assistance from the FBI, she worked with other officers to break the codes, which involved the use of the Greek alphabet to detail specific sexual acts with children, in mind-numbing detail.

Leaver's task, in preparing the case, was twofold: to show what Hamilton had done to the three Vietnamese boys who were prepared to testify, and to paint the overall picture of his addiction. Constables Jim Moores and Terry Green of the analytical section of the Sexual Assault Squad helped create charts and graphs that organized Hamilton's activities into sequence, to enable the Crown prosecutor to focus on specific abuse pertaining to the three victims on whom charges were based. To present the pedophilic overview, Leaver had Hamilton's handwritten letters to Harvey typed and bound in a large three-ring binder that was presented to the Crown on Monday, August 17, 1992.

The pressure on investigating officers is formidable: prosecuting Crown attorneys are only as good as the evidence enables them to be, so the case against Hamilton would succeed or fail on Leaver's investigative work — and on the slim, scared shoulders of the boys. "I had to provide the evidence and build the whole picture or he'd get away with it and go back to teaching as if nothing happened," she says. Yet no matter how well she did her job, she had to face the real possibility that the case could collapse: the three victim witnesses might not show up, or even if they did, they could fall apart on the stand. Hamilton's defence lawyer might have an easy time of it, presenting his client as a good samaritan who volunteered to help newcomers to Canada, and was thanked for his efforts by "false allegations" drummed up by a "witchhunt mentality." Leaver had to show that, in her words, "this man is a committed pedophile who is a danger to children *all the time*. The object of the exercise, as in all sexual assault investigations, is to prepare such a strong case that the accused will see the writing on the wall and plead guilty, so the victims don't have to testify."

Shortly after Alex Hamilton was arrested and released on bail, he breached a bail condition that he was not to have contact with children. Living with his parents in Barrie, he drove to Toronto, accompanied by his mother, and visited his Queen Street West hunting grounds. He spotted Tong* (one of the three complainants) in a phone booth and, according to Tong, squeezed into the booth, said he was afraid to go to jail and insisted the boys had to change the stories they'd told the police. Tong also said Hamilton instructed him to phone him. (Some pedophiles masturbate while talking to children on the phone and keep voice recordings of children on their answering machines, as masturbatory aids.)

Tong was upset by Hamilton's demands and called Detective Leaver, who rearrested Hamilton for "obstruct justice" because he had approached an alleged victim and tried to interfere with the case. Leaver wanted him held in jail, but at the bail hearing she was asked by the justice of the peace: "Were these all Asian boys?" referring to Hamilton's victims. Leaver said they were, "and the J.P. just sort of shrugged." As if Asian kids didn't really count? Leaver can't say, but she was appalled at the ease with which the J.P. let Hamilton go. At the same bail hearing, a man arrested on drug-trafficking charges and rearrested for selling drugs while on parole was refused bail by the same J.P. In the eyes of the criminal justice system, Leaver notes, the abuse of drugs is worse than the abuse of children. The outcome of Hamilton's bail hearing was that his parole conditions were altered: instead of having to be accompanied everywhere by his mother, he was now leashed to his father — an odd arrangement, confining a forty-six-year-old pedophile to the care of the parents who'd raised him, without any questions about his upbringing.

Before the bail hearing, Leaver and two other officers visited Hamilton's parents in Barrie, an hour's drive north of Toronto: Leaver wanted to get a statement from Mrs. Hamilton about her stroll along Queen Street West with Alex. Leaver also had a search warrant for the senior Hamiltons' house. One of Alex's victims had described being taken to Barrie in winter, along with another boy, on the pretext of having to help shovel snow while Alex's parents were in Florida. On one of these trips, a boy alleged, Alex had brought out a stack of pornographic materials that were stashed in a box in the basement behind the furnace. Leaver wanted to find the box.

Seated with the senior Hamiltons in their spotless middle-class living room, accompanied by two male police officers, the search warrant secure in her briefcase, Leaver contemplated a strategic decision: across from her, an enraged Alex Hamilton senior was breathing hellfire and damnation at police officers in general and at Leaver in particular. A large, stocky man with a big square head, prominent jaw and bulldog glare, he was on the verge of exploding.

Leaver was thinking fast: "He was furious, he called us pigs, accused us of making a mess of his son's house, which we hadn't; we had the pictures to prove it. Anyway, I had to make a choice. Was I going to execute the search warrant and possibly get more evidence or have this man go nuts and maybe have a heart attack?" Leaver believed, at the very least, that Hamilton senior would attempt to obstruct them, if not assault them, if they tried to search the house; she was also worried about his health, given his fury around protecting his son. "I decided it wasn't worth the aggravation."

Leaver and the other two officers said their goodbyes and set off for the Barrie police station, where Alex junior was being held on the "obstruct justice" charge; Alex senior followed in his car. Leaver had second thoughts and asked the officers to drop her off so she could talk to Mrs. Hamilton, who was the only witness to the Queen Street West incident. Leaver needed a statement from her. Mrs. Hamilton was relatively friendly, in the absence of her husband, and chatted about her walk along Queen Street West with Alex. She recalled the scene vividly and remembered exactly what she and Alex had worn; her description of her outfit exactly matched Tong's evidence, an important corroboration if Alex junior should deny he'd spoken to the boy. Mrs. Hamilton also located the phone booth her son had entered, at the exact corner on Queen Street where Tong said it was. The only detail that had escaped her attention was the boy inside the phone booth. (Later, at the bail hearing, she admitted seeing Alex talking to an

Asian boy.) The two women moved into the kitchen, sat down at the kitchen table, and Mrs. Hamilton began to talk more personally: "I can't face my neighbours," she said, admitting her son had a problem and needed help — at which point the front door burst open and Hamilton senior "came flying in, screaming," Leaver says. "He was having a total fit." Halfway to the police station, he'd realized Leaver wasn't in the car with the other officers and had raced back to his house, desperate to stop her from talking to his wife.

"Calm down," Mrs. Hamilton said, "she's a nice woman," but he didn't hear.

"What the fuck are you doing?" he screamed at Leaver, hurtling toward her. "You're trying to destroy my son." Leaver was no sitting duck: she'd already gathered her gear and was backing around the table, away from him; she got herself into the front hall just as he whipped around the table after her. She was moving fast to the front door; he'd left it open. He bore down on her and gave her a hard-hitting push that propelled her outside. At that moment, Leaver's partners screeched to a halt in front of the house, having realized they'd lost Hamilton senior en route to the police station.

Disclosure of police evidence to Hamilton's lawyer, Peter Maloney, was set for Friday, August 21, 1992. Maloney got to see some of his client's trophy snapshots of little boys, reams of decoded child-sex data and diaries of trips to the Philippines. Through the fall and winter of 1992–93, Hamilton's case crawled through the criminal justice system. As the date for the preliminary hearing approached, Leaver became increasingly concerned that her three victim witnesses were experiencing such severe emotional distress that they wouldn't make it to court. She met privately with a Vietnamese community leader who promised to talk to Tan about the importance of testifying. But Tan, Tong and the other boy received no therapy and there was no victim-witness coordinator in the downtown Toronto court who could help prepare them for their ordeal. Leaver and the Crown attorneys who prosecuted the case did their best to support the boys, but it wasn't enough.

One week before Hamilton's preliminary, Leaver had to drop her third victim — "he can't speak, he's totally terrified" — and subpoena her second, Tong, who was planning not to show up; she would have been left with just Tan, and as every police officer knows, it's very difficult to get a conviction in child sexual abuse cases with only one victim. These are tough judgement calls: when victim witnesses try to back out, should they be forced to appear or allowed to disappear, and with them a case in which the state has already invested a great deal of time, effort and money? In this instance, the Vietnamese families' reaction to Hamilton's pedophilia — the shocked disbelief, the desire not to know — didn't help the victims. But if the case went to trial, Leaver intended to support her remaining two witnesses by reinterviewing boys she'd identified, who had, like the boys in the Gallienne case, been too afraid to make a statement.

On Monday morning, January 11, 1993, at Toronto's Old City Hall, Alex Hamilton and his parents waited outside a third-floor courtroom. His thinning hair combed across his balding head, Alex was a scrawny figure next to his burly, grey-haired father. Alex faced a total of thirteen charges, including two charges of sexual assault against Tan and Tong, two charges of "invitation to sexual touching," two of sexual interference and two of "counsel to commit sexual assault"; plus the charges of attempting to obstruct justice and failing to comply with bail conditions; plus a charge of conspiracy to commit sexual assault related to the information in his letters concerning sexual activities in the Philippines.

Out in the corridor, Detective Leaver had her arm around a Filipino teenager; it was Tan. As they passed by Hamilton and his parents, Tan trembled; his fear was palpable. "I know I'm doing the right thing," he told Leaver, "but it's really hard." FBI Special Agent John McCarthy paced the halls. He'd been brought in from Pennsylvania to testify about the origins of the case. Heidi Siu, a journalist from the *Overseas Chinese Newspaper*, sat on a wooden bench. "Chinese parents cannot permit children to speak about this scandal," she said; she understood the victims' dilemma. "This is a disgrace to the whole family."

A little man in an ill-fitting suit, Alex came to court as if to work, his head filled with facts and figures and an amazing recall of detail — how much he'd paid the boys on specific occasions, etc. — ammunition he would use to get his lawyer to challenge tiny inaccuracies of his victims' testimony. At the end of the day, after the two boys had testified and submitted to gruelling cross-examinations by the defence lawyer, they were devastated, unable to explain why they "let" Hamilton do it. Leaver was worried about them. "You start questioning yourself," she says. "Should you put kids through it? Is it worth it?"

The preliminary hearing dragged on past its allotted three days, and was rescheduled for February 17, the first available date when all parties could attend. On February 17, Leaver was involved in a rape and murder investigation, so Hamilton's preliminary was put over to March 25. On it went, through the summer of 1993, as prosecuting Crown attorneys Mary-Ellen Hurman and Chris McGoey endured months-long waits for legal clarification from Manila concerning Filipino laws against child sexual abuse — important information relating to the charge against Hamilton for "conspiracy to commit sexual assault."

By September 1993, Hamilton's lawyer, Peter Maloney, had indicated his client would be interested in pleading guilty; Maloney and the Crown entered into plea bargaining, a common procedure that can be initiated by the Crown or the defence. The courts are dependent on plea bargains, for better or worse, because of huge backlogs that clog the system. A guilty plea is considered a sign of remorse; the accused, having admitted his crime and spared his victims from testifying, therefore deserves reduced charges and/or a lighter sentence — that's the rationale. But a guilty plea offers the accused a strategic advantage: a judge or jury doesn't get to see victims reliving the abuse on the witness stand, and without a vivid sense of the damage done, they may be more lenient.

In early October, Hamilton pleaded guilty to two charges of sexual assault, two charges of "invitation to sexual touching," two charges of sexual interference, the attempt to obstruct justice and the failure to comply with bail conditions. The charge of conspiracy to commit sexual assault was dropped. At sentencing later that month, Peter Maloney, in submissions before Judge William Babe, said that Hamilton was "willing to undergo any assessment or treatment the Court orders, even though he and I both believe…that there is no treatment [for pedophilia] and that people who come before Courts offering treatment as a method for overcoming a certain basic built-in instinct are offering the Court an illusion in order to permit the Court to delude itself…."

Maloney acknowledged that Hamilton's "natural inclinations" led him "to do things that are contrary to the laws of the country...his diaries and his letters are a frank admission of his yearnings — his desire to be involved with young men...." Maloney, a well-known gay activist, did a major disservice to the gay rights movement: he blurred the line between pedophilia and homosexuality, fuelling anti-gay rhetoric that stereotypes homosexuals as pedophiles. As we've seen, Hamilton was not interested in "young men." His "age preference" was prepubescent boys, as documented in his letters, diaries and journals. "What you hear in the diaries," Maloney said, is Hamilton's "anguish" that "what he most desires is unattainable in this country...and therefore he wants to go where he won't be prosecuted for that activity which he enjoys...." As if exploiting poverty-striken children in Third World countries is acceptable.

Maloney argued that his client had suffered enough, having spent the past year under house arrest, his reputation ruined by media publicity and by the Barrie Police, who'd broadcast information that a convicted pedophile was living in the neighbourhood. In regard to Hamilton's crimes, Maloney's argument was dismissive; there was no abuse, he suggested, just "trivial conduct," playing with genitals. As for the law that children under fourteen cannot consent to sex, Maloney scoffed: "To say that a person under fourteen can't give consent is an absolute utter myth. It's simply a legal fiction."

Crown prosecutor Mary-Ellen Hurman noted that Maloney's attempt to present Hamilton's pedophilic lifestyle as normal was not acceptable; society, she said, does not accept the sexual abuse of children as normal.

On November 2, Judge Babe sentenced Hamilton to fifteen months in jail and to a lifetime prohibition order banning him from working or volunteering with children, and from hanging around playgrounds or schoolyards. These were the small victories: Hamilton went to jail (though he could be out within five months) and he lost his teaching certificate for having lied about his criminal record.

On the legislative front, a law was passed making the possession of child pornography a criminal offence. The targets of the reforms, developed under then Justice Minister Kim Campbell, were underground networks of pedophiles who share and circulate child pornography. As of August 1, 1993, it is illegal in Canada to possess, produce, sell or distribute pornographic films, magazines, videos or computer-generated images that involve or depict people under eighteen. The maximum penalty for simple possession is five years in prison, with a ten-year term for selling or distributing child porn. In the autumn of 1993, Detective Bob Matthews led the first police raid in Toronto under the new law and seized a massive collection that included two thousand home-made child porn videos. By January 1994, eight people allegedly involved in child porn production and distribution had been arrested.

But the frustrations in this area of criminal justice are manifold — particularly in terms of the wild discrepancies in sentencing. Ned Hanson, the founder of the Toronto Boys Choir and a friend of John Gallienne's, was convicted in the early 1990s of sexually abusing boys in the 1960s and received a suspended sentence. Douglas Kennedy, a school principal in Cobourg, Ontario, received two years less a day for sexually abusing a pre-teen boy from 1988 to 1991. (Kennedy was a friend of the victim's parents, and when the boy disclosed the abuse to his father, the father drove to Kennedy's home and beat him with a baseball bat, breaking Kennedy's legs. The father received a six-month jail sentence.)

On the other hand: in January 1994, James Cooper was sentenced by an Ontario judge to thirty years for sexually assaulting five former stepchildren and one of their friends between the ages of seven and fourteen. And Kurt Schmidt, a convicted pedophile who, like Alex Hamilton, had targeted Asian children, faces a dangerous offender application brought by the Crown prosecutor. If the application is approved, Schmidt could be held in prison for an indefinite period — which could be the rest of his life — on the grounds that his behaviour shows a long-term commitment to the sexual exploitation of children that is not likely to change. It was Schmidt's collection, which included a huge cache of hundreds of home-made child porn videos, that precipitated the Crown's action. The bulk of Alex Hamilton's collection was never found; the police suspect he was tipped off by Mark Harvey.

The criminal justice system is riddled with bias and inconsistencies. It tends to treat crimes against property more severely than crimes against persons. Sex crimes remain the one area of criminality in which the offence is often judged not by the behaviour of the perpetrator but by the response of the victim. Offenders who belong to social elites continue to receive lenient treatment from judges, who may disapprove of the way victims deal with being sexually assaulted: if the victim didn't disclose right away, or turned to drugs, or became promiscuous, or began lying or shoplifting — all common reactions to sexual abuse — the defence lawyer usually has an easy time of it.

But there are signs of change. Detective Leaver is optimistic that people are waking up to the strategems of perpetrators, and starting to listen to children. Still, investigating child sexual abuse can be the hardest beat for police; they bear the brunt of confronting a crime that is often treated as a minor offence in court. They see the collections, the videotapes of children being tortured, the damage done to victims who can't speak about what they've endured. It is the police, working on the frontlines, who confront the ruthless egotism of offenders and the societal denial that protects them. It is officers like Wendy Leaver who are listening to victims and carrying their experience into the broader world, into schools and universities, educating us all. To end these horrors, we need to know.

3

Diagnosing the Abuse:
Dr. Marcellina Mian

*Never jump to conclusions. Remain calm during a
disclosure. Our job as professionals is to absorb the
impact, like a guard-rail, to contain the damage and
reassure the children that they will be fine.*

— Dr. Marcellina Mian
Pediatrician and director of the
Suspected Child Abuse and Neglect (SCAN)
Program

DR. MARCELLINA MIAN walked up University Avenue from her office
at the Hospital for Sick Children, crossed College Street in the shad-
ow of the Ontario Legislature and, crunching autumn leaves in her
path, sped into the Medical Sciences building at the University of
Toronto. Slipping into a first-year class already under way, she leaned
against a concrete block wall, waiting to go up next. At the podium,
Detective Wendy Leaver was finishing a lecture to medical students;
in the back row sat Robin Badgley, the head of the Badgley
Commission on the sexual exploitation of children — a subject taught
to University of Toronto medical students by a multidisciplinary team
that includes Badgley, Leaver and Mian. The fledgling doctors in jeans
and T-shirts didn't know how fortunate they were in their teachers, and
how unusual such a class was in the history of medicine; they belong

to the first generation being formally educated to detect the signs and symptoms of child sexual abuse.

"The life goal of pedophiles is access to children," Leaver said. "Pedophiles believe children want to be sexually involved with adults and they've organized their lifestyle to provide them with access." The students stared at Leaver with uncomprehending eyes, as if they couldn't believe their ears. "There's the Pedophile Information Exchange. If they're going to California, they arrange to get children en route. But don't think they look like 'creepy perverts.' You will come in contact with pedophiles in your practice; they could be your most charming patients, the last people you'd ever suspect."

Leaver was followed by Dr. Mian. Physicians, she said, are like most people: they're very uncomfortable dealing with child sexual abuse. "They aren't trained to look for signs of abuse and they ignore the symptoms and behaviour patterns that signal abuse." In a June 1991 article in *The Canadian Journal of Diagnosis*, she'd listed specific indicators that by themselves don't prove a child has been abused, but do signal a need for attention: persistent sexualized behaviour with other children and with toys, excessive masturbation, age-inappropriate knowledge of sexual activity, pronounced seductive or promiscuous behaviour. Non-specific indicators include aggressive or overly compliant behaviour, pseudo-mature behaviour, poor peer relations, non-participation in school and social events, hyperactivity, nightmares, clingy or fearful behaviour, bedwetting, sleeping problems, eating disorders, depression and suicidal feelings; also substance abuse, self-destructive behaviour, running away from home; and fear of men.

Mian described a recent case in which a family doctor discovered that a child under the age of five was infected with gonorrhea, a sexually transmitted disease. The little girl's father also had gonorrhea, but the physician failed to consider the possibility that the father could have sexually abused his daughter. When Mian was called in for an assessment, she was told by an insistent physician that this was "a good family," and by an adamant wife that her husband was "a good man." The wife was certain she must have harboured the infection and passed it on to her daughter in the bath, and the physician appeared to believe her.

"What's going on?" Mian asked the class.

"The mother's trying to protect her child," said a female student.

Mian shook her head, no: "What the mother is doing is typical of incestuous families; she's protecting her marriage, not her child." Mian underlined the extreme level of denial in the physician and the mother, both of whom had rallied to the side of the abuser and failed to protect a small child who would likely be abused again. "The power of the mind to deny abuse is very great," she said. Yet even these first-year medical students knew that gonorrhea is not an airborne or water-borne infection; the child couldn't have been infected by sharing a bath with her mother.

Because doctors don't want to believe that people they know would sexually abuse a child, they may neglect a child who is at risk — and ignore their scientific training. "In the family of a child with gonorrhea, it's amazing how many times a father, uncle or brother asks for, and is given, an antibiotic for a sore throat without an examination," Mian said. "The physician hasn't bothered to culture the infection." It seems obvious: if a child has a sexually transmitted disease, and an adult family member requests an antibiotic supposedly to cure a minor ailment, the adult should also be tested for a sexually transmitted disease. But all too often, physicians don't ask the obvious questions, don't do the obvious tests — and so children are exposed to further harm, even though there is a legal requirement that medical professionals must report any suspicion of abuse. Physicians will also collude, in Mian's experience, with an infected husband and not reveal the gonorrhea to a wife who is also a patient. Physicians have an ethical responsiblity, she emphasized, to care for all their patients equally. (The law requires doctors to report cases of sexually transmitted diseases to public health officials, who notify all known contacts; in Mian's opinion, it's a reasonable short-cut, and the humane thing to do, to notify a spouse directly.)

She turned off the overhead lights and clicked on a slide projector. For a moment, in the darkened classroom, she spoke into the beam of light: the sexual assault of children is more common than diabetes or asthma or many of the problems family physicians deal with every day, yet most doctors receive no training in the examination of sexually abused children. Then the slides began, images flashed on the cement wall, enlarged colour photographs of the anuses and vaginas of abused

81

and normal children. It was a shock to see the vulnerability of human flesh so graphically displayed. One picture showed a child of about two years bleeding from her vagina; in another, Mian indicated anal tissue that had been torn by penetration and had healed, forming visibly thickened folds or clefts around the edges; she compared a normal fleshy hymen on a prepubertal girl to a girl whose vagina had been penetrated and the hymenal rim injured. "Children who have not been abused do not usually have their hymen gape open," she said. Little girls are born with a hymen; its absence indicates penetrating damage of some sort. However, not all sexually violated children show signs of abuse. SCAN and other centres pick up physical evidence of sexual abuse in 40 per cent of cases. In one study, eighteen offenders admitted to vaginal penetration, but seven of their victims (39 per cent) had normal physical examinations. In other words, penetration had occurred in 39 per cent of the cases in which the abuse was not detectable. A lack of medical evidence doesn't mean there was no abuse; and children who don't remember pain weren't necessarily unhurt. "They feel the pain at the time of the abuse, but they dissociate from it, split off from it, and watch what happens from somewhere up on the ceiling," Mian said.

Within the criminal justice, pediatric and child protection fields, Dr. Mian is a formidable presence, widely regarded as one of the foremost experts in the country; if adults are sometimes intimidated by her, children are not. "The minute you meet her, you know she can see," says one of her former patients. "She's a knight in shining armour; she gives you hope; she's not afraid of the truth." Born in Egypt to Italian parents, Marcellina Mian grew up, she says, "with a keen sense of fair play, which is what abused children don't get." She spent her teenage years in Montreal, earned her medical degree from McGill University in 1970 and embarked on her pediatric career in the United States; her mentor was Dr. William Rowley, whom she describes as "a wonderful child advocate." Dr. Rowley now practises medicine in an inner-city ghetto near Boston, working with economically disadvantaged families. An innovative physician, he established the child abuse teams at the New England Medical Center and at North Shore Children's Hospital in Salem, Massachusetts.

In the 1975 case that initiated her into the field of child abuse, Mian was part of a medical team at the North Shore Children's Hospital called to resuscitate a four-month-old infant in shock from a severe beating by his mother. "The mother was outside talking to the police while we were trying to bring the baby back to life," Mian said, "and the whole time I was thinking, *How could anybody do this to her child? She must be a monster.*" The baby died, and Mian was delegated to tell the mother, whom she assumed to be a truly evil person. Instead, Mian found a seventeen-year-old single parent who was devastated by her baby's death. Disowned by her family when she got pregnant, abandoned by her boyfriend, the teenage mother had dropped out of school and into a deep depression; that day, the baby had been crying and she had started pummelling him, shouting, "Don't cry." The more she hit the baby, the more he cried, until finally he was silent.

And so the young doctor learned about the two sides of abusive parents: the monstrous part that can hurt a child and the terribly vulnerable part that regrets the abuse, that's trapped in its own pain. Later, she would encounter another type of perpetrator: "There are evil people in this world who enjoy making children suffer. I know, now, that they exist, but I don't know what to say about them." Then there are non-offending parents who collude with abusers, and those who refuse to believe their children: "A mother will say, 'I don't believe it, it couldn't have happened; I know my child, my child would have told me.' Well, that's not the way it works."

Mian moved to Toronto in 1980 to become a staff pediatrician at the Hospital for Sick Children, one of the best-known institutions of its kind in the world; a year later she was appointed head of the sexual abuse team, and in 1984 she was named director of the SCAN Program, which now sees nearly a thousand children a year — maximum capacity — and is swamped with referrals from the Children's Aid Society, police, physicians and other agencies. SCAN assesses for physical abuse and neglect as well, but the majority of cases are determined to involve sexual abuse; 80 per cent of the victims SCAN identifies are female, though more males are coming forward. SCAN doesn't keep a waiting list — Mian doesn't want referral agencies to relax "because they've got their children on our list" — and is sometimes forced to turn away new referrals. "We've got to keep push-ing the pressure outward into the community for increased services," she says. "Child sexual abuse is still regarded as a rare phenomenon; what we've got is an epidemic on our hands." The good news is that more children are receiving earlier protection and better treatment, greatly enhancing their prospects for recovery. "It's clear that many abusive adults were abused as children," Mian says, "but I am more often amazed at how well people turn out in spite of the horrible suf-fering they've endured. I see the amazing resilience of children; it is quite incredible that they can still be so delightful despite the terrible experiences they've had."

The SCAN team consists of three physicians, three social workers, one nurse, one art therapist, a coordinator and two intake secretaries, with one team member on call twenty-four hours a day. The SCAN assessment process is carried out in two formats, "brief" and "full." Requests for a brief assessment usually come from a doctor or parent who has concerns that a child may have been abused; this assessment involves a physical examination by a SCAN physician followed imme-diately by an art therapy session, and is done to advise parents or pro-fessionals whether there are grounds to suspect or validate abuse, and whether to pursue further investigation. The full assessment is quite different: it's usually court-ordered, after the Children's Aid Society has carried out its own investigation. It takes about four months to complete, involving interviews and cross-checking with the child and all the major players in the child's life. If one key figure, such as a parent who may be the suspected perpetrator, refuses to participate, SCAN refuses the case — because the assessment may then be con-sidered biased; the lawyer of the accused might argue in court that the assessment wasn't valid because his client wasn't part of it, and another investigation could be ordered. Multiple assessments are traumatic and, in Mian's opinion, another form of societal abuse, particularly if clinically unnecessary.

More children, however, can be seen by SCAN in the brief assess-ment process. Having made a disclosure or aroused suspicion of abuse, they typically arrive at the hospital with a parent or social worker. Mian insists that everyone who comes in contact with the children and their families, from receptionists to physicians, be sensitive and supportive. "When we're in a vulnerable state, we want the people around us to get it right the first time." For victims and parents alike, the disclosure has the same import as the revelation of a life-threatening illness. "What children say about the abuse can bring down their entire world," Mian says. "They've probably maintained the secret for a long time, and likely have ambivalent feelings about the abuser, whom they may perceive as the only person who's given them attention or affection." Children don't understand that they've been pawns in a scenario that is all about an adult's needs for power, control and erotic gratification, but they do know it's a deadly secret; to tell it "is an enormous thing, earth-shattering, cataclysmic for everyone involved," Mian says.

The SCAN approach is designed to make the child's entry into the medical system a positive experience, guided by professional neutrality. In the seventies and eighties, when the first waves of disclosures emerged, children were rushed to hospital emergency rooms in squad cars with sirens blaring, and were terrified by a process in which adults either reacted hysterically or didn't believe them. "Now we know the first priority is to stay calm and not traumatize the child any further," Mian says. If children disclose within twenty-four hours of being abused, they should be taken to the hospital so forensic evidence (sperm, blood or other signs of abuse) can be collected before they are given a bath. If the disclosure comes more than twenty-four hours after an assault, there's no need to alarm them with an emergency trip to the hospital. If they disclose at bedtime, and they're safe for the night and feel settled, Mian advises letting them go to sleep and bringing them in the next morning.

Once at the hospital, children may encounter physicians who have no idea how to deal with sexual abuse — which is why Mian expends considerable energy educating her colleagues. They usually don't know how to ask the child about what's happened; the child may sense the doctor's discomfort, think there's something wrong and clam up, leading the doctor to believe that nothing much happened. Or physicians may use inappropriate language in a way that hurts the child: Mian described a recent scene in a hospital emergency room, with a medical resident examining a child whose father admitted having had intercourse with his daughter. "Did it hurt when Daddy made love to you?" asked the resident. Mian told him, later, that his terminology was inappropriate, and he acknowledged that he hadn't known what to say, and hadn't wanted to ask, "Did it hurt when Daddy raped you?" Mian recommended that he speak in clear, non-judgemental language: "Did it hurt when Daddy put his penis inside you?"

At the beginning of the brief assessment process, Mian conducts a physical examination that can last ten minutes or half an hour, depending on how the child feels. At SCAN, everything depends on how the child feels; team members are careful to treat children with respect. Being examined, having their genitals looked at, may make them feel embarrassed, ashamed, vulnerable. Mian doesn't say, "Here's the gown, take off your clothes, I'll be back." Instead, she begins the examination with them fully clothed, letting them take control of the experience. She gives them choices, asks if they want the curtain pulled, if they want to be examined on the table or on their mother's lap. She pays attention to body language. If she gets the impression the child doesn't want the mother in the room, she'll suggest the mother go and have a cup of coffee and come back in fifteen minutes.

Language is important. Professionals should avoid animal imagery; they should not tell a child to lie on the table in a frog-leg or doggie position. Abused children are sometimes called dogs or bitches and may have had dog collars tied around their necks. Some physicians ask children to hug them, in an effort to be friendly, but they should not ask for affection; children may have had to gratify adults without consent. "If a child wants to hug the doctor, okay," Mian says. Nor should doctors tell children how cute they are. "Don't say what lovely blond hair and blue eyes they have, or what a cute outfit they're wearing. Compliments may conjure up the flattery of the abuser. Do reinforce the strong, healthy child. If they jump up on the table, tell them what a good jumper they are. When the doctor listens to their heart, tell them what a strong heart they have. Children who've been abused are afraid of being torn and broken and disfigured; they may be bleeding. Reassure them that they're perfect human beings, normal and healthy like other children." In most cases, the medical exam won't prove or disprove anything, "which is why we have to be so careful in our assessments."

The criteria for evaluating whether abuse has occurred are complex; the most important components of the diagnostic process come from the child's behaviour, symptoms and account of what happened. The fundamental rules are simple: never jump to conclusions; let the child lead the process. Children who've been brought up in psychologically abusive homes, or exposed to sexual activity among other family members, or subjected to neglectful or alcoholic caregivers may be disturbed or may have inappropriate sexual knowledge but may not have been sexually abused. Some children come out of such chaotic environments that the precise nature of the problem may be difficult to discern — which is why the neutral approach is so important. It means careful listening to, and observation of, children without leading them in any predetermined direction. SCAN's brief assessment statistics bear out the team's caution: sexual abuse is confirmed in 25 per cent of cases, and not found in another 25 per cent, with further investigation and follow-up recommended for the remaining half.

SCAN team members constantly assess the validity of the child's disclosure, if there is one, examining the child's symptoms, the medical findings and family dynamics; they monitor behaviour following disclosure, assess motivation, cognitive development, memory and ability to distinguish truth from fantasy; and they analyse who stands to gain and who stands to lose. Disclosure, Mian underlines, is a gradual process — as was the abuse. Diagnosis takes time. Generally speaking, distressed children who've disclosed become more upset initially but gradually calm down and feel relieved of the burden of the secret, especially if they've been well received.

Abused individuals of any age usually tell their story through "incremental disclosure," revealing snippets to various people, a friend, a teacher, a babysitter — someone outside the perpetrator's circle. This is a process of sending up "trial balloons," saying as much as they think their listener can hear, gauging the response, seeing how much trouble they get into, letting out as much as they can without feeling too much pain. "The mildest stuff usually comes first," Mian says, "the worst comes later, when they feel safe enough to tell."

It is common for children to disclose after seeing a TV show or performance about sexual abuse; schools that have instituted plays about "good touch" and "secret touch" have become a major receiving ground for allegations. A play can trigger disclosure by making it clear the victim is not responsible for the abuse. Critics of such projects are concerned that children may be susceptible to a "me too" reaction, inventing false allegations to gain attention, but Mian has never known a young child to make up tales about sexual abuse as an attention-getting device; children may tell lies to get themselves out of trouble, but they do not lie to get into trouble. In fact, it's common for children to retract their allegations in the face of angry or upset parents. The response of non-offending adults is crucial to the child's ability to say what happened. If they are perceived by the child to be closely allied to the abuser, the child may be afraid to tell. If a parent erupts, "Oh my God, this is the most terrible thing I've ever heard," or "Joe's my best friend — he would never have done such an awful thing," the child clams up. "It's important," Mian says, "that adults remain calm during a disclosure and reassure the child that she or he will be all right."

The SCAN team uses, as one of its evaluation criteria, the concept of the "Accommodation Syndrome," as defined by Dr. Roland Summit, a psychiatrist and head physician at a busy UCLA medical centre in the suburbs of Los Angeles. Summit has written extensively on what he terms "the hidden world of child sexual abuse," which is so prevalent in his view, as to be a "normative experience," and so "developmentally toxic" that it forces untold legions of children to dissociate from reality, using complex mental processes that are only just beginning to be understood. "We are all players in a strange charade in which everyone assumes the role of the untouched," he observes — while every extended family, every church group, every workplace is inhabited by the "walking wounded," silenced and isolated in a culture dedicated to denial.

The Accommodation Syndrome is Summit's analysis of how children usually cope with, and disclose, sexual abuse. "It's an enigma to us, a mystery, why children don't tell right away about being abused," Mian says. But if your house is robbed, you tend not to talk about it, because you don't want to be told, "You mean you didn't put bars on the windows? You mean you didn't install an alarm system? You mean you didn't...?" It's human nature. If something bad happens, we tend to blame ourselves — or feel we will be blamed. Nobody likes to admit to being betrayed. Nobody likes to appear a fool.

The first phase of the Accommodation Syndrome is secrecy: children understand they're not supposed to tell, and they don't. "The terrifying reality of child sexual abuse," in Dr. Summit's words, is that "it happens only when the child is alone with the offending adult.... Contrary to the general expectation that the victim would normally seek help, the majority of victims in retrospective surveys had never told anyone during their childhood."

The second phase is helplessness: what can children do when they find themselves being sexually abused by an adult who is bigger, stronger and more powerful than they are, who is determined to do it, regardless of how they feel? The child can do nothing but submit. The prevailing reality for most victims, Summit writes, is "an unprece-dented, relentlessly progressive intrusion of sexual acts by an over-powering adult in a one-sided victim-perpetrator relationship." Which makes it very difficult, he adds, to see children being attacked in court by defence lawyers and discredited by judges because they "let it hap-pen" and didn't protest the abuse at the time it occurred.

The third phase, entrapment and accommodation, describes the trauma bond, which is one way human beings — from hostages to pris-oners of war to incest victims — cope with abuse. "Inside the pysche, it's easier to believe that the people in charge of you are good, not malevolent," Mian says. Instead of seeing the abuser as bad, children come to think *they're* bad, accommodating the abuse in such a way as to believe they have some control over it. It's the victim mentality: *I'm bad, I'm wrong; if I do things right, if I look right, talk right, walk right, it won't happen.* Summit writes: "The desperate assumption of responsibility [by the child] and the inevitable failure to earn relief set the foundation for self-hate.... In the classic role reversal of child abuse, the child is given the power to destroy the family and the responsibility to keep it together.... Maintaining a lie to keep the secret [becomes] the ultimate virtue, while telling the truth would be the greatest sin."

In the fourth stage, partial/fragmented/delayed disclosure, chil-dren reveal a tiny piece of information, usually telling the least bad thing that's happened; it may be disguised, as in "I had a friend who..." or "I had a dream that..." or "I heard about someone who..." If the adult listener says, "Don't be disgusting" or "We don't talk about things like that" or "Oh my God, he touched you where?" the child is not going to say that Daddy had intercourse with her. And so children are isolated by the abuse, wanting to tell, sending out signals and clues that disappear in a sea of denial. Most adults, Summit writes, "cannot believe that a normal, truthful child would tolerate incest without immediately reporting or that an apparently normal father could be capable of repeated, unchallenged sexual molestation of his own daughter. The child of any age faces an unbelieving audience."

In the fifth phase, recantation/retraction, children typically say they've lied, made it up or dreamed it. Recanting is usually a sign of the child's ambivalence toward the abuser, and fear of destroying the family. In Summit's experience, recantation is triggered by the upheaval caused by disclosure. In the turbulent aftermath, the abuser — parent, teacher, choirmaster — abandons the child who is often catapulted from the role of favourite to outcast, and labelled a liar; the family is fragmented, the child blamed, and all the care and concern are lavished on the perpetrator. Studies show that the majority of children who recant later reaffirm their allegations, once they've recovered from the shock of disclosure and abandonment, if they receive support.

Dealing with children who may have endured horrendous abuse, the professional must not overreact, Mian says, but listen to what they have to say without telling them how to feel. Don't dismiss their fears, don't say, "Don't be silly." Don't say, "It wasn't that bad — he just touched your breasts." The touching may be as upsetting to one child as intercourse to another. If they're scared, let them say so; fear is defined by the child, joy is defined by the child, horror, love — the professional's job is to listen and reframe, if necessary. A teenage incest survivor who'd been sexually abused since infancy told Mian that she'd had "the best orgasms" with her father, and missed them. If the professional reacts with disgust — "Oh my God, you must be sick, orgasms with your father" — the girl is hurt further. The fact is that children habituated to sexual activity from an early age may become addicted to sex; it's not their fault. Mian told the girl that it was "understandable" she missed sex even though she didn't want it with her father, "and we can work on that." It's a particularly disturbing element in some cases — the mix of physical pleasure with psychic pain, the child's feelings of love entwined with hate — and professionals need to be clear within themselves that the child is not to blame.

Yet children are often consumed with shame and guilt for "letting" the abuse happen. Mian will reframe the situation by emphasizing how young and powerless they were at the time. Absolving them of guilt helps to unravel the trauma bond; if they continue to see their perpetrator as blameless and themselves as bad, they remain stuck in an abusive dynamic, hating themselves. Physicians need to be aware of their power in helping children deal with these issues: doctors are perceived as authority figures, and they can play an important role in assuring children that they didn't do anything wrong.

After being examined by Dr. Mian, the child is taken along the hall to the office-playroom of Jacquelyn Jay, the SCAN team's art therapist. The sequence is important: the medical examination may trigger feelings and memories that can be revealed in artistic form. Abused children are usually guarded in their speech, but they are more expressive in their art. Jay offers them an assortment of tools and toys to play with: crayons, paints, clay, sandbox, doll house, anatomically correct dolls. (The parents — if they've accompanied the child to the hospital — will be interviewed separately by SCAN social workers.)

Jay's job, as she sees it, is to create an environment where children feel they can take control and do or say whatever they want without fear of negative repercussions. The children she sees come in three streams: for a one-hour session in the brief assessment process, for repeated sessions in the full assessment and for ongoing treatment for up to two years.

Is it really possible for children, in a one-hour session with an art therapist, to reveal deep dark secrets they've never told anyone before? "Yes, absolutely," says Jay. If they are comfortable and can concentrate on what they're drawing or painting, and if they've been triggered by the physical examination, they're likely to display, in their art, anxieties and preoccupations they could never share in direct conversation with an adult.

The approach is gentle. Jay aims for pleasant neutrality: "When I see children, even if they've given a complete disclosure, I work on the basis that I don't know what's happened to them." That's important, she says, because sometimes parents may have projected concerns about sexual abuse onto a child who is indeed anxious — but hasn't been sexually abused.

She begins by confirming that Dr. Mian has checked the child's "outside parts." Jay reviews the names of all the body parts, to make sure she knows the words the children use; she assures them they're fine and explains that she's the person who'll help with their "inside feelings." She ascertains that they understand colours and feelings, and then asks if they'd like to draw, paint or make clay figures, whatever they want. "We *never* suggest things and we are scrupulous about providing an open atmosphere in which children can express their concerns without interference. It's such a serious charge, child sexual abuse; God forbid you should wreck someone's life without just cause."

In Jay's experience, it is extremely unusual, although not unknown, for children to fabricate false charges. There have been custody disputes where one parent has pressured a child to say that the other parent "touched my private parts." But such allegations fall apart under the scrutiny of trained professionals. There are other cases on record where the courts didn't believe the child's allegations and awarded custody to the father, who, it turned out, continued to sexually abuse the child for many years. There are also cases of sincere adults who've occasionally misinterpreted children's statements or behaviour. Jay has seen children who were overstimulated and seemed to have precocious sexual knowledge. "They were exposed to pornography at home, they'd witnessed parents or siblings engaged in sexual activity, they were deprived of affection, but as we discovered, they were not directly sexually abused."

Discerning the truth takes time, since children may not have the words to say what was done to them and certainly aren't bursting to blurt out the secret. "They will often give you a lot of cheery chat to hide their pain and make you like them," Jay says. Because many abused children have had to block off the secret part of their lives, they are unable to express themselves; craving adult approval, they often don't have opinions or preferences. Not allowed to have needs of their own, they survive by fulfilling the needs of others; they may feel empty at the core, and their artwork is likely to be pervaded by a sense of doom — especially if the abuse is predictable and the child is consumed with anticipatory dread.

Through art and creative play, however, these children can reveal themselves; art expands their vocabulary in an unselfconscious way, allowing them to express the inexpressible. "Once children reach the age of representation — around three or four or five, depending on the child — they are able to make art that they have strong personal concepts about," Jay says. Their process of communicating in this context is a little like Hansel and Gretel, lost in the woods, leaving a trail of crumbs behind them. The art therapist follows the trail of artistic clues and gently engages the child in conversation about the images — without, it must be underlined (as SCAN team members always emphasize), suggesting ideas to the child.

By themselves, of course, their artworks aren't proof of abuse, but they're pieces of the puzzle. Jay picks up a clay figure that depicts a boy seated on a stump. The figure looks like an upright corpse, and it has a secret: the little artist who made it fashioned an intricate link between the body of the boy and the stump he sat on. Jay lifts the boy's rear end; he has a plug up his anus. "This little boy was sodomized and he has exactly replicated in this figure what his childhood was like." She selects another clay figure from a tray filled with expressive creations; this one is a severe-looking blackbird mounted on a black nest. The bird conveys a funereal sense of gloom. "This is how Sally* felt," Jay says. "She was like the mother bird sitting on the nest, being sexually abused, with nothing in the nest, no eggs, an empty home, and painted black, like death." Having created the sculpture, Sally was able to talk about it.

For Jay, the joy of the work is in seeing children relieved of their burden. For most of them, the process extends beyond the art therapy playroom, and their involvement with the SCAN team often reaches from the hospital to the courts.

At 1:45 p.m. on a rainy August afternoon in 1992, Dr. Marcellina Mian arrived at the Whitby courthouse in a rented car, accompanied by Jacquelyn Jay, who was driving. Instead of pulling straight into a parking space, Jay turned the car around and parked front end out — a basic security precaution. If Mian was threatened after court by irate relatives of an accused offender, which has happened, she could make a quick getaway. She prefers not to drive herself to court, and always arrives in a rented car. She has to be careful. "You take my child away from me and I'll get yours," one father roared, after Mian testified, on the basis of a lengthy assessment carried out by the SCAN team, that she believed he had sexually assaulted his daughter. Her professional opinion, recommending that the child be removed from the father's home, would carry considerable weight with the Children's Aid Society, police and courts. Within the criminal justice system, Mian has earned a reputation as the pre-eminent expert witness in child sexual abuse cases.

Entering the courthouse, Mian was whisked off to the Crown prosecutor's office. "Thank God she could come," said Penny Contreras, the victim witness co-ordinator, who'd had a bad morning in court; despite Contreras' best efforts preparing a four-year-old child to testify, the little girl had been terrified when she entered the courtroom and saw the accused. "She froze on the witness stand," Contreras said. "She told the judge she 'forgot' what happened; she just wanted to get out of there as fast as she could." This was the prosecution's worst nightmare: a case collapsing because the victim — the only witness — was too scared to speak. Did the Crown try to have the child testify on closed-circuit TV? "I wish. That's a luxury we don't have here," Contreras said.

Crown prosecutor Janice Smith was counting on Mian's testimony to explain the child's behaviour. As an expert witness, the doctor was not required to have first-hand knowledge of this particular case; her role was to frame the child's behaviour in an informed context, illuminating her symptoms, analysing her cognitive abilities and discussing some of the paradoxical aspects of children's responses to abuse.

As well, to bolster the prosecution, Smith had filed what she termed a "Khan application" to allow the child's out-of-court statements to the police, to her mother and to a babysitter to be admitted as evidence. Without a special ruling, these statements would be considered hearsay and would not be admissible; but the rules governing children's evidence had changed with the Khan case. In 1985, fifteen minutes after a visit to Dr. Abdullah Khan, a Toronto physician, a child three and a half years old told her mother that the doctor asked if she wanted a candy and told her to open her mouth. "He put his birdie in my mouth, shook it and peed in my mouth," the child said. The mother called the police. A wet spot on the girl's shirt was found to contain a mixture of semen and saliva. Dr. Khan was arrested. At his trial, the judge ruled that the little girl was not competent to give evidence and refused to allow the mother's statement on the grounds it was hearsay. Dr. Khan was acquitted. The Crown appealed; the Ontario Court of Appeal ruled that the trial judge had erred and should have allowed both the child and her mother to testify. Dr. Khan appealed to the Supreme Court of Canada and lost.

The Supreme Court's 1990 ruling, written by Madam Justice Beverly McLachlin, concluded that "hearsay evidence of a child's statement on crimes committed against the child should be received, provided that the guarantees of necessity and reliability are met...." In other words, the mother's statement about what her child said was both necessary and reliable. "The child had no motive to falsify her story, which emerged naturally and without prompting," McLachlin wrote. "Moreover, the fact that she could not be expected to have knowledge of such sexual acts imbues her statement with its own peculiar stamp of reliability. Finally, her statement was corroborated by real evidence." A new trial was ordered and Dr. Khan was convicted and sentenced, *in absentia*, to four years in prison. (He skipped out on $50,000 bail put up by his wife and was apprehended a year later, in March 1992, by the FBI, who tracked him to Atlanta, Georgia. He was returned to Canada and incarcerated. The College of Physicians and Surgeons revoked his licence to practise medicine in August 1992.)

Dr. Mian took the stand at 2:20 p.m. The first thirty minutes were taken up with a survey of her curriculum vitae, presented by the Crown prosecutor to establish the doctor's credentials as an expert witness; judges give greater weight to testimony from experts than from ordinary people and must therefore be assured that the expert's status is of the highest order. The judge was informed that in 1984, for instance, the year Mian joined the SCAN team, she was appointed to the Metropolitan Toronto Special Committee on Child Abuse, was president of its board of directors for the next five years while sitting on the Ontario Hospital Association child abuse protocol committee and a Ministry of Health and Welfare working group on abuse and family violence, and so on. The prosecutor also listed dozens of professional articles Mian had written; research findings derived from her own studies; international conferences at which she'd presented papers; training seminars she'd conducted for physicians, judges, lawyers, Crown attorneys, Children's Aid Society workers, etc. She "had knowledge of" up to a thousand cases of child abuse every year, the majority involving sexual abuse, and she testified, on average, once a month at various trials.

The judge declared her "eminently qualifed." Prosecutor Smith launched into a "hypothetical" case, which was in fact the case before the judge, asking Mian to comment and place the facts in a context informed by expert knowledge. Smith asked Mian to assess the cognitive ability of a child aged three years, nine months (at the time of the abuse). Mian said children of that age "have a good sense of themselves, generally." They know numbers, colours, where they live and who's in their family. They also have a very concrete way of looking at things, and she illustrated her point: she had asked a three-year-old what street her house was on and the child looked at Mian as if the doctor were stupid. "It's not on the street," the little girl said, "it's on the sidewalk." Of course she was right, Mian added.

Three- and four-year-olds do not have a good sense of time; "yesterday" could mean last week or last month, and if they said something happened "three times," it could have happened twenty times; "three times" meant, at the very least, "more than once." However, three- and four-year-olds have a good sense of their surroundings and of specific events, especially traumatic events. "The research shows that everybody, children and adults, remembers traumatic events more clearly because of the emotional impact," Mian said, unless they've been so devastated by the events that they've completely repressed what happened.

Smith wanted to know if children normally fantasize or make up stories about sexual abuse. Mian was clear: "Sexual material is not something we normally expose our children to," she said. "Detailed knowledge of sexual function is not something young children ordinarily have, nor do they fantasize about it. Children from three to five are generally quite disgusted with anything to do with the bathroom and they're very unlikely to fantasize about anyone touching them" [in the genital area].

Smith laid out her "hypothetical case." Suppose Mian had to assess a child aged three years, nine months, who'd gone to the same babysit-ter for a year and a half. Suppose Person B came to live in the child's home and after a few months the child's behaviour began to change, she began to have nightmares, became clingy, anxious and cried, and told her mother she didn't like Person B. Suppose one day the babysit-ter separated the crying, screaming child from the other children, sat her down in the living room and said, "What's wrong?" The child didn't answer; they watched TV for ten minutes, the child complained about two older cousins who picked on her, as a way of leading into what was really on her mind, and then she said, "I'm afraid of B." The babysitter asked why. "He comes into my room at night and touches me," the child said. The babysitter asked where Mom and Dad were when B touched her. "In bed, asleep." Where did he touch her? The child pointed to her breasts and her crotch.

Mian's initial response demonstrated that she did not jump to con-clusions: "A new person was introduced into the child's home; maybe she saw B as a rival. The child was showing distress: maybe B was overbearing, overly friendly and cutesy, or maybe he was mean, or maybe she was being sexually abused." Up to the point of the child's disclosure, Mian said, her symptoms were non-specific. "Then she said B came into her room and touched her: that's a disclosure of sex-ual abuse that needs to be assessed."

Prosecutor Smith asked why the child didn't disclose to her own parents. "B was staying in the house at her parents' invitation," Mian said. "Her parents might have told her to be good to B and she might not have felt safe telling her parents."

Smith continued: when the babysitter told the parents, they took the child the same day to the hospital and then to the police, where the child was interviewed by Detective Debbie White of the Durham Regional Police Sexual Assault Squad. Smith read from the child's police statement, made with the parents present; this was one of the "hearsay" statements that Smith hoped to have admitted as a result of the Khan application.

Detective White: Why were you at the hospital?
Child: I was sick.
Detective: Where?

Child: My belly, it was nervous.

Detective: Why?

Child: Because B touched me on the boobies. (And she pointed to her vaginal area and made a rubbing motion.)

Detective: What's that area called?

Child: Bum.

Mom interjected: She also calls that birdie.

Detective: How many times did he touch you there?

Child: Two times last night.

Mian's response was that it sounded like a good interview. "The questions are based on what the child said and the officer didn't lead her." This was a crucial point: anyone to whom a child discloses has to be careful not to "contaminate" the evidence by appearing to suggest what the child should say. As for "two times last night," that means it happened more than once, "but that's all we can say."

Detective: Does B live in your apartment?

Child: Yes. (She looked sad.)

Detective: When you say B touched your bum and your boobies, where were you?

Child: In bed.

Detective: What were you wearing?

Child: A nightie. (The child then drew a diagram of her bed and showed how B had lain down on her bed.)

Detective: What did he use to touch you?

Child: A pencil.

The fact that the child can draw the scene strengthens the credibility of her statement, Mian said. As for the pencil: "When children say something was used to touch them, we are very picky about clarifying exactly what it was. Children will say they have been poked by needles when it was a penis. When I hear 'pencil' I hear round, hard, longish, maybe sharp, or maybe squishy and rubbery. It could be a pencil, a finger, a penis." Detective White should have asked the child what kind of pencil.

Smith moved on to "incremental disclosure." Eight months later, the child revealed another incident. She was watching TV with her mother and a show came on about a girl who was sexually abused. Asked if she wanted to change channels, the child said, "No, that's what B did to me. He wanted me to touch his dicky bird. Yuck." The mother said, "Do you want to talk more about it?" The child said, "No." The mother reassured her: "If you do want to talk about it, that's fine. I love you; you're a good girl."

The issue around the girl's second disclosure was critical to the case: the accused's lawyer had suggested that the child, in making another statement that was different from her first, had lied. If B had tried to make her touch his penis, why hadn't she told the babysitter or the police officer at the beginning? Prosecutor Smith asked Mian the crucial question: was the child's second statement inconsistent with her initial disclosure? "No," Mian said. "It adds to the credibility of the previous statement. It's a different statement, and maybe next month, or if she were in therapy, she'd tell you about something else he did to her."

At 5:00 p.m., the judge set another date for Mian to return to be cross-examined by the defence lawyer. Six weeks later, on October 6, 1992, she was back in court and defence lawyer Carol Lettman began the cross-examination. Lettman questioned Mian's qualifications, combed through the various studies and articles produced by the SCAN team and queried the doctor about how she did her research and how she conducted SCAN assessments in excruciating detail. The strategy backfired: instead of undermining Mian's credibility, Lettman's prolonged interrogation merely served to enhance the doctor's reputation. And forced Mian to return yet again.

Leaving the courthouse at the end of another long day, she betrayed a touch of annoyance; she was frustated by the enormous waste of time and resources in the criminal justice system. "All those hours, all those lawyers, all that money spent and nothing accomplished," she said. "Now you know why doctors don't want to be expert witnesses."

The trial continued to drag on so long — from August 1992 to August 1993 — that midway through the process the defence lawyer tried to get the judge to dismiss the case because of delays; the judge rejected the defence submission and eventually ruled in the Crown's favour on the Khan application, allowing the child's hearsay evidence — her statements to her mother, her babysitter and the police officer

— to be admitted. The accused was eventually convicted and sentenced to nine months in jail; he could be released after serving one-third of his sentence, which meant he would likely spend no more than three months behind bars.

Some cases hit closer to home. In the early summer of 1992, Mian was called to Brown Elementary, where her own children had gone to school. The red-brick institution, on the brow of the Avenue Road hill between Rosedale and Forest Hill, is an elite public school within the Toronto Board of Education. Brown was in a state of crisis. One of its most popular teachers, John Freestone, had been charged with sexually abusing a pre-teen boy twenty years earlier, and the school community was up in arms — in defence of Freestone. "You've got to understand that John Freestone is a wonderful teacher, maybe the best teacher my kids ever had," said David Peterson, a former premier of Ontario. "He took the kids on trips to Ottawa, he created interesting projects, he was engaged in their lives. Then the kids come home with a letter saying Freestone's been kicked out of school and my God! The shit hit the fan!"

Mian could not have been faulted for expecting a best-case scenario at Brown. Much of the preventive work she'd done in the past decade, particularly her involvement in the Metropolitan Toronto Special Committee on Child Abuse, had been aimed at enlightening students and teachers on child abuse issues. Brown's pupils had received a broad range of enriched programs; they'd seen the play *Journey to A.M.U. (All Mixed Up)*, developed by Catherine Stewart and produced by the Metro Special Committee to teach the difference between healthy touching and secret touching. Brown's teachers had special training to sensitize them to children who might want to disclose. The Toronto Board of Education had developed a progressive new policy, Standard Procedure 54, for dealing with children's allegations of abuse by teachers, and had the foresight to assign Vicki Kelman, its in-house child abuse expert, to deal with the allegations against Freestone.

Kelman has impeccable credentials. She worked with Mian on the Metro Special Committee, formed in 1981 in the wake of the murder of Emanuel Jaques, a twelve-year-old shoeshine boy whose body had been found in a garbage bag on the roof of a Yonge Street sex shop.

He had died in a production of child porn that turned into a deadly orgy. Metro chairman Paul Godfrey (now publisher of the *Toronto Sun*) was horrified by the Jaques case and supported a concerted effort to eradicate child abuse. The Metro Special Committee focused on the systems that have a direct impact on children's lives, drawing together a network of senior officials from the fields of criminal justice, child protection, mental health, education and medicine. Mian chaired the committee's board and Kelman was a frontline worker as ripples of change began to reverberate through schools, police forces, hospitals and courts.

And here they were, so many years later, at Brown School, where the principal, John Degraaf, had received a phone call in March 1992 from Barry,* a man in his thirties. Barry said he'd been molested as a child by Freestone. Degraaf did what he was supposed to do: he informed his superintendent and the police were called. Barry was interviewed by the police on Friday, April 10, 1992. His story was this: he'd been in treatment for alcoholism a couple of times in his adult life. The third time around, a counsellor posed a question no one had ever asked, in all Barry's years of turmoil: Were you ever sexually abused as a child? Barry's answer was yes. In 1969, at the age of eleven, he'd joined a Leaside baseball team coached by John Freestone, who was then in his twenties. Freestone took a special interest in Barry and became a regular visitor to the boy's home. After Sunday-night dinner, Freestone would go upstairs to Barry's bedroom to say good-night. Freestone began giving Barry backrubs, and gradually escalated to masturbation and oral sex — in Barry's bedroom, with his parents downstairs. Barry was a prisoner in his own home, terrified his parents would find out. By the fall of 1973, after four years as Freestone's "special friend," Barry was an isolated, destructive teenager. He dropped out of North Toronto Collegiate after grade twelve and was kicked out of his parents' home for his raging, boozing ways. Through his twenties, he numbed the pain with alcohol, stumbling through a string of dead-end jobs, going nowhere fast.

On Monday, April 13, Freestone was called into the principal's office, told he was under investigation and sent home, on full pay. On Wednesday, the day charges were laid, Vicki Kelman talked to all the grade four, five and six students at Brown, explaining that a grown-up man alleged that when he was a child, he'd been molested by Freestone. Kelman made it clear that she didn't know if Freestone, who taught grades five and six, was guilty, and that it was the job of the criminal justice system to investigate and determine the truth. She said that she'd answer any questions they had, and that if there was anything they felt uncomfortable about, they could talk to her privately.

The letter informing parents of the charges against Freestone was sent home with the students that afternoon. The next day, three children disclosed having been sexually touched by Freestone; they said he'd come up behind them at various times, in class and on the playing field; that he'd held them in a tight hug that felt more like a grip, and pressed his erect penis against their backs. They were afraid of him, they said, but couldn't stop him. The school called the police. And in the week between Wednesday, April 15, when the letter was sent home, and Wednesday, April 22, when the school held the first parents' meeting, the situation exploded. The parents didn't know about the new set of allegations, since charges hadn't yet been laid, and those closest to Freestone were furious that he'd been removed from the school. "What's happened to the presumption of innocence?" was their rallying cry.

Before the Toronto Board of Education could intervene, the pro-Freestone faction emerged as the dominant force. They formed the Ad Hoc Committee for Room 40/41, named after Freestone's home room, led by Atalanti Moquette and her banker husband. They called a meeting on Tuesday night, upstaged the Wednesday-night school meeting, usurped the school's leadership role — and within weeks, in the depths of the recession, raised more than $10,000 toward Freestone's legal fees. This was the worst thing the parents could have done, in Mian's opinion: "Such a strong show of support for Freestone right off the bat silenced the children. If the parents *wanted* to shut the children up, they couldn't have devised a better plan." That's precisely what some parents did want, according to Principal Degraaf, who said that "quite a few" took him aside and advised him to "just drop it, leave it alone, Freestone's a good math teacher, and sometimes it's the price you've got to pay. "

At the first school meeting, on Wednesday night in Brown's library, David Peterson was shocked by the vehemence of Freestone's supporters. "They were goddamn mad and mean, and there was a very strong defence of John Freestone. There was one rough tough father — I thought he was going to pound someone. It was potentially a bit of a mob scene. God knows I've seen difficult crowds thousands of times in my life [as a politician], but this was different; there was a level of emotion that was very scary."

The school officials hung back and let Kelman take the brunt of the collective rage. Principal Degraaf was profoundly ambivalent: he thought Barry was telling the truth, but Freestone was his friend, and he failed to show leadership when it was needed. "I feel guilty about that [meeting]," DeGraaf said later. "I wasn't sure what my role was." It was left to David Peterson to speak in support of Kelman. "I felt I had to," Peterson said staunchly. "Things were getting out of hand."

Called in to attend a subsequent meeting that was just as stormy, Mian observed that the parents were so busy defending Freestone they'd forgotten about their children's safety. Parent after parent stood up and said, "I've been in his classroom, he's a marvellous teacher, he's wonderful with the children, he's our friend," and Mian had to tell them, over and again, that their experiences with Freestone were irrelevant in terms of whether or not he'd sexually abused children. "You can't determine whether someone's an abuser by watching him in class," she said. Freestone's behaviour at a family dinner party, or at an outing to the ballet, did not illuminate his private sexual practices.

Mian was blunt. "This is how most institutions and individuals respond to allegations of child sexual abuse: with anger and denial, as you are doing. Unfortunately, it's a normal, defensive reaction. Your first responsibility is to your children. If they're angry at how Mr. Freestone is being treated, let them tell you; if they're sorry for him, hear it; if they have other things to tell you about Mr. Freestone, let them speak. If you the parents are angry at the school and protective of John Freestone, your children won't tell you if he's been abusing them. Pay attention to your children."

The three girls who'd disclosed were ostracized by Brown students and staff when the second set of charges was laid. One of the teachers — a close friend of Freestone's — called the girls "dirty liars." Principal Degraaf asked the students if they wanted to donate money from a bake sale to Freestone's defence fund. The complainants had contributed to the bake sale, and were hurt by their principal's show of support for the accused.

In the year it took for Freestone to come to trial, he was employed on full salary at an administrative make-work job at the Toronto Board of Education. His defence lawyer succeeded in separating the two sets of charges — a move that was highly beneficial to the accused. There were two trials; Barry's — the one with the strongest likelihood of producing a conviction, because the charges were more severe — came second. In the girls' trial, in September 1992, the judge was not allowed to know about Barry's allegations or the circumstances that had triggered the girls' disclosure. The judge found the girls to be credible witnesses, the *Toronto Star* reported, and said he believed they were telling the truth, but he gave the benefit of the doubt to Freestone, noting the teacher's unblemished record, sterling reputation and support from colleagues and parents. Freestone was acquitted on charges of sexual interference.

Later that month, Freestone was back in court for a preliminary hearing into Barry's allegations; Barry testified and was cross-examined by the defence lawyer. The case crawled through the system, and finally, eight months later, on May 3, 1993, Freestone stunned some of his supporters by pleading guilty in a court appearance that lasted all of three minutes. On June 14, he was back again for sentencing, supported by the ever-faithful Principal Degraaf and Atalanti Moquette, whose blank faces registered no reaction to Barry's wrenching victim impact statement, which he delivered himself from the witness stand.

Defence lawyer Bill Markle introduced a medical assessment that referred to evidence of "homosexual pedophilia" and "borderline personality disorder" but indicated that Freestone had "placed careful controls on himself." The judge, declaring he had no evidence the accused was a danger to children, sentenced Freestone to twenty-one months in an Ontario reformatory; he was handcuffed and taken away to jail. On January 12, 1994, Freestone became eligible for parole but did not apply. His earliest possible release date is August 14, 1994, when he will have served two-thirds of his sentence. By serving two-thirds of his time, he will not have to submit to supervision upon his release.

At Brown School, the rancour of battle hung like toxic fog in the air. What went wrong? "The parents got caught up trying to sort out whether the teacher was guilty or not," Mian says. They had normal working parents' guilt. They refused to acknowledge that anything bad could invade the perfect world they believed they'd created for their children, and they behaved, Mian says, "like typical non-offending parents in an incestuous family." They felt, "I'm an intelligent person with good judgement, I would not send my child to be taught by a pervert, therefore my child's teacher cannot be a pervert." In Mian's view, everything that happened at Brown was predictable: "The abuse of children has been going on for centuries. If it was easy to stop, we would've done it." The Toronto Board of Education acted responsibly, in her view, and the parents behaved normally, but not in a child-oriented fashion. "Hopefully, the climate at Brown School will change. We've got to focus on adults being responsible for their actions, and we've got to start protecting children. This is an epidemic, yet we still, as a society, act as if it isn't happening."

There are no easy solutions. Generally speaking, the law is pro-family and pro-parent, not pro-child; professionals still neglect children at risk, though doctors and teachers are legally required to report any suspicion of abuse. Expert assessment is available from physicians like Dr. Mian at the Hospital for Sick Children, but more services are desperately needed. And denial is widespread — in churches, schools and other institutions where abuse occurs. Institutional cultures that have harboured a perpetrator are, like families, profoundly infected by the abuser's stratagems to gain control, which include the long-term manipulation, co-option and sometimes the collaboration of co-workers and other non-offending adults. Officials tend to identify with perpetrators — "Oh my God, he can't be bad, he's one of us" — and make excuses for them. On some level, some people always know. But just as we confronted a social practice that was a major cause of mayhem on highways — drunk driving — so we can educate ourselves about child sexual abuse. What's at stake is not only the well-being of hundreds of thousands of children but also of our entire society.

4

Prescott:
Breaking the Cycle

*Empowering the children, that's what we're trying to
do. When the children are supported in saying what
was done to them, the trial can be part of the healing process.*

— Crown attorney Des McGarry

THE CHILDREN WERE the final witnesses called by prosecutor Des
McGarry in the 1991 trial of Billy Elliott, twenty-six, who pleaded not
guilty to seven counts of sexually abusing three children. Lucy* was
nine, her brother Freddy* seven (Joey,* six, was deemed too young to
testify), when they were among the first children in Canada to give
evidence on closed-circuit television. Billy Elliott, curly-haired, blue-
eyed, wearing a beige suit, slumped behind plexiglass in the prisoner's
box as members of the jury watched Lucy and Freddy "live," on specially installed television sets, in an innovative procedure that allows
children to testify outside the stern intimidation of the courtroom.

Lucy and Freddy's initial disclosures to their foster parents in 1989
precipitated Project Jericho, a five-year joint investigation by the
Ontario Provincial Police, the Prescott Police and the county's Family
and Children's Services. Together they uncovered the massive Prescott
sexual abuse case. (The code-name Jericho was chosen to honour

Joshua, a baby who the police believe died. "Joshua led the battle of Jericho, and the walls came tumbling down," says OPP Detective Rick Robins, referring to the Bible story. The body of the baby Joshua was never found, but various witnesses described seeing him killed; the investigation into his death continues.) Linked by kinship and friendship ties, Prescott's perpetrators abused their own children, their neighbours' children and their grandchildren in a multi-generational network that was staggering in its reach and its routine violation of hundreds of victims. Some were terrorized in nightmarish ways that can only be termed ritual abuse. The police had evidence that Billy Elliott had been in the habit of digging up bodies in the graveyard, pulling the heads off skeletons and engaging in makeshift basement rites in which adults disguised in costumes sexually abused children; sometimes the activities were recorded by videocameras.

In 1989, after the first arrests arising from Lucy and Freddy's allegations, nine Prescott-area men and two teenage boys were charged with sex-related crimes. In January 1991, the total number of accused perpetrators reached thirty-one, including a handful of women, charged with sexually abusing sixty-two children. By December 1992, forty-two people had been charged with sexually abusing 150 alleged victims. Prescott was reeling, and the local papers were filled with horrendous stories as offenders were convicted and sent to jail. But it would get even worse. A year later, at the end of 1993, 225 alleged victims had been identified and fifty-five people charged; half the accused had been processed through the courts, with a 93 per cent conviction rate.

"This is not a unique situation in terms of abuse," says Pam Gummer, the child abuse project coordinator with Family and Children's Services. "Prescott is unique in terms of outcome." Out of horrific revelations a strategy was forged, linking police investigators, child protection workers, foster parents, a designated Crown prosecutor, a victim-witness coordinator and a therapy team; supported by Ontario government funding, they demonstrated — for the first time in North America — that early intervention can make miracles in children's lives. The Prescott case is a best-case scenario.

Prescott, Ontario, population 4,200, is a picturesque town on the edge of the Pre-Cambrian shield, on the north shore of the St. Lawrence

River, an hour's drive east of Kingston. Tucked away in the green hills of the south shore is Ogdensburg, New York, so close across the thin blue line of river that it beckons youthful swimmers in a summer rite of passage. Prescott is an old town, settled in the 1700s, distinguished by the stone houses that anchor its shady streets. But it's pockmarked by poverty. "White trash" is what folks call these families, descendents of Scots-Irish farmers who eked out a meagre existence on rocky ground before migrating into Prescott. Here, with little education and fewer skills, many of them have survived on welfare for generations.

"Rich people hide their secrets more easily," said Stephen Heder, then head of the county's Family and Children's Services. "They tend not to get caught. The poor live in each other's pockets and have no secrets." But poverty's lack of privacy was of little help to Lucy, Freddy and Joey for quite a few years. According to the locals, "everybody knew" about the "inbreeding" among the "hillbillies." John Morris, publisher of the *Prescott Journal,* said with glib assurance: "When we were kids, we all knew who these people were and what they were doing and who to avoid." When the scandal broke in 1990, "there were no big surprises," said Anne Kindervater, a Prescott town councillor. "People said, 'Oh yeah, well, I could have guessed *that.*' You know, when you see a grown man walking down the main street holding hands with his seventeen-year-old daughter in a certain way, you kind of wonder." But why, if everybody knew, hadn't anyone intervened? "There was a lot of apathy," Kindervater shrugged. "People suspected but they didn't want to get involved. It took a couple of children to come forward and say, 'This happened to me,' it took foster parents who listened, and social workers and police officers who cared, and then it snowballed. It took a new generation to stop it."

Maureen McDougall is part of the new generation. She was a neophyte social worker when she first visited Lucy, Freddy and Joey in 1988 at the home they shared with their mother, Nancy,* and her boyfriend, Billy Elliott. McDougall's notes from July 26 state: "The home was very dirty, unkempt, scraps of food on the floor, a lot of flies in the house, broken chairs in the kitchen, rotten food in the fridge, clothes lying around everywhere, window screens pushed out, human excrement on the stairwell, the children's beds urine-stained with no sheets, dirty diapers lying in a closet...." It wasn't difficult to determine, she told the court, that "this was a high-risk family." Joey was three and couldn't speak; Freddy was four and his words were garbled; Lucy, at six, was intelligible but hyperactive, as were her brothers. Lucy had already been removed from her home by child welfare officials, placed in foster care and then returned to Nancy. There was a court order for "supervision" in a state-supported attempt to keep the family together, although the three children had been "found to be in need of protection" even before Billy Elliott moved in.

McDougall was diligent in attempting to supervise: she made twelve home visits to Nancy's house during the summer of 1988. Nancy had been on welfare all her life; she was a woman "of limited intelligence who needed assistance with life skills, grocery shopping, budgeting, meal planning," McDougall testified. Nancy treated her children badly, yelled at them and called them "ignorant brats" or "dirty animals," but the social worker saw no evidence of other forms of abuse until one day she saw Lucy rub her pubic area as if she were in pain. McDougall made an appointment for Lucy to be examined by a doctor. Nancy objected strenuously, and on August 25, 1988, the day before Lucy's medical appointment, "Nancy was so upset she was shaking and trembling," McDougall testified. "She stormed inside the house — the children were outside with me — and yelled that Lucy didn't have to go to the doctor and that if I took Lucy to the doctor, she, Nancy, would run away with the kids. I told her I'd apprehend the children [remove them from the home] if she didn't co-operate."

The Prescott police were on standby the next day when McDougall and her supervisor, Pam Gummer, drove to Nancy's house. The children were there, and the two social workers took them into Kingston to see the doctor. From that day forward, as a result of the medical examination — which indicated that Lucy and Joey had been sexually abused, and raised questions about Freddy — they never resided with their mother again; less than a year later, on June 15, 1989, the children were made wards of the Crown. But they didn't tell anyone what had happened to them — not until they found the Johnsons.

Susan* and Steven Johnson* lived in a rambling, four-bedroom farmhouse in a village near Prescott. They had three children of their own and a desire for more. "We'd talked about adopting since Willy* (the youngest) was born," Steven says, "but we thought we wouldn't be allowed; we already had kids, we weren't rich or famous...." In the early years of their marriage, Steven worked as a hospital orderly while Susan managed the home front, doing freelance writing and picking up part-time jobs on the side. On one of those jobs, with Family and Children's Services in Brockville, she was assigned to work with three developmentally delayed children who were up for adoption. They were not the sort of children many people were eager to claim, but Susan was entranced by them. The Johnsons applied to become adoptive parents, went through the home-study procedure and were approved. Then Family and Children's Services decided the children would be better off with a childless couple. "We were heartbroken," Steven says.

But not for long. Two days later, Family and Children's Services called again: "We have three others," said the child-care worker, sounding apprehensive, "but they have *real* problems." The Johnsons were asked if they wanted to watch Lucy, Freddy and Joey play through a one-way observation window before making a decision. The Johnsons said no. "That bothers me," Steven says, "the thought that I would examine them like specimens and say, 'Oh no, the behaviour of that one seems odd to me, I won't take that one.' When you have children, you take what you get and love them for who they are. I feel very strongly about that."

In early July 1989, a social worker brought Lucy, Freddy and Joey to meet the Johnsons for the first time. The children burst out of the car, calling them Mom and Dad, "and we didn't know what hit us," Steven says. He has a hard time describing the impact of their arrival: it was like an invasion of buzzing hornets, a whirlwind.... "Like watching a movie speeded up, they moved so fast," Susan says. "You couldn't see their faces." One of them said, "We're going to stay here *for eber and eber.* "

The children had been removed from the house Nancy lived in with Billy Elliott a year earlier; they'd been in two different foster homes and they were healthy and well fed. But they were developmentally delayed, with severe behavioural problems, and experts couldn't predict whether they would ever catch up to their age group. That their prognosis was uncertain did not affect the Johnsons, who were informed that the children had been neglected and abused. Joey, a cherub with blond curls, grunted but could not say words. "He was only four," Steven says, "and he wasn't a bad boy, he wasn't angry or aggressive, just impossible to control, and falling, falling down everywhere." Lucy, seven, and Freddy, five, were poorly coordinated and had difficulty expressing themselves. They all obsessively touched, grabbed and manipulated every object they could reach, "the way babies do," Susan says. With their eldest almost through high school, the Johnsons were familiar with normal child development; it was disconcerting, and wildly disruptive, to encounter baby behaviour in larger children. It was as if they'd never learned to explore the world. "They'd missed everything in terms of developmental stages," Susan says.

When the children moved in, on July 28, 1989, they were like wild animals attempting to adjust to domesticity. The first six months were difficult, beyond anything the Johnsons can describe. Every moment of every day was taken with watching every move the little ones made, stopping them from pulling things over or hurting themselves. They couldn't concentrate on quiet tasks, couldn't sit still at the dinner table, dove into food compulsively. One night after supper, Steven found Freddy on the kitchen floor, eating out of the garbage can. Steven had just emptied the birdcage into the garbage. "You're eating bird poop," he told Freddy, who turned green and never ate out of the garbage again.

At night, after they'd finally got the little ones settled down, the Johnsons held mini-conferences until one in the morning, just the two of them, talking about how they felt, what they'd done, what worked, what didn't, how the little ones responded, the problems they were having in trying to blend the two families of children. They had re-adjusted their roles: Steven was the stay-at-home parent while Susan had a full-time job as a journalist — and they worried about neglecting their older children because of the all-consuming needs of the younger ones.

During that first summer, the Johnsons took the three children to the beach as often as possible, to let them run around and burn off energy. One afternoon, after they had played in the water for hours, Steven took Freddy and Joey into the change room. Susan was waiting outside with Lucy; Steven emerged looking as if he'd seen a ghost. What had happened inside? Steven had taken off their bathing suits, an innocent action on his part that triggered "a sexual reaction" in Freddy and Joey, "as if they were robots and this was what they'd been trained to do when they were undressing with a man." They began to play with their penises and they tried to touch Steven's genitals through his clothes. Steven recoiled. He didn't get angry, but his message was clear: "I just told them I was going to dry them off and get them dressed and put clean clothes on them and then we were going home." He figures he did the right thing: "It never happened again. I guess they got the message, because that was the end of it."

"We didn't know about sexual abuse, I'm ashamed to say; we didn't know the symptoms," Susan says. "Just once I saw Joey do something. I'd gotten the kids all dressed up to go to my brother's wedding, and we got in an elevator, Joey and I, at the reception, and there was a man in the elevator. Joey turned to him with a sweet smile and patted him on the genitals." Susan blushes at the memory. "I removed Joey's hand and we all pretended it hadn't happened."

Soon she wouldn't be able to pretend. After a few months in their new home, Lucy and Freddy started relaying odd snippets of events from their earlier life. The Johnsons had no idea what to make of the horrific information they were hearing; their social worker advised them to make notes, and Susan did, recording incomprehensible details that sounded like torture. The Johnsons discovered that the children were unable to sleep through the night. At the slightest unexpected noise, they'd sit up, eyes wide open in terror, unable to speak. One night Lucy was sick and vomited in bed. "She was too terrifed to tell us," Susan says. "She lay there all night in stinking sheets, poor little thing."

The disclosures came in bits, disjointed statements, disconnected fragments. "I'd think, 'That's it, we've heard it all, it can't get worse,' and then we'd hear more, and it would be worse," Steven says. Susan grips the arms of her chair and makes a shrieking primal-scream face. "There were times we had to call the social worker late at night and say, 'Help, we can't take this.' " But the disclosure period didn't last long. It was like a balloon that burst; out the stuff came, over a period of six months, and then it stopped, as if the children had said, "Here, take it, it's yours, I'm going off to be a child." At almost the same time, the information the Johnsons had passed to the social worker (in the form of written notes kept by Susan) was communicated to the police, "and it became an investigation and we were told not to talk to the kids about it at all," Susan says. "I worry about that — I hope they didn't feel we were shutting them down...." Steven interjects: "The police wanted to make sure we weren't perceived as having put ideas in the kids' heads or words in their mouths."

Pam Gummer was sent to the Johnsons' house to conduct the first official investigative interview with Lucy and Freddy. She noted that the children had blossomed since she'd accompanied Maureen McDougall to remove them from their original home. Gummer approached her current task with professional detachment. The questions uppermost in her mind concerned the Johnsons: had they put ideas into the minds of the children? Was it possible the children had really disclosed the unspeakable things the Johnsons said they had? It is critical that experienced investigators be brought in during the initial assessment stage, in order not to proceed on false allegations. Gummer is a seasoned frontline professional, and she'd once encountered a case, in a divorce dispute, in which a woman had claimed her daughter had been sexually abused by her estranged husband. Gummer's suspicions were raised by the mother's attitude and confirmed by the little girl, who was unable to say anything more than "Daddy touched my private parts." The child couldn't provide any contextual detail; there was no sense of where it happened, how it happened, no emotion, "none of the odd touches that make a real story," Gummer says.

But the stories of Lucy and Freddy were unlike anything Gummer had encountered in nine years as a child welfare worker. She was stunned to hear the words coming out of the children's inarticulate mouths. They flooded her with details, emotions, strange settings and unbelievable scenarios that such limited children could hardly have invented. Afterward, driving back to Prescott, "I was in a daze, I couldn't concentrate and I had to pull off to the side of the road," Gummer says. "I thought, this can't be, these kids are talking about such bizarre and twisted fairy tales." Yet she felt instinctively that they were telling the truth.

And when those fairy tales did prove to be true, many townsfolk weren't surprised. This strangely knowing response reflects the paradoxical nature of sexual abuse wherever it occurs: it's a deep dark deadly secret that some people are always aware of — like Dean

Grahame Baker, the senior minister at St. George's Cathedral, who had been informed of various instances of John Gallienne's sexual molestation of children. In the Prescott case, it took the disclosures of only two children to get action. The police followed the leads offered by Lucy and Freddy in every possible direction — and practically everything the children said in that first interview with Gummer was later corroborated by physical evidence and statements from many other witnesses and victims. (Gummer would play a central role in the investigation, along with police officers Gary Sluytman and Rick Robins, whose initial probes led to setting up the Project Jericho team.)

At the beginning, Lucy and Freddy's stories of cult-like rituals, videocameras and groups of adults in costumes with animals dragged in, and of a baby being murdered, were "unfathomable," Gummer says. When Freddy told her about being placed in a hole in the ground and left for hours, she couldn't imagine what he was talking about. Lucy described monsters that jumped out from behind the washing machine in the basement and sexually assaulted the children and made them drink "yucky juice" which they were told was blood that came from dogs killed by Billy Elliott's father. Then the police found a trapdoor under the floor of the house, and a six-foot-deep hole beneath it that was littered with scraps of food. At her own trial, Nancy admitted she'd watched Billy and her two brothers-in-law dress up in sheets with eye-holes cut out and sexually abuse the children. When Billy Elliott's parents, who were also charged with sex-related offences, sold their house, the couple who bought it landscaped the garden; digging up the yard, they found masses of animal bones buried in shallow graves. Billy's father, it turned out, had been charged by the local Humane Society with cruelty to animals. And one day Billy bragged to Gummer that he'd dug up bodies in the graveyard.

When Billy Elliott went to trial in 1991, he was one of the thirty-one men and women charged with sexually abusing sixty-two children. Among his co-accused were friends and relatives, cousins, uncles, aunts and in-laws. A short, sturdy fellow who, unlike most of his crowd, had been regularly employed, he'd worked at a feed mill earning six dollars an hour. He had a grade-nine education, was basically illiterate and had been a ward of the court temporarily during his own troubled youth. Billy had acknowledged to a social worker before his trial that his mother had engaged him in an incestous relationship when he was a boy.

In court, Elliott pleaded not guilty to sexually assaulting Lucy, Freddy and Joey. Crown Attorney Des McGarry warned the jury of seven women and five men that some of the evidence they were about to hear might disturb them. "You will hear that some of these acts occurred in the home with other adults present, sometimes dressed up in costumes.... I anticipate the children will refer to them as monsters." The prosecution began with testimony from medical experts. One doctor said that when he met Joey three years earlier, in August 1988, the little boy walked up to him and began to rub the doctor's groin with his hand. The doctor pushed Joey's hand away and told him not to do that, but Joey persisted. His "sexually oriented play" and apparently affectionate behaviour showed "a fixation on genital matters which is extremely unusual for a three-year-old boy." Joey was also obsessed with mouths, "and wanted to stare into people's mouths," which may have been related to all the oral sex he had endured.

The 1988 medical examination revealed clear evidence of anal penetration. Joey had an anal skin tag, the result of a healed fissure caused by "tearing of the anal margin," which, "after the age of one, was usually indicative of anal manipulation by...an object big enough to cause a tear in the anal opening." Most children resist anal examinations, but Joey did not. His anal muscles did not contract; he had reduced anal reflexes, and just lay there quietly. With Freddy, then four and a half, the assessment focused on his "unusual" affectionate behaviour, "being very open to strangers," and his utter lack of personal boundaries, though the physical findings were inconclusive. A pelvic examination of Lucy showed that she "did not have a hymenal ring, which meant she was not a virgin.... She was a fairly passive child; she just lay there with her legs open...as if this had happened before and she wasn't fighting any more." The condition of her vagina, at the age of six, was "very suggestive of chronic penetration."

During a recess in the trial, Steven Johnson brought Joey to the foyer of the courtroom. A tiny boy in a red-and-white-striped T-shirt, Joey hugged everyone within reach. He grabbed the legs of Des McGarry and, in an obsessive fashion, made the police officers and social workers pick him up and hold him. "Joey's indiscriminate affection," Maureen McDougall said later, "is typical of many victims. Children who have been sexually abused lack boundaries and can become walking targets for offenders." It's not that they like or want abuse, it's just that they don't know anything else.

Cecil Miller took the stand. A tall, gangly scarecrow of a man with a long mournful face, no front teeth and tattoos on his hands, Miller had already pleaded guilty to seven counts of sexually assaulting thirteen Prescott children, ranging from a twelve-month-old baby girl to two-year-old Joey to a seventeen-year-old mentally disturbed teenage boy. At the age of thirty-seven, Miller was serving a seven-year sentence at Kingston Penitentiary, where he was doing time with Lorne François, the elderly pedophile who'd been his "mentor." Known around Prescott as "Horny Lorny," François had initiated many of the children who had grown up to become perpetrators and had now been convicted. François hadn't taken kindly to the criminal proceedings. After his conviction, he'd turned to Maureen McDougall and Pam Gummer and said, "I'll kill you bastards."

Miller was more mild-mannered. He was born in Prescott, "lived there all my life," he said to the judge in a burst of pride that was at odds with his miserable existence. Born into an alcoholic family, he was socialized into a lifestyle of intra- and extra-familial abuse of staggering proportions. As a child, he was treated like the village idiot; he was the weird kid everyone taunted and teased and threw snowballs at. He dropped out of school in grade nine, unable to read or write, and, like most of the offenders in this case, had been dependent on the welfare state his entire adult life. He was the stereotypical pervert, the creep who hung around schoolyards and made no secret of his perversions.

Miller told the court about visiting Billy Elliott one day. Miller went upstairs to get cigarette papers and saw Billy in the bedroom with little Joey. Joey was two years old and his diaper was on the floor. "Billy had his dick in Joey's bumhole," Miller said. On the witness stand, he made humping motions, to demonstrate what Billy was doing to Joey; he indicated that the act was a normal, everyday occurrence, something he and his friends did to pass the time. "Joey just lay there,"

Miller said. "I watched Billy bumfuck Joey and then I went and done it, I stuck my dick in little Joey. Billy was on the bed and watched me do it. Then Billy sucked my dick and I sucked him and then we come downstairs for a coffee and a smoke."

Judge David McWilliam announced to the jury that he had approved Des McGarry's request to allow Lucy and Freddy to give their evidence on closed-circuit TV. After a day of arguments (from which the jury had been excluded), Judge McWilliam had been convinced by McGarry's presentation, with expert witnesses, that the interests of justice would be better served if Lucy and Freddy were allowed to tell their story outside the courtroom. David Wolfe, a psychology professor at the University of Western Ontario and director of research at the Institute for Prevention of Child Abuse in Toronto, said Lucy wanted very much to testify, and believed it was important to say what had been done to her, but was afraid to see Billy Elliott. "She said she's afraid he'll touch her private parts." The children's heightened anxiety at having to confront Billy would only deepen their confusion about the criminal proceedings, he said. "It's very difficult for children to stand up in court and be heard; it's hard for them to concentrate on answering questions with all these people staring at them."

Courtrooms are frightening places — they're designed to be — and they operate on an adversarial basis intended to provide antagonistic adults with a level playing-field on which to thrash out their differences in the search for truth and justice. But by virtue of their youth, inexperience, lack of knowledge and fear of adult authority, children are overwhelmed in court. When forced to confront their perpetrator they often faint, cry, urinate on the witness stand or become mute. Uncontrollable flashbacks may be triggered by the sight of the offender. The actual experience of abuse can contain a deeply buried "near-death" sensation, induced by the shock of overpowering violation, that makes many children feel they're going to die; later, the act of recounting the abuse may be accompanied by a tidal wave of fear that carries, for the child, the same threat: loss of control, which means death.

Until recent changes to the law, children were routinely retraumatized as they were shuffled through the maze of the court process, surrounded by strangers, meeting one Crown attorney at the preliminary hearing, a different Crown at the trial, asked to bare their souls again and again, questioned with cruel dispassion, confused and frightened at every turn. The system is still inimical to children in many jurisdictions, with Crown attorneys required to prosecute in packed courtrooms and child rape victims marched up to testify in front of their perpetrators, who may be surrounded by family members glaring daggers at the child for having "destroyed the family" by telling the truth.

But 1988 amendments to the Criminal Code and the Canada Evidence Act set the stage for greater accommodation of children. Three new offences were defined — sexual interference, sexual exploitation, and invitation to sexual touching — which allow police to charge individuals who've sexually harassed children by engaging them in "sex games" or other activities that lead up to but don't necessarily include molestation or penetration. The new legal definition of "sexual exploitation" protects young people between the ages of fourteen and eighteen, who are vulnerable to sexual demands made by trusted adults — teachers, coaches or babysitters — and recognizes breach of trust in this context as a criminal offence.

The necessity of corroboration of children's evidence was done away with — an important step, since the crime of sexual abuse usually occurs when the perpetrator is alone with the child. Defence lawyers are prohibited from introducing evidence about the victim's sexual reputation. And children are allowed to testify without having to see the accused, using a screen or closed-circuit television. The court is also allowed to accept as evidence police videotapes of children's statements about abuse, which can be shown to judges and juries so that children don't have to endlessly repeat the story of what was done to them.

The result is that children are being heard in court as never before. Approval of the so-called Khan application, as we've seen, means that their hearsay evidence — statements they've made to other people about the abuse — can be admitted. And a barrage of modern studies shows that children as young as three can furnish as accurate an account of events as adults. Ronda Bessner's 1991 Ontario Law Reform Commission report on child witnesses demonstrates that children are "remarkably resistant" to "suggestive comments" about events in which they've participated, that their memories are as good as adults' and that they're as capable as adults of differentiating fantasy from reality. In other words, the notion that children are creatures of fantasy, lost in a world of imaginative monsters, is an outdated stereotype.

An equally significant advance is the development of the victim-witness assistance program, which Janet Lee became involved with in the early 1980s in Ontario. Seconded as the victim-witness coordinator in the Prescott case in May 1990, "for six months, I thought," Lee is still on the case three and a half years later. Her job is to prepare children to testify in court. She does *not* talk about their evidence; her focus is on how the system works. She takes children into empty courtrooms, shows them where the judge sits and explains the function of the adults who will be present: "The Crown attorney's job is to help children tell their story; the defence lawyer's role is to defend the accused and raise a reasonable doubt in the judge's mind that maybe the accused didn't break the law." The child's responsibility, she emphasizes, is to tell the truth. Lee advises them, going in, that "we don't know the outcome and can't promise you anything, but the police believe you. You're the one who knows what happened, because you were there. Your only job is to tell the truth."

It sounds simple, but it isn't. Children have no concept of what the legal system is all about and they're "scared out of their minds," Lee says, "that being in court means they're bad." Their fear is compounded by their distress at having to recount devastating events. "It's hard enough to describe in great detail in front of other people your first intimate sexual experience, especially if it was a humiliating one, a rape or something you feel ashamed of," she says. "Imagine if you had to describe it in a strange setting to a roomful of strangers who judged you. Imagine if you were the victim and you were treated like the criminal."

The most difficult part for victim-witness coordinators is preparing children for cross-examination by defence lawyers. "It doesn't matter what the defence lawyer says to you, as long as you stick to what you know," Lee tells her young clients. "If the defence lawyer says something that's wrong, correct him. He doesn't know what the truth is; you do. You were there; he wasn't. Straighten him out. If there's a long pause and you've answered the question, just wait for the next question. If he says something and tries to get you to agree, and you don't know what he's talking about, say so. Never agree to anything you don't understand. Say, 'I don't know' or 'I don't understand' as often as you need to."

What she can't tell children is that they're being thrown into the ring with a criminal defence lawyer skilled in the art of tearing witnesses apart. Adult rape victims report that being cross-examined by the defence lawyer can be almost as traumatic as the rape; what, then, does cross-examination do to children?

Here is a typical example — it's what *didn't* happen to the Prescott children — with two teenage witnesses, an older brother and a sister three years younger. They look big and strong; the boy is now taller than the perpetrator, and the power imbalance that existed when the boy was seven, and his sister four, and they were both afraid of Kirk,* their babysitter's teenage son, is no longer visible.

The boy testifies first. He represents a prosecutor's worst nightmare: a victim who doesn't want to speak, who communicates in monosyllabic outbursts. His story emerges painfully slowly. He was in grade two when the abuse started. He'd returned to his babysitter's house after school and he was taken upstairs to Kirk's bedroom, where Kirk pulled down the boy's pants. "All I remember is that I was on my knees," the boy says, his voice barely audible. Moments pass. "I was sucking his penis." Eyes downcast, he seems to shrink with every word. Kirk, in the front row of the courtroom pews, glares menacingly at him.

Kirk ejaculated in his mouth, the boy says; on another occasion, he was made to lick Kirk's bum; down in the basement recreation room, Kirk "stuck his penis in my bum. It hurt." Another time, the boy saw Kirk get on top of his sister and stick his penis in her vagina. The sister will later testify that Kirk raped her when she was five years old and continued to rape her regularly until she was nine.

The defence lawyer, Judy Rekai, takes over, cross-examining the boy with a barrage of sneering questions and insinuations that are part of the standard arsenal used against victims in court: *Why did you keep going to the babysitter's house if you were so scared? Why didn't you tell the babysitter? Why didn't you tell your mother?* (It is the adversarial system that is responsible for this harsh treatment of victims, not individual defence lawyers. The system, as currently constituted, treats attacks on victims' credibility as an acceptable means to determine the truth.) Rekai asks the boy what time of year it happened, when it happened, how many times it happened. Children can never recall these details — they don't keep lists of abuse dates — and their natural tendency to obliterate the events from memory is used by the defence to the accused's advantage.

"I don't remember," the boy says. "Oh, you don't remember," Rekai says coolly. This will become a taunting refrain: "You don't remember…you don't remember," implying he made the whole thing up. "You say Kirk told you to lean over the table. Did he *force* you to lean over the table? What were you doing *before* you leaned over the table? Oh, you don't remember!" With every angry question, the boy slumps lower, visibly crushed. His answers are muted "no's" or "I don't remember's."

"What *do* you remember?" demands Rekai.

"Just the assault," he says.

"I'm sure you didn't know the word *assault,*" she says furiously. "Who told you the word *assault*?" She's implying that he's been told what to say.

"I don't know."

"What *do* you remember?"

"I remember his penis in my bum. It hurt."

The defence lawyer frowns ominously. "How do you know it was his penis."

"I don't know."

Now she acts really angry: "Why did you say it was his penis if you don't know? Who told you to say that…? What did you feel?"

"A stabbing sensation in my bum…"

"And you kept going to Mrs. Brown's* house every day, winter and spring, summer and fall, and you never said anything to anybody?" Rekai acts incredulous, although the boy's behaviour is typical of victims. "Weren't you concerned about your sister? You were the older brother — weren't you supposed to watch out for her? You say you saw Kirk have intercourse with her and you never said to your mom, 'Something happened.' Don't you care about your sister?"

"Yes."

"He didn't do anything to force you, did he? He didn't *force* you to lick his bum…. What about the first incident — he didn't hurt you in any way, did he? Your memory is very hazy, isn't it? You don't really remember much about what happened, do you?"

The defence lawyer's strategy in such cases is to break the victim's spirit and get them to agree to anything, just to get off the stand. All Rekai has to do is establish a little bit of doubt in the judge's mind — a task that would be relatively easy if there were only one victim. In this case, the boy's testimony is reinforced by his sister, and in the end, Kirk is convicted.

In the Prescott case, the defence lawyers couldn't attempt such aggressive cross-examination: there were too many victims, too many corroborative witnesses, too many perpetrators who had pleaded guilty and testified against each other. And the children received a level of support, from court preparation to long-term therapy with a specialized treatment team, that enabled them to grow through the process.

Billy Elliott sat in the prisoner's box and watched the members of the jury adjust headsets over their ears. The judge had just informed them that he was ready to go to the videotaping room (in the same courthouse), where he would conduct an inquiry to determine whether Lucy and Freddy understood an oath. TV monitors in the courtroom were turned on, showing a plain room with a table. On screen, the defence lawyer, wearing black court robes, sat on the left. A little nine-year-old girl in a pale blue dress walked on with a woman (Susan Johnson) wearing a red dress. The little girl sat down in a chair facing the camera, swinging her feet under the table, her legs too short to touch the floor. The judge appeared, screen right, a large figure in black robes.

Judge: Hello, my name is Judge McWilliam.
Lucy: Hello. (Soft voice, like a mouse.)
Judge: How old are you?
Lucy: Nine.
Judge: How many brothers and sisters do you have?
Lucy: I have one sister and four brothers. (The judge is momentarily confused, and the lawyer explains that Lucy has included her Johnson foster brothers and sister, all of whom she names in chronological order, by age. She appears bright and articulate.)

Judge: Where do you go to school?

Lucy: Cambridge school.

Judge: I went to Cambridge too, in England. (Lucy doesn't respond.)

Judge: What's your favourite subject in school?

Lucy: Recess. (Big laugh from the judge. He asks about her teacher, her friends, and then he hones in to determine whether she understands enough about God to allow her evidence to be sworn.)

Judge: Do you know what a church is?

Lucy: When we open the Bible and sing a song.

Judge: Do you go to church?

Lucy: Sometimes.

Judge: Why?

Lucy: I don't know.

Judge: Does it have anything to do with God?

Lucy: Yes.

Although she agreed with his suggestion that "God is a good person," Lucy was not able to describe God's characteristics in sufficient detail to satisfy the judge. In the hierarchy of evidence-giving, sworn testimony carries the most weight; the next step down is to promise to tell the truth, and the judge determined that Lucy could tell the difference between fairy tales and reality, between made-up stories and the truth; he decided that though her evidence could not be sworn, she could promise to tell the truth, the whole truth and nothing but the truth. "Yes, I do promise," Lucy said.

Crown attorney Des McGarry took over: speaking gently to Lucy, using simple, concrete language, he led her back through the stages of her life, back to Billy and Nancy. At the mention of their names, Lucy leaned forward on the table and put her face in her hands.

"Where did these things happen that we're here to talk about today?" McGarry asked. She told him, "Upstairs in the bedroom." (She couldn't bring herself to talk about what happened in the basement.) What sort of things? "Bad stuff they did to us in our private parts." What private parts? "My vagina and my bottom. Billy put his fingernails in my private parts, in my vagina and my bottom. Nancy hurt me too." Did she see Billy's private parts? "He hurt Freddy's and

Joey's private parts; he moved his private parts to one side and another on Freddy's and Joey's." McGarry finally got her to name Billy's private part: "His dick," she said. "Billy put his dick in my vagina." How did she feel? "Angry. I didn't like it. I said no but he went ahead." Did it happen more than once? "It happened lots of times.... One time Nancy tied my hands behind my back and Billy put tape over my mouth...." Were there any other people there? Lucy named other people who had participated and who have since been convicted.

The defence lawyer's cross-examination of Lucy was relatively mild — due to the overwhelming evidence against Billy Elliott. Nevertheless, the defence tried to raise questions about Lucy's ability to recall her past. Who lived in her house, Lucy was asked. "Me and Nancy and Billy and Freddy and Joey and Josh." This was the first mention the jury had heard of Joshua; the police had been searching for his body for months — though there was no official record of his birth. "Josh," Lucy repeated, "he was the baby but Billy killed him." The defence lawyer moved along quickly, not wanting Lucy's story about Josh to come out. The police speculated that Nancy — who had also been sexually abused as a child — might have become a cult "breeder," giving birth at home to babies who "disappeared." (Another baby she had with Billy, after Lucy, Freddy and Joey had been made Crown wards, had also been taken into custody.)

Freddy's testimony was sparse. He was being asked to recount events that had happened three years earlier, when he was four years old and living in a nightmarish world. Twisting around in the chair facing the camera, he tried to describe what Nancy and Billy had done. "They hurt us." What part of you? McGarry asked. "My penis," Freddy said, spitting out the word like a poisoned jellybean. Did Billy hurt any other part of you? "I don't know what you mean." Did you see Billy's penis? "Yes." Tell me about that. "He put it in our mouths and our bottom, me and Joey." Did you see something happen to Lucy? "Yes...I don't remember." Where? "Down in the basement." He named other adults who had been present (who have since been convicted, including his mother). What did they do in the basement? "Lots of stuff." But he couldn't bring himself to say any more.

It was enough to convict Billy Elliott, who was sentenced to seven years in jail for sexually assaulting Lucy, Freddy and Joey. Billy subsequently received an additional eighteen-month prison term for sexually abusing two relatives when they were children. Nancy was convicted and received two years less a day. Billy's parents were convicted; his mother got fifteen months for "aiding and abetting" a sexual assault, his father two years less a day for sexual assault. So far, sixteen accused have been found guilty and twenty have pleaded guilty. Of the 225 alleged victims, 145 are children and eighty are adults reporting abuse as kids. Forty-two children are "in care," apprehended by child protection authorities. In addition to the fifty-five adults already charged, the police report that another fifty alleged perpetrators are under investigation.

In the summer of 1992, the Johnsons were in the process of completing formal adoption procedures for Lucy, Freddy and Joey. Their eldest son, Mark,* had just won a graduate scholarship. "Do you mind if we brag?" Susan grinned. She and Steven relished Mark's embarkation into the adult world and the maturation of their teenagers while "the three little ones" settled down. Everyone was astonished by their progress. "You know what this means?" Steven said. "You can't put limits on what these children can achieve."

Lucy was always the easiest of the three, polite and acquiescent, but Susan realized that she was "without a self; underneath, there was nobody there. It was as if we looked inside her soul and nothing was alive." This was said kindly, with compassion. Like many survivors of sexual abuse, Lucy knew how to be invisible. In order to endure constant, intolerable violation, she'd perfected a disappearing act: her inner self was a deserted landscape from which all signs of life had been obliterated. The Johnsons' great gift to Lucy — the gift so many victims yearn to receive — was the most valuable prize of all: being seen.

Living with the Johnsons, Lucy slowly came out of hiding and gained confidence. "Now, three years later, I see her developing a self," said Susan, who took particular delight when Lucy argued about watching certain TV programs, or staying up late. "She stands up for her opinions, she feels like a somebody. She actually believes she's entitled to be herself and stand her ground and not let anyone push her around, which is amazing for her." She has also developed a goal: she wants to be a hairdresser. "That was our initial way of communicating,"

Susan said. "She'd brush my hair and stand behind me so she didn't have to look at me, and we'd talk. That's how we got to know each other."

When she first arrived at the Johnsons', Lucy didn't know how to play with other children, and was teased in the schoolyard because she was so awkward and withdrawn. She had difficulties manoeuvring around people, perhaps because she was still highly dissociated, and crashed into adults and knocked other kids over. But as she calmed down, she became more aware of space and of her own body, and more articulate in her speech. Like Freddy, she used to start sentences in the middle; her thinking was chaotic and it was hard to tell what she was talking about. She was now more coherent and socially adept, making friends with children close to her own age and able to have disagreements with them, which she hadn't had the confidence to do before. And she enjoyed school. These were huge developments for a child who'd been so alienated that, despite her intense need for approval, she couldn't connect with her peers. "Lucy's become a really happy person," Susan said. "She's happy to *be,* to have toys and friends and birthday parties." Lucy had just turned eleven, and Becky,* the Johnsons' teenage daughter, thought her mother should explain the biological facts of life to Lucy. "Becky says, 'Mom, it's time!' So we're kind of setting the stage, telling Lucy how we're women and that's special. Lucy has a terror of blood [related to ritual abuse] and we're worried about that, but I'm hopeful things will work out."

Freddy was the wildest and most uncontrollable. He had no self, like Lucy, but in a different way. "His eyes were glazed over," Susan said. "It was like you couldn't catch a glimpse of him — he was always yelling and leaping." When Freddy's hyperactivity dissipated, he became too compliant for a time, and was now finding the middle ground. The great discovery for Freddy was books. The Johnsons read to him every night: "It was as if he couldn't get enough, he was starving for stories," Steven said. Then Freddy came home from school one day and he could read! "He was really excited," Steven said, "we all were." Freddy was learning almost at his age level — a remarkable achievement for a boy who a few short years ago had been so grossly neglected and abused that he appeared irrevocably damaged.

Talking about the children's progess, Susan became a little tearful: "Freddy's going to grow up to be a fine man, he'll be as honest as the day is long, he'll be kind, he won't make headlines but he'll be the sort of man people respect. Joey, on the other hand" — she smiled — "Joey's got a touch of the devil. He's mischievous and charming, but I'm afraid he's going to get stuck playing the clown." Joey was seven and had just learned to ride a tricycle. His legs weren't very strong; he didn't get to walk much as a baby. Testimony from Billy Elliott's trial revealed that the children were sometimes tied to furniture or lowered into a basement cistern, a deep hole in the ground with water in it, and left for hours. The big breakthrough for Joey, Susan said, was that "he has real feelings now. He had no feelings at the beginning; he couldn't have cared less about our reactions. Now, he'll cry if we get angry at him, and that's a big step forward."

Inevitably, the children have undergone a battery of assessments and examinations by professionals: doctors, speech therapists, psychologists. For Steven, this was the hardest part: "I couldn't handle all the so-called experts treating the kids like specimens. I'm glad that's finished." Yet there was no avoiding ongoing interventions: at school, just before Lucy had to go to court to testify, she told a playmate what her parents had done to her. Lucy's friend told her mother, who called the principal. "Something terrible is happening to a child at this school," said the mother. "She's being horribly abused by her parents." It was, Susan said, "a very awkward situation." The principal couldn't discuss the court case with the woman but he assured her Lucy was being looked after. "I felt bad for Lucy," Susan said, "because she got the message she wasn't supposed to talk about what had happened, and that's not fair to her. She'd been silenced as a victim and I didn't want her to be silenced again. These children are heroes and the world should know it, but how can anyone know they're heroes if they can't talk about what they survived?" On the other hand, Susan didn't want them exposed to neighbours "thinking they're weird. The kids will go through their teenage years in this community, they'll go out on dates with our neighbours' children, and I don't want them to be stigmatized. That's the awful double bind the kids are in."

For the Johnsons, the most difficult symptom of abuse to deal with — because it was so persistent — was the children's eating disorder.

They still ate uncontrollably. Steven took them to a picnic, and they ate so much that they vomited. At home, they would finish a big meal and sneak into the kitchen, to raid the fridge. One morning after breakfast, Lucy downed a bowl of cold Kraft dinner left over from the night before. One night Susan made a batch of fudge, stored it in the freezer and later found Lucy vomiting in the bathroom; she'd eaten the entire batch of frozen fudge and made herself sick.

"It doesn't have to do with physical hunger," Susan said. "It's another kind of starving." When they lived with Nancy and Billy, the children were treated like animals, fed erratically or not at all, made to eat scraps off the floor, tied up, left alone, starved, literally, for food and adult approval; the only attention they received that wasn't verbal or physical abuse was sexual violation.

"The kids will lie, cheat and steal for food," Susan said. They were getting into trouble at school for stealing other kids' lunches, and Lucy had been suspended for a day for refusing to abide by disciplinary measures relating to her food thievery. Susan and Steven were working with the children's teachers to set firm boundaries. When Susan found out that Lucy had stolen chocolate bars from a local store, they went back to the store and Lucy apologized to the shopkeeper and paid for the chocolate bars. When Lucy did it again, Susan asked the shopkeeper to ban her from the store for a few days.

The Johnsons tried to reassure the children that they were safe. Steven slipped in messages as often as he could "about how they have the right to be respected and they can say no to things they don't want to do, they have value and worth just being themselves." The children's "affection boundaries" were still fragile; they physically touched people in inappropriate ways and were often too eager to be liked, too desperate for approval. Susan might intervene if Joey climbed all over a stranger, but it was awkward: she would tell Joey not to sit in Mr. X's lap, Mr. X would say, "Oh that's all right, I love kids," and Susan would want to say, Shut up and follow my lead. There's something going on here that you don't know anything about.

Then, every once in a while, the children would make great strides. One day Susan noticed that Joey, who'd been scribbling in an uncontrolled manner, was doing very fine detailed colouring inside the lines of a colouring book. "All of a sudden you see it, he's got this new skill, and you watch him concentrate with a new sense of purpose and you know it means something. I'm not an expert, I don't know the terminology, but something good is happening. You play it by ear; you do what works. It's taken three years, and it's really just now that we can see progress. We love them. They're beautiful kids."

This is a story of hope. Lucy, Freddy and Joey bear the scars, but their wounds are being tended. Because they were heard, other children were saved. They still sleep wrapped in their sheets like shrouds, as if they're trying to protect themselves, and they will continue to require therapy, at different stages, as they grow up. But they're out there now, running around the playground, skipping and jumping and laughing, and no one would ever guess what they've been through. They've come out of hiding. They belong in the world.

5

The Path
to Healing

Behind the wall we erect to protect ourselves from the history of our childhood stands the neglected child we once were, the child who was abandoned and betrayed. It waits for us to summon the courage to hear its voice.... It has a gift for us...the gift of truth.

— Alice Miller
Breaking Down the Wall of Silence

THERAPEUTIC TREATMENT FOR SURVIVORS of child sexual abuse is a relatively new field. Less than two decades ago, incest was regarded as such a rare phenomenon in the Western world that it was estimated to occur in one in a million families — a figure that was cited as recently as 1975 in *The Comprehensive Textbook of Psychiatry.* American sociologist Diana Russell concluded, less than a decade later, that of the one in three women sexually abused in childhood, according to her study, 16 per cent were victims of incest. Russell's figures were replicated in 1992 by the Women's Safety Project, a random survey designed by the Institute for Social Research at York University, Toronto, in which 17 per cent of women reported an incest experience before the age of sixteen. But somehow, traditional psychiatry remained preoccupied with "intra-psychic neuroses," and failed to grasp the truth: that many clients' problems were caused not by imaginary disorders but by childhood sexual abuse.

In one sense, the Prescott children were lucky: their abuse was identified by police and social workers, often before the children understood it themselves, and they received treatment. From 1989 to the end of 1993, they came to a therapy playroom in a renovated greystone warehouse in Prescott. There were sixty children, aged three to eighteen, including Lucy, Freddy and Joey, and they came to therapy to try to learn to be children, in a program operated by Beechgrove Children's Centre, developed as a model of early intervention that is being studied throughout North America. The three-woman treatment team was linked with the key players in the children's lives — social workers, teachers, police officers, foster parents and families of origin; half the children were in foster care, and the therapists also ran support groups for foster parents.

The hardest part for the children, at the beginning of treatment, was being labelled, singled out, pointed at. Nobody wants to be a victim, and these children were no exception. At school, they were whispered about and revictimized, as if the crimes committed against them were somehow their fault. "They felt a lot of shame about all the lurid publicity," says Ruth Campbell-Balagus, a team therapist. "They hated the glaring headlines, the stories about that awful Prescott place, the details of what happened."

They would arrive for therapy and just sit in the playroom, surrounded by toys, not knowing what to do. They didn't know how to play, didn't trust adults, couldn't show feelings. "They wanted us to think they were happy, and that's all they wanted us to think," says Bridget Revell, another team therapist.

Dr. Susan Meyers, who has a Ph.D. in psychology and was the senior member of the team, describes a typical client, ten years old, who arrives for her session, says, "I'm fine," and makes it very clear she's not interested in talking about abuse or going to court. "She prefers going places in her head," Meyers says. "She'd created a magic tree that she went to when terrible things happened, and she wanted to stay in the magic tree, feeling good." Court times were crisis times. To testify meant having to admit the abuse had happened, which made the child feel that her world was caving in. Better to be in the magic tree than in court, with people staring at you and saying you made it up.

Despite their fears, the children's experience with "the system" transformed their lives. "Going to court turned out to be a positive event for most of our kids," says Campbell-Balagus. "Being able to tell their story, being believed and seeing the abuser punished for having done a bad thing was incredibly empowering." But in order to understand what had happened to them, they needed therapy.

"Sexual abuse stops children from growing in certain core emotional ways; they can't reach out, they're too afraid," says Campbell-Balagus. "When the abuse starts, certain aspects of development stop, and that's what we have to do in therapy — find those blocked places, go back and start over." In the natural maturation process, children learn to define their personal boundaries, negotiate with others and cope with strong emotions — anger, disappointment, sadness, frustration, happiness. They go through the terrible twos, the tantrums, the aggression, the obsession with autonomy, all essential stages in the growth of the self; they defend their turf, say no to everything, glory in their emerging sense of "I'm me!" and learn to feel they are valued for the unique little persons they are. Their self-esteem is fragile; children are extraordinarily dependent on adults for survival and approval, and learn what's right and wrong from the behaviour of the trusted authority figures in their lives.

Basically, adults can do anything they want to a child. If a perpetrator touches them sexually, children can't possibly be expected to know what's happening, and they certainly aren't equipped, developmentally or physiologically, to cope with adult sexuality. Overpowered by the sexual frenzy of the offender, many children dissociate involuntarily, or become frenzied themselves, or go into psychic hiding, or rage uncontrollably, or become passive sex toys. Whatever strategy they use, it has the same outcome: the end of normal growth. Instead of learning to handle their emotions and negotiate with the world around them from a position of autonomy, they are forced inward, required to deal with a reality for which there's no social context. Not allowed to speak about what is happening to them, they try not to feel; it's too painful, too confusing, and so they numb themselves, withdrawing from the world, trapped in the trauma bond.

Campbell-Balagus had a client, Jenny,* a pre-teen girl who displayed no feelings, no interests, no wishes. Like many of the Prescott victims, Jenny was so accustomed to being violated that her own lack of boundaries seemed normal to her; so accustomed to servicing other people that she was unable to make choices. Children who aren't allowed to say no don't learn how to say yes. Campbell-Balagus would ask Jenny if she wanted to draw or paint or play with puppets and the girl would shrug: "I don't know, I don't care."

The breakthrough came one morning when Jenny said she wanted to go outside for a walk; it was the first time she'd suggested an activity, and Campbell-Balagus seized the opportunity. That walk was the best therapy they could have done. They walked by the river and Jenny saw a family of ducks. She quacked like a duck, as if she were two years old — "Abused kids need to go back through stages they've never experienced," Campbell-Balagus says — and then she went down a slide. The slide was wet and she got mad at the therapist because her pants got dirty; it was nine in the morning and she didn't want to go through the day with dirty pants. "Jenny felt, I think, that I'd put her in a situation that wasn't safe."

What was so positive about this, in therapeutic terms? Jenny expressed her feelings; she had asserted herself, she had taken the risk of being angry — which revealed a degree of trust in Campbell-Balagus — and they were able to have an important conversation that brought them in closer contact. Campbell-Balagus explained that if she had known the slide was wet she would have told Jenny, and she assured Jenny it was okay to get dirty: "You're a kid, kids play, kids go down slides and sometimes slides are dirty and kids get dirty and that's okay." Many abused children are afraid of doing the "wrong" thing that in their eyes causes the abuse; Jenny needed to be reassured that she hadn't done anything wrong.

As they walked along the street, Jenny said a man was staring at her. "He likes me," she said. Campbell-Balagus asked if Jenny knew the man. Jenny shook her head: no, she didn't know him. The therapist wanted to know how the man could like her if he didn't know her. "He's staring at my bum," Jenny said. This was another spontaneous situation rich with therapeutic possibilities; they talked about boundaries and interacting with people and how you don't have to talk to people you don't know. It was a conversation they couldn't have had in the abstract, because Jenny didn't understand abstract concepts.

The anarchy of abusive families often extends to the public

domain. If there are no rules at home, why bother to pay attention to society's rules? No one in Jenny's family had taught her about traffic signals. When they reached an intersection, Campbell-Balagus had to explain that Jenny should stop on red, go on green, and look left and right before she crossed the street. On the other side of the street, Campbell-Balagus said she was getting cold. Jenny didn't understand why. The therapist explained that they'd passed from the sunny side to the shady side, and that when she was in the shade she got cold, and she showed Jenny the goosebumps on her arms. They crossed the street again, back to the sunny side, and Jenny looked up with a big smile: "Now you're warm"; they crossed to the shady side and Jenny was triumphant: "Now you're cold." It was as if a light went on inside that little girl. The discovery of a benign natural order can come as a revelation to an abused child. For the first time in her life, perhaps, Jenny experienced a rhythm to life that was safe.

One misconception many people have about the healing process is that victims must talk about the abuse. For children, therapy works in oblique angles. "Our goal is not to make them regurgitate every sordid detail," Bridget Revell says. "They don't have the coping mechanisms to deal with it, and they can be retraumatized or desensitized if they're made to recite events with no emotion attached." In order to grow, children need to be able to feel again; in order to feel, they need to communicate the pain, and be recognized for what they've endured. That's best done through play, art and puppet games. In play therapy, therapists model behaviour, teaching children how to express feelings, showing them that they have boundaries and can safely interact with others without being violated.

Learning to express anger in safe ways is an essential piece of the process. Mike,* like many abused children, refused to show any feelings at all, in an attempt to control himself; then he'd blow up at minor irritants. The resulting temper tantrums caused him problems at school, in the playground, at his foster home; he was on the road to becoming a serious troublemaker, not because he was inherently bad, but because he had good reason to be angry: sexually abused as a child, he'd been taught that getting mad was bad. "He pushed all his feelings down," Revell says. "Then something would upset him, he'd lose control and later he'd promise he would never get mad ever again in his whole life." This is the vicious cycle that many abusive men are trapped in; they batter their wives, feel remorse, promise never to do it again and are inevitably triggered again; the cycle can be broken by uncovering the root cause of their rage, which is often some form of childhood violation.

But knowing the source isn't enough; Mike had to learn how to safely express his anger, stand up for himself and set boundaries. Over many sessions, Revell helped him visualize his temper; they made friends with his "temper lion" and talked about what made the temper lion come out. Then Revell invented the "Get Mad Quiz Game," based on the structure of a TV game show. Each side, his and hers, had three team members played by puppets, with a puppet judge who ruled on whether the answers were right or wrong. They took turns being the judge. Revell tape-recorded questions such as: *Is it okay to get mad? Is it okay to throw food when I get mad? Is it okay to tell people when I get mad? What's one thing that makes you mad? What did your dad do when he got mad?*

Revell would turn on the tape-recorder: "When you get mad, is it okay to break your toys?" The Revell puppet would answer, "Yes, I can smash all my toys if I want because they're my toys." The Mike puppet would crow, "Wrong!" The bad little boy who never did anything right was elated when he won the game, which served a twofold purpose: to build self-esteem and teach appropriate ways of expressing anger.

Among the therapists' favourite tools for dealing with anger and control issues are dolls and puppets. "It's really important that the kids learn to feel in control, because they've been so invaded," Campbell-Balagus says. She had a little client who wanted to play doctor, with the therapist acting as patient. "That could have caused boundary problems — I didn't know what she wanted to do to my body — so I encouraged her to examine the [anatomically correct] doll; I spoke through a puppet, playing the part of the patient, so she could talk to the puppet, not to me." Such role reversals, with the child occupying the adult power position, allow victims to re-enact scenarios in which they've been abused, express their fury and remain in control; they learn to feel safe in the here and now.

It is a natural human response to avoid pain — everyone does it, psychopaths to the ultimate extreme of cutting off emotion so completely that they feel nothing, and can cause pain to others without remorse. Meyers had a client, Tom,* "a little guy who'd been invaded all the time and was an expert at shutting people out." She was stuck; she couldn't get anywhere with him. Tom was all action and no talk, a bully who was so busy defending himself that he couldn't relate to anyone. Meyers would ask how things were going at school and he'd say, "Perfect, no sweat." Then his teacher would tell Meyers that Tom had been so disruptive in class that he'd been kicked out three times that week.

One day out of the blue, Meyers invented a story about a knight who lived in a village caught in the middle of a war. The knight made himself a suit of heavy armour that helped him survive the war. Then the war ended and the villagers went out to plant the fields but the knight was still clanking around in his armour; he was too hot, he couldn't bend down, he was trapped in his armour....

"The knight died, didn't he?" Tom interjected.

"Well," said Meyers, "it's really sad. He needed that armour but he got stuck in it, and that story reminded me of you. You got hurt and you needed armour to protect you but now it's getting heavy and rusty...."

"So?" said Tom.

"So," she said, "why don't you make a suit of armour that you can put on when you want and take off when it's too heavy?" He liked the idea, and she helped him construct a handsome suit of cardboard armour, which she kept on a special shelf in her office. "The point was to respect his armour, because he really needed it — he suffered serious abuse committed by multiple perpetrators — and to honour him for being brave enough to consider taking it off."

With each child the breakthrough takes a unique form, arising indirectly from some form of play. Digging in the sandbox or painting pictures, playing with anatomically correct dolls or talking through hand-puppets — with the child choosing and leading the activity — the therapist watches for "the teachable moment," those spontaneous happenings in which children experience a burst of insight that moves them forward.

Sammy,* one of Meyers' clients, had been sexually abused from infancy, and was so habituated to sex that he engaged in sexual activity indiscriminately, with children or adults of either sex. As Sammy approached puberty, Meyers worried that he would become a sex offender. "He was twelve years old and he would be humping the mat [in therapy session] just because he felt like it; it felt good." Like many of the Prescott survivors, Sammy was developmentally delayed (attributed to deprivation, neglect and abuse, not organic causes), which made him at once very vulnerable and very dangerous.

Meyers' task was tricky: without shaming or blaming him, she had to try to help him understand that his behaviour was inappropriate: it wasn't that *sexuality* was bad, but that he'd been overpowered by adults' sexual needs and had "got stuck" with sex in a way that blocked his growth. Sammy had been set up and didn't know it; he hadn't done the things other kids do, hadn't been allowed to explore the world, to play baseball, be a child. He had no sense of personal boundaries. At twelve, he was a big boy functioning at the level of an eight-year-old, whose activities were limited to sex. A decade earlier, Sammy would have been labelled "retarded" and put in a class for "dumb kids," where he likely would have molested other children and launched a career as a pedophile.

Sammy had "no cognitive awareness," Meyers says, "of being a victim." He didn't understand concepts of consent, violation or power imbalance. "He's like a lot of the adult sex offenders I've dealt with. *They just don't get it,* they don't see that they're hurting kids — *because* they were hurt as kids. They've cut off the part of themselves that was victimized. They can't feel anything apart from the sexual addiction." And as they get older, they find their predilections reinforced by mainstream culture, movies and rock videos that glorify violent males who dominate younger, weaker sex objects.

Meyers made no progress with Sammy until one day he arrived for a session very upset. It was the first time she had seen him show spontaneous emotion. What awful thing had happened? Bobby had stolen Sammy's baseball cards. This was it: the teachable moment. Meyers asked Sammy why he didn't like what Bobby had done. "Because they're *my* baseball cards and I didn't say he could have them," Sammy cried. He was devastated — and he was feeling! Meyers comforted him and gently talked to him about the concept of theft; she made the connection that Bobby taking his baseball cards without permission was like Daddy taking his body without permission, since a child is unable to withhold consent from a powerful adult. Sammy needed to understand that his father had taken something that belonged to Sammy, and that it wasn't fair to Sammy to have his body used whenever his father wanted. It was a revelation to Sammy that his father had done something wrong. Understanding that he'd been powerless to stop the abuse, Sammy could begin to reclaim himself.

Admitting their own helplessness is the most painful step for survivors of any age — and the most necessary. If a parent was the abuser, children need to believe they are loved by Mom or Dad; to realize a parent committed terrible crimes against them — acts that have nothing to do with love and everything to do with the abusers' obsessive self-absorption and blindness to others — is to acknowledge a kind of death. To accept that they weren't safe with their own parent, or with a trusted authority figure, is a terrifying step for children. Yet the end of the illusion is the beginning of recovery. The acceptance of the truth is, ultimately, liberating.

Bridget Revell describes one small moment when painful truths were acknowledged and a child grew. In a therapy session, seven-year-old Sarah* was playing house; she instructed Revell to act the role of the child. Sarah took charge as the mother. Revell said, as the child, "Where's my dad?" Without skipping a beat, Sarah said, "He's in jail." (Which was true.) Revell asked why. "He touched you," Sarah said. She marched to the blackboard, drew intricate diagrams of two little girls and explained where they were, what they were wearing and what the perpetrator was doing to them. She was telling her story. "She couldn't have done it if she'd been talking directly about herself," Revell says, "and it would have been too threatening if I'd asked her what her father had done to her, but this way, in play, she was able to distance herself from the abuse while sharing what happened."

Revell then took a risk, based on the work they'd been doing in therapy. Still in the role of the child, she asked: "Why did he do that to me? Did I do something wrong?" Sarah was vehement in her response: "No, you didn't do anything wrong, it was him, it was his fault, he was the bad one, not you!" Then, as if to prove her point, she picked up the play phone and announced she was calling the jail. *Ring, ring, ring:* "What?" she said. "You're letting him out so soon?" Revell was amazed that a seven-year-old understood, with adult-like awareness, the disturbing reality of short sentences for sexual offenders. Sarah kept on talking: "He says he's learned not to do it any more? You can't believe a word he says. Oh, I see. You're giving him pills." She hung up the phone. "They're giving him pills," she said firmly, "so he won't tell lies any more."

This vignette demonstrates how far Sarah had come: she was able to acknowledge the abuse, identify the perpetrator and recognize that he'd been punished for being bad; she made herself safe by giving him pills so he wouldn't lie any more, even though she knew she couldn't trust him. She had, in her own way, taken back control over her life. "That's the essence of trauma, losing control," Revell says. "This is what healing is all about: being able to look back and say, yes, I was helpless then, and now I'm safe."

The Prescott treatment program "graduated" dozens of children "who've done the piece of work they needed to do," Meyers says. They're free to move on and grow emotionally, having been recognized for what they've suffered. The therapists held individual graduation ceremonies and commemorated each child's accomplishments. Meyers did a body tracing of a five-year-old girl to show how much bigger she was, and told her, "You've grown in a lot of ways: you can do somersaults now, you can sleep with just the nightlight on and you're living with a new mom and dad." The little girl had come into therapy when she was three, and now she needed to ride her tricycle with other kids, go to kindergarten and have fun. For a boy whose graduation involved being adopted, the therapists videotaped a session with his biological mother, who explained that she loved the boy but couldn't look after him because of her own problems. The tape was given to the child so he could watch it as many times as he needed, to understand that he was adopted not because he was bad, stupid or unlovable (as he initially thought), but because his mother loved him enough to want him to have the kind of life she couldn't give him. "What these kids need more than anything is what Lucy, Freddy and Joey have with the Johnsons: to be safe and cared for, to go out into the world and be children," Meyers says. "They've already had too much involvement with adults, and we don't want to 'therapize' them to death."

Alice Miller, the world-famous Swiss psychoanalyst, broke from Sigmund Freud's orthodox canon, and from psychoanalysis itself, in 1988. "I was forced to take this step," she wrote in *Thou Shalt Not Be Aware: Society's Betrayal of the Child*, "when I realized that psycho-analytical theory and practice obscure — ie., render unrecognizable — the causes and consequences of child abuse by (among other things) labeling facts as fantasies...." Miller came to believe that behavioural symptoms are a sign language of distress. Hyperactivity, extreme with-drawal, substance abuse, self-mutilation, promiscuity, suicidal obses-sions, eating disorders — all have a specific function: "to express the unconscious trauma" in a disguised form that no one — neither client nor therapist — can understand. Yet when repressed trauma is commu-nicated and understood, symptoms disappear and healing begins.

So it was for Shirley Turcotte, who, like many Prescott children, grew up disordered and dissociated. Her story illuminates the efficacy of good therapy. Lucy, Freddy and Joey can't talk about their experi-ence of evolving through layers of protective dissociation, but Turcotte can; she can also turn the process inside out and explain it from the professional's perspective. Today, she's a well-known therapist who specializes in the treatment of adult survivors. The therapist's role, she believes, is not to be a guru, not to make clients dependent: "Everything I know, I encourage my clients to know, so when they wake up at two in the morning and they're flashing back or flooding, they can look after themselves, because that's what it's all about." The therapist's job is to listen well, be flexible, innovative, and unafraid of clients' behaviour, dreams or memories. Therapists must not dictate to clients what their problems are, and must never interfere in their clients' process of sorting out memories and dreams.

Turcotte sprang to international prominence with the 1987 release of *To a Safer Place,* a National Film Board documentary based on her unpublished autobiography; a film crew followed her from her Vancouver home on a journey to Manitoba, to confront the ghosts of her past. Turcotte's father was Métis, the son of an aboriginal man and a white woman; her mother was of Russian descent and from a

Mennonite background. Shirley is the second of six children, three girls and three boys. At the age of six months she was taken to hospital in shock; she'd been sexually abused, and she'd dissociated. Like many of the Prescott children whose exploitation began in infancy, Turcotte would store memories of pre-verbal abuse in her body, though it would be many years before she understood what body memories were — that various aches, pains, rashes and areas of numbness were trying to tell her something.

As time went by, she split into many different parts, "which was a brilliant way to survive the next fourteen years," as she puts it. She was later diagnosed as having multiple personality disorder, a dissociative technique that some abused children develop spontaneously, allowing them to fragment reality into dozens of different pieces or "alters," in order to bear the unbearable — and to stay sane. She is grateful for her ability to split, grateful to have had a hiding place in the basement where she "left" her body when she was being sexually assaulted, "grateful it was so black and white, he was so clearly the bad guy, the evil one; I didn't have to deal with the confusion of the seductive perpetrator, which is so hard for so many survivors." (In 1961, her father was convicted of sexually abusing Shirley and one of her sisters. He received a suspended sentence, after which "the abuse got worse," she says.)

Turcotte also had amnesia, as many abused children do, and couldn't remember huge chunks of her childhood. Not remembering can be a dangerous thing. The last time she babysat in her youth, she was twelve years old. The baby cried and she couldn't stand it. "I took a pillow and put it over the baby's face." She managed to pull out of the trance before anything happened, and never babysat again, "but I hated myself for the longest time, and I was afraid to have children." She didn't understand that she was re-enacting a buried memory. "I needed to retrieve that baby, that part of myself, from its frozen state, I needed to empathize with the crying baby self I abandoned, in order to live." The impulse to do "awful things" is common among survivors, she says; the therapist's job is to help clients track back to the source, which may be a memory of abuse. "We're trying to get the unconscious memory into the conscious mind so it can be integrated." This means breaking the trance, gently encouraging survivors to emerge from their dissociative cocoons. "I don't know how to express the sacredness, the delicacy of this task. It's like walking on eggshells."

So it was for Harvey Armstrong, a fledgling psychiatrist who first encountered Turcotte almost twenty-five years ago. She'd escaped her father's house when she was fourteen and had been placed in foster care. A runaway who slashed herself, Turcotte was institutionalized and kept trying to die. At seventeen, she was referred to Dr. Armstrong, a University of Toronto psychiatric intern who knew nothing about child sexual abuse but was sensitive enough to sit back, listen and follow his patient's lead. Covered with scars, fixated on what she now terms "suicidal ideation," Turcotte was emerging from the dungeon of her childhood. To this day, she remembers very little of her nine years in therapy with Armstrong, because he was talking to her "alters" — pieces of herself that she wasn't conscious of and that he didn't yet realize were parts of a multiple personality.

Today, Harvey Armstrong is a specialist in the treatment of children, adolescents and their parents, as well as adult survivors of child sexual abuse. He is an associate professor of psychiatry at the University of Toronto, a staff psychiatrist at the Hospital for Sick Children and a much-sought-after expert witness (on behalf of victims) in child sexual abuse cases. But in the late 1960s, having been taught nothing about child sexual abuse during medical school or psychiatric training, he was utterly bewildered by Turcotte as she switched personalities, talked in the voices of children of various ages and hallucinated. He was frightened that he might not be able to bring her back from the living nightmares that seemed to engulf her; she was remembering buried trauma, on the path to releasing it, but Armstrong didn't understand, then, how the process worked. Few did. Many psychiatrists would have consigned her to the back ward of a psychiatric hospital, labelled "personality disorder" or "schizophrenic" or "manic-depressive," and plied her with drugs that would have reduced her to a zombie state.

Instead, Armstrong listened; the more he heard, the more she told, and a pattern emerged. In order to see it, he — like Alice Miller — had to break out of his training in Freudian orthodoxy, which held that children fantasized about sex with parents. He asked senior psychiatrists how they treated sexually abused children, "and they looked at me as if I was crazy. They'd never heard of it; it didn't happen. Nobody [in the medical profession] was prepared to acknowledge it was a problem." He tried to find academic papers, studies or statistics in the field, and came up empty-handed.

Armstrong had no choice: "Basically I kind of went along with Shirley and she taught me." After nine years, she "graduated" from therapy, "outgrew crazy," as she puts it — or, as Alice Miller would say, her symptoms disappeared because the trauma had been expressed. She moved to Vancouver, became a telecommunications technologist, got married and began her activist work with survivors, which led to more education and a new career. She became a registered clinical counsellor in British Columbia and discovered she'd invented, as a survivor, many of the techniques she was being taught to use as a therapist. She was already an expert at psychodrama and role-playing. As a child, she had no toys, no TV, no normal socialization or dinner with the family; all she had was being down in the basement with her brothers, acting out the violent behaviour of their father. One of her brothers would puff himself up and rant and rave like an idiot, and "we'd get to see how awful and stupid Dad looked." They would beat him up and chase him out of the room. Through role-playing, they took back control and redressed the balance: they saw that he was the pathetic weak one, and they were real, human, sane.

When her professional expertise was established, Turcotte asked Harvey Armstrong if they could shift their relationship from patient/doctor to friend/colleague. He agreed, and introduced her to his wife, Mary Armstrong, with whom Turcotte established a close relationship. Over time, Turcotte came to regard the Armstrongs as her spiritual parents; they speak of her with parental pride and maintain close personal and professional ties.

Operating out of an expansive suite of offices shared with a group of colleagues in mid-town Toronto, the Armstrongs preside over a mini-empire of therapeutic ventures that range from group therapy to retreat weekends and the Centre for Focusing Inc., operated by Mary Armstrong. Since 1971, Harvey has been involved with native communities, and is frequently to be found far off the beaten track, in Sioux Lookout and points north, training aboriginal leaders to provide therapy for their own people, an interest he shares with Turcotte. (He won two major awards from the American Psychiatric Association, for his work with aboriginal people and with teenagers in crisis.) Apart from his private practice, Armstrong's time is increasingly taken by Parents for Youth, which he formed to help parents (in a group therapy setting) deal with out-of-control teenagers. The groups attract successful adults with an average income of $80,000-plus a year; the one area of their lives where they perceive themselves to be failing is as parents. Armstrong finds, in the majority of these families, at least one parent who was abused in childhood, didn't know how to establish boundaries and thus set up their children to become tyrants. Children who haven't had firm limits set for them are deprived; at a deep level, their needs haven't been met, and they keep pushing, unconsciously seeking the reassurance of limits. If the parents are treated, the children get better.

Mary Armstrong, meanwhile, had studied with Dr. Eugene Gendlin, a professor of psychology at the University of Chicago and founder of the Focusing Institute. Gendlin has two Ph.D.'s — one in philosophy, the other in psychology — and proposes the revolutionary view that "clients *know it all,* not therapists," as Mary Armstrong puts it. His emphasis is on working through blocked emotions to recover knowledge stored in the body — an approach that appealed to Turcotte, who trained with both Gendlin and Mary Armstrong.

Mary Armstrong does not make diagnoses or "suggest" to clients what their problem may be, and thinks it's bad therapy to do so. "I don't know anything about clients until they tell me; I don't know where they're going until they get there." Many people who enter therapy are middle class and high-functioning; they are often depressed and/or angry without knowing why; they may be suffering from migraines, insomnia or bowel disorders; and they've decided to look inward. In the sixties and seventies, if they were lucky, they could have received benign analysis from a Freudian psychiatrist, sophisticated dream interpretation from a Jungian, or psychodrama directed by a Gestalt therapist. As helpful as these approaches might have been, clients often ended up going in circles, unable to break through their inner defences to what Turcotte calls "the core wound." The therapist's job is to help them get there by opening themselves to their own knowledge, in a safe way, working through the dissociative layers without being flooded by traumatic memories.

Mary Armstrong's particular interest is the phenomenon of dissociation: "It blows my mind, frankly, how the human mind operates in the face of trauma. It is absolutely fascinating that we are able to cut off whole parts of our personalities in situations where reality is intolerably painful." Dissociation seems to be an instinctive ability some people are born with, like a gift for music. Not everyone can do it. "My personal theory is that a lot of children who die unexplained deaths were sexually abused and did not have the ability to dissociate. When you think about a little girl or boy who is raped by Daddy at night and comes downstairs in the morning to eat cornflakes with the abuser as if nothing happened — these children have *erased* the abuse; it is their ability to split that allows them to grow up and function and go through most developmental steps without being overly depressed. It is an incredible skill." Some clients uncover memories of practising: lying in bed at night, or daydreaming by day, they may have made themselves very small or put themselves up on the ceiling or out in the trees, or developed tricky mind games, practising for the moment when the abuse starts and the dissociation takes over.

But dissociated memories weigh heavily on the soul. "It's like having too big a mortgage on your house," Mary Armstrong says. "It catches up to you in adult life. The split in consciousness is stored in the body and the body demands healing." If there's no psychic resolution, there will likely be physical symptoms that can lead to disease.

Defences can be stubbornly held, difficult to dismantle and so deeply ingrained that many people aren't aware of them. In childhood, the defences were necessary; in therapy, Armstrong encourages clients to develop rapport with the mechanisms that protected them. "Clients need to be able to say, 'Thank you very much, you served me well, you saved my life.' " But as clients begin to retain glimpses of buried memories — triggered by disturbing dreams, or odd images or remarks — they approach the trauma zone, where they usually encounter massive resistance. Armstrong works *with* resistance, never against it. "Never use a battering ram to push through the blocks. It's an important insight for clients to see how resistance works and that it's there to protect them from knowing. Then maybe they can move forward and get in touch with the child's fear." As they cross the borderline from not knowing to knowing — which one survivor described as like entering an abandoned Nazi concentration camp; though it was deserted, it carried the echoes of screams and feelings of terror — the process of integration begins. It can be characterized as short-term pain for long-term gain. It's about building a relationship with the dissociated child abandoned so long ago.

"I am Lust," Shirley Turcotte says, approaching a volunteer who has been drawn from the audience and instructed to keep Turcotte at bay. "Lust keeps coming at you, it never gives up." Turcotte is on stage at the Ontario Institute for Studies in Education, leading a sexuality workshop at a sold-out conference for professionals, dealing with child abuse. She is acting out "the traumatic bond" that exists between a sexually abused child and the perpetrator. She wants to give her audience a visceral understanding of the dilemma of a child who is targeted as a sex object by a powerful adult.

"Oh darling, I love it when you push me away," Turcotte croons seductively, trying to grab the volunteer, who defends herself against the unwanted advances. "You excite me when you're angry," Turcotte says. She is relentless; the audience is riveted; the volunteer, a hip-looking woman with short dark hair, in black jeans and a white T-shirt, gradually loses her equanimity.

"I'm Lust, I'm an addict, I'm never going to stop," Turcotte says, prowling the stage. If we're going to talk about sexual abuse, she seems to be saying, let's experience a piece of it, and realize it's not fun. The audience is feeling it, as is the volunteer. The more aggressively she tries to push Turcotte away, the more intense is Turcotte's leering, grasping pursuit. Then the volunteer twists around suddenly and, she thinks, triumphantly: she happens to be trained in Wen-Do, a women's self-defence technique, and she's immobilized Turcotte in a powerful hold.

"Okay, she's got me," Turcotte says, "and I've got what I want." There is a strange silence in the huge crowd. "We're stuck in this place," Turcotte explains. "We're trapped in the traumatic bond — *this is it* — she can't get rid of me because *she can't let go.*" The audience emits a collective gasp and the volunteer's victorious smile fades;

Turcotte has tricked them all. Now they can see it: the volunteer is stuck in the defensive stance, her body rigid with tension. "This is where I was stuck with my father for years," Turcotte says. She recalls her father's eyes when he was going to abuse her — an image that haunts many children, that they may associate with a dragon or a devil. "He mesmerized me, I would be paralysed, hypnotized. I couldn't escape; there was no way to stop him. It took me a long time to get rid of him. It was hard to learn not to take him everywhere I went."

She speaks to the volunteer, who still holds her: "How do you feel?"

The volunteer grimaces: "Shaky."

"How do you get rid of me?"

"I don't know."

"It's a stuck place to be." One of her first goals in therapy is to "get the offender out of the room." With most clients, the damage was done in the past; abusers generally have no power in the present. The task for adult survivors is "to get back to the self, break the traumatic bond, release the pain and move forward." Turcotte releases the volunteer and allows herself to be chased away without further ado. The volunteer sits down and Turcotte returns to the stage. "You can spend the rest of your life holding off the offender, trapped in the traumatic bond, or you can let go."

Adult sexuality is profoundly shaped by child sexual abuse. Taught that human contact means sexual contact, survivors may be confused about how to interact with people. Like Lucy, Freddy and Joey, they may have trouble establishing "affectional boundaries"; they may sexualize all relationships, without knowing why, and engage in sex with married colleagues or bosses; or they may withdraw from human connection and become workaholic loners. They may be promiscuous and pretend to adore sex when in fact they are unable to be present in their bodies during the sex act; they may masturbate compulsively, or vacillate between sexual addiction and aversion.

In adult sexual relationships, survivors need to be in control; they need to be able to select when, where and how they make love. Turcotte suggests they begin slowly — "Today it's okay for you to hold my hand" — and gradually let themselves be present in their bodies.

However, when memories surface, accompanied by overwhelming rage and grief, it may be impossible to continue a sexual relationship. They may have difficulty breathing, feel like choking or vomiting, spitting as if there's semen in their mouth — which Turcotte encourages them, very gently, to experience, understand and expel, as part of unravelling the trauma bond.

Abraham* was a workaholic lawyer of sixty-seven when he came to see her. He was suffering from acute anxiety attacks, convinced he was going to have a heart attack and die. For years he'd sought out psychiatrists and medical specialists in a desperate bid to discover what ailed him, and in therapy with Turcotte he talked nonstop, with a hypochondriac's encyclopedic knowledge about everything that was wrong with him. Turcotte noticed that when Abraham spoke he took sharp breaths between sentences, sucking in air, panting — in fear? She amplified the sound of his breathing and it reverberated around the hall in waves of shock. In therapy, she asked him to exaggerate the sound, to make it louder, to feel it. Over time, the sound led to the memory of Abraham being anally raped as a child. Now he understood why he'd been so addicted to work; if he paused long enough, he might have to remember. At last, the four-year-old in Abraham was safe enough to look at the trauma. "It's never too late to heal," she says. "And never too late to remember."

She takes questions from the audience: "Are you still having memories," a woman asks, "or does it ever end?" Turcotte is not ready to talk about the second round of memories, which catapulted her deeper into the terror of her childhood. "When you have years and years of amnesia, as I do, you can expect to have memories periodically, for the rest of your life, to be healing for ever. Healing is about being comfortable with the process, being empathetic, loving and gentle with yourself, being non-judgemental about whatever is ready to surface and letting it come." Being a survivor of child sexual abuse is not a disease, she notes. "The ways we've survived — repression, dissociation, multiple personality — are creative responses; and we're in process all our lives, just like everybody else. Life is a process."

The part of the process she has not discussed publicly is ritual abuse. It's a taboo topic. "People react toward ritual abuse today just as they did ten years ago when we started to talk about sexual abuse: with disbelief," Mary Armstrong says. Many of the Armstrongs' professional colleagues thought them "perverse," as Harvey puts it, to bring up such a "fringe phenomenon" as child sexual abuse years earlier; today, many mental health professionals take a similar attitude to ritual abuse. Yet for the past five years, Harvey and Mary Armstrong have been hearing gruesome reports about ritual abuse from clients who don't know each other, who've been brought up in different parts of North America, but whose stories are horribly similar. "It's unbelievable stuff, though we believe our clients," Mary Armstrong says.

Ritual abuse does not have to involve Satanic worship; cults can be small or large, based within families, communities or quasi-religious groups, organized with crude informality or using more sophisticated procedures drawn from, and distorting, biblical teachings. The practices are handed down from generation to generation, acted out on a spectrum that, at its low end, is exemplified by the Prescott case. Billy Elliott dug up bodies from a graveyard and pulled the heads off skeletons; adults dressed in masks and costumes terrified children, who were sometimes bound and gagged; Billy's father killed animals in front of children and they were forced to drink the blood — at least that's what their abusers told them it was, and that's what they believed.

"It's not my interest, ritual abuse," Harvey Armstrong says. "It just keeps coming at me and I feel an obligation to pay attention since my colleagues aren't too interested." However, centres of expertise are developing, and Armstrong cites St. Luke's Presbyterian Hospital in Chicago, where psychologist Roberta Sachs specializes in treating ritual abuse survivors using a form of play therapy. In the Prescott treatment playroom, there was a sandbox where children could play out, in the sand, the inner traumas that preoccupied them, which they couldn't have otherwise expressed. Sachs, understanding that many adult ritual abuse survivors also can't find language for the horrible things that have been done to them, began to use a sandtray — a sandbox on legs, small enough to make the adult player feel big, dominant and in control.

Armstrong pushed a cassette into his VCR and Roberta Sachs appeared on the TV screen, explaining that the tape had been produced by St. Luke's as a training tool for therapists. "The sandtray frees up a part of the mind that can't express itself in a verbal way," she said. "Clients can position figures in ritual abuse ceremonies or show the groupings of the MPD [multiple personality disorder] alters." As clients construct their inner world in the actual space of the sandtray, the therapist can help them process the emotional content; by manipulating the scene and the "people" in it, they are able to maintain control while expressing the trauma.

The video cut to a sandtray, with the client's hands arranging tiny dollhouse figures — children, adults, babies, monsters, animals, furniture and implements — in the sand. Harvey Armstrong stopped the film for a moment, with a warning: "What you're going to see is typical of ritual abuse survivors. You may find it very upsetting. You're going to see a client go down through layers of dissociation and describe a series of intolerable degradations that forced her to dissociate."

The camera was fixed on the sandtray. The only visible parts of the client were her torso and hands; she was white-skinned and sounded like a well-educated American. She placed a row of dolls, dressed in black capes and hoods, on the sand in an area she'd organized to resemble a classroom, with little blackboards, desks and shelves full of toys. "These are god monsters," she said, fingering the hooded dolls. "I thought they were teachers at first, then I found out they weren't. I was three years old." Her voice regressed to the wispy lisp of a three-year-old. "They made us take off our clothes. I was cold. I hated it."

She ripped the clothes off a girl doll and acted out her words: "A person held me down, he was twisting and pushing into me, he pulled my head back, I bit my lip." She started to cry, couldn't talk, bashed a hooded figure into the naked girl doll. "They flipped me around, I don't know, they forced me down, it felt like they were chewing on me, clawing on me...." She sobbed hysterically, then she screeched, a heart-stopping scream. "They stuck things inside me, I banged my head real hard and it hurt and I didn't care. I felt so dirty." Sachs' voice was gentle and soothing: "That's an awful thing for a three-year-old to go through."

The client screamed: "They smeared stuff all over us...."

Harvey Armstrong spoke: "It was probably feces or blood."

"It smelled terrible," the client cried. "I hated it, I hated it. Parts of animals, all cut up, they made me eat it...." She let loose a terrifying shriek. "I threw it up, I hated it."

Armstrong turned off the tape. "Children who are put through these tortures are often given cult names in the brainwashing process so that when they're adults they can be reactivated in the cult." He's had clients in therapy with him for a couple of years, and he didn't know they were participating in rituals. The clients weren't deliberately deceiving him; their dissociative splits were so profound that they didn't know where they'd been. Armstrong has had clients who said they were going away for the weekend; and when they came back they found bruises on their inner thighs, or they had sore penises or vaginas and didn't know what had happened. Victims can be "let go" to get an education, establish themselves in professional roles as teachers or doctors, then "called back" to recruit more victims and participate in rituals. "These things are going on right here in Toronto and they're a lot more common than any of us would like to believe," he said.

If survivors try to escape the cult, their "alters" may try to pull them back; the alters may feel like aliens, but they're one-dimensional trance states, split-off parts that contain a slice of memory or a sequence of abuse. To the host personality, these parts may feel like complex, dominant beings, but they're very limited in their abilities. "Some know how to fuck, others know how to fight, some are passive and acquiescent, others aggressive and angry, and some hate the others," Armstrong said. The parts of a multiple personality can be totally different from each other; they can have different prescriptions for their glasses, different allergies, different sexual preferences. Armstrong worked with a female client who had "protector males" (alters) who thought they were six foot three and three hundred pounds and liked to throw their weight around. She also had child personae who were tiny and terrified.

Coming to terms with multiplicity can be a frightening process. To feel the disjointed edges of other selves moving in and out of the "mainframe," experiencing the fluidity of identity and the strangeness of discovering unfamiliar aspects of oneself, can make many survivors, their doctors and families think they're crazy. They're not, Armstrong says; they reflect a normal human response to intolerable abuse.

He showed another sequence of Sachs' tape. "I would go to church and I would hear the litany in my head — *I am the bad seed, I deserve to be punished,"* the client said, constructing a scene in the sandtray. "They brought home dead animals, birds, squirrels. They taught Katie what she was supposed to do." Holding miniature dolls, moving them around with agitated purpose, the client described how Katie, a younger self, "shattered into thousands and thousands of pieces and she never returned home." Her voice regressed to an earlier age; she whined and cried: "I couldn't see anything 'cause I was very, very scared and I couldn't breathe so I went away [dissociated]." She picked up a little boy doll. "His job was to scoop out the eyes of the dead baby on the altar." Sachs assured the client she would never have to do that, ever again. The client confessed that "when they asked me who killed the babies, I said, 'Me did it. Katie didn't do it, I didn't do it — *me did it.*"

In another sequence, a client described how she'd turned herself into an animal so she "didn't have to do it as a human being. It's kill or be killed." Then she shifted into another persona who didn't recognize Sachs; the client tried to slash herself and then threatened Sachs "Don't you dare hurt anyone," Sachs said, wrestling her down. "I'm not going to let you hurt yourself. You're not in a cage any longer, you're not an animal, you don't have to fight for your life. There, take a deep breath, let somebody come through who knows it's safe here, I'm right here, it's safe, I see you, I believe you." Weeping, the client said she wanted to die. Sachs reassured her: "You didn't have a choice then. You have a choice now. To die now would make a mockery of your survival."

For therapists, hearing such revelations is an occupational hazard. Carrying the secrets of people who've been horribly abused causes immeasurable stress. Professional confidentiality prohibits therapists from talking about their work with friends or family, yet they need to relieve their psychic burden; they also need to set firm boundaries with clients who are extraordinarily needy.

Turcotte learned the hard way about setting such boundaries. For years she worked on the edge of burnout before realizing she wouldn't be able to help anyone if she didn't look after herself. She also noticed that she wasn't the only one with this problem. "As we're able to hear more, survivors are able to say more — *thank goodness, and oh my God!* if you know what I mean. There's very little support for us. What we need to know we *can't* learn at university. We have got to change the way we do business." Turcotte reorganized her Vancouver practice. The result is a strict regimen: she sees a maximum of six clients a day for three weeks of every month, and quits precisely at

5:15 p.m. every day, when she hops on her bicycle and rides to the Pacific ocean. She guards her private time zealously. "I am *not* a caretaker. When you're with me, you have my attention one hundred per cent, three times a month. That's it."

The fourth week of every month is spent in aboriginal communities or speaking at conferences. Turcotte is a member of the Manitoba Métis Federation and proud of her heritage; she teaches aboriginal counselling techniques at the University of Manitoba and runs two-year courses for indigenous healers in remote communities, where child sexual abuse is a legacy, in part, of religious residential schools that aboriginal youngsters were forced to attend.

She has a two-year waiting list and screens carefully, on the phone and in person, before making the long-term commitment — "as long as is necessary" — to take on a new client. She sees people from every social and economic stratum — lawyers, doctors, architects, prostitutes, poor people, gays, lesbians and people with AIDS. Most are survivors of child sexual abuse and need more time than she can give — which is why she sets up weekly support groups for clients who need more interaction. She attends the first few meetings, teaching them to set boundaries, share time and put limits on when they can contact each other outside the group. Then she tells them, "This is your group, you run it." For those who are especially needy, Turcotte creates a buddy system: she asks clients who've been with her a few years, whose treatment she's "sponsored financially" — people she hasn't charged — if they'd be willing to "buddy up" with a newcomer for one hour a week. She specifies that it's for support, not therapy. Again, firm boundaries are established — one hour a week of talk, no more — and the rest of the time, if new clients need emergency help, they're directed to call a hospital or crisis centre.

Turcotte stopped keeping notes on clients after her files were subpoenaed in sexual assault cases; since she couldn't guarantee confidentiality, and was opposed to defence lawyers and accused offenders searching through victims' private therapy files, she decided she would have no notes to be subpoenaed. Nowadays, she encourages clients to keep their own therapy journals, "but it's up to them. I don't keep track."

However, therapists need to keep track of each other, through peer supervision, which Turcotte strongly recommends. It's essential to monitor the therapeutic process. She provides supervision for other therapists and participates in her own supervision group with two colleagues a minimum of every second week. This is their only opportunity to talk about their work and share their strong reactions to certain clients, their strengths, mistakes and difficulties.

One of the questions she is always asked, at professional conferences, is how to deal with clients who mutilate themselves. Turcotte herself was a slasher, and speaks from personal experience. The first thing therapists should understand, she says, is that most slashers have been cutting themselves (often with knives or razor blades) for many years, and there's no point getting into a panic and pressuring them to stop. As with any client behaviour that appears undesirable, Turcotte's approach is the opposite of what the client's accustomed to: instead of being disgusted, she is interested. She wants to explore the self-mutilation, to find out where it leads. Clients may mutilate themselves because it's a habit, a learned coping mechanism to drown out unbearable emotional pain; it may be easier to cut themselves than deal with a current problem; or slashing may be connected to a repressed memory that needs resolution. "The key is to not get locked in to one interpretation. How many ways does one have to look at this? *All* the ways."

She will ask why a client wants to slash that particular wrist in that particular way, wondering what the injury reminds the client of. She asks clients to draw pictures of their bodies and show her where they want to cut; she encourages them to act out self-injurious impulses on inanimate objects, to express that energy in a safe way: to slash the phone book instead of their arm, to make sounds, to follow the impulse back to the source — which is usually a scene of abuse. Once the memories are integrated into the conscious mind, the self-injurious behaviour usually stops.

One client gouged her body and got what Turcotte calls "tissue memory" in the form of hives and rashes. Turcotte expressed interest in the hives and rashes, and eventually the client followed the physical sensations back to an itch associated with a memory of being abused in itchy grass, and the gouging stopped. In another case, a client got little red dots all over her body; she scratched obsessively and welts appeared on her arms and legs. The scratching led back to a memory of being chased through stinging nettles. But Turcotte cautions therapists not to jump to conclusions: one client compulsively slashed an area around her neck; her obsession with cutting in that one place led to the memory of *witnessing* someone else having her throat cut.

She has a lot to say about memories. "Memories can collapse on top of each other. Clients may remember something they saw happening to someone else, they can pick up images and feelings from different events, so it's important to step back, let the memories flow without interference and let the client sort them out." Therapists must *never* tell clients what their memories mean, and they must remind clients, as the memories unfurl, that they're only remembering. Turcotte repeats certain phrases, like mantras, for clients to cling to: *It's all right to remember. It's over, you're safe now, it's not going to happen again. Remember you are remembering, you are not re-living. The feelings of terror belong to the past. You are no longer the child you were when that happened to you.*

She had a client, Barbara,* who was "extremely together," the sort of person who would "impress you as a woman who had it made, if you met her on the street." But in private, in therapy, Barbara was practically catatonic. When Turcotte asked about her mother, Barbara would hunch into a self-protective huddle. She was terrified of her mother; abused as a child, she still believed her mother was trying to kill her, and nothing could shake her conviction.

Turcotte took direct action. Fortunately, the mother lived nearby, and for a therapy session, Turcotte drove Barbara to see the mother-monster, who was now a feeble old woman. It wasn't a particularly dramatic visit; Turcotte talked to the mother about her children; the woman complained bitterly and said what rotten kids they were. "Don't you think it's strange that your kids are still afraid of you?" Turcotte said. Like most abusers, the mother was in total denial about what she'd done to her children and viewed herself as the injured party. Although she demonstrated no empathy for her daughter, the visit was a great success, therapeutically speaking. Turcotte did for Barbara what she'd desperately needed as a child: for an adult to stand between the child and the abuser, to break the spell. "Barbara needed to see that her mother couldn't do anything to her any more. Her mother was a blind old woman who'd tortured her children but her power was gone and her children grown up." That visit was the beginning of Barbara's recovery and the end of her terror. The myth of the monster had been broken.

That evening, delivering the keynote speech for another meeting of therapists, Turcotte continues her theme: the need to demystify the monster. She thought she'd confronted her personal demons, she says, but after the release of *To a Safer Place* she entered a darker underworld than she had known existed. She was, at the end of the eighties, a celebrity; the film had been televised across North America and won all sorts of attention and awards. It had also triggered an onslaught of death threats, hate mail, obscene messages left on her answering machine by masturbators, and dire warnings "not to tell." She became depressed, and the suicidal ideation returned: driving across the Lion's Gate Bridge in Vancouver, she wanted to crash over the edge, into the sea; while walking, she wanted to run into traffic. She had severe headaches, lost time, regressed back into her multiplicity. She became afraid of having a bowel movement, fearing something was attacking her anus; she felt she was choking, fearing that something awful was going into her mouth.

One morning she awoke to find her bed shaking; after checking to make sure that she wasn't dreaming, and that there wasn't an earthquake in Vancouver, she realized she was hallucinating. "Ten years ago, a hallucination meant I was crazy; now it means my body wants to tell me something, wants to heal, wants to live." Her voice drops: "What shook like that so long ago? It is not real that the bed is shaking now but it is real that something shook like that and she, the earlier part, is frozen there. What shook like that, where she is trapped?"

It was a truck that shook, rattling down a bumpy gravel road, taking Shirley the child, shoved into a shiny blue chest, "to that place where they did dripping bloody sexual things to children in the name of God." She pauses for a long time. "I am a survivor of a Christian cult." Her parents belonged to a group connected to a hospital run by priests and nuns, who participated in the ritual abuse. Her sister Linda was able to validate her memories, which "was a blessing." It is hard for people to believe the unbelievable when they have no one else to confirm that it really happened.

For fourteen years she'd been out of therapy — "I thought I was fixed" — and there she was, needing help again. "It was hard to live through it. My marriage didn't survive it. I nearly didn't survive it."

Through 1989 and 1990, the psychic fury raged, as the younger parts who'd experienced the ritual abuse — the cult alters — released their memories. Anibo, a little two-year-old alter, came up with a knife, wanting to kill. Anibo was aligned with the cult. "She was so fierce, she roared, she was the wrath of God — and I had to sit beside her. I couldn't stand her, she couldn't stand me." But Turcotte learned to tolerate Anibo's presence and was eventually able to embrace her as "one of the most interesting parts of me."

She found out that the threatening messages and strange packages had been sent by cult members. She hallucinated two robed figures at the end of her bed, pulling at her feet to take her where they'd taken her a long time ago, when she was little and had no choice; this time, she was able to fight back. "I'm old enough and strong enough now to neutralize them with my mind's eye. I can kick them in the head and toss them out of my house. I am not the same person now that I was then. It is our fear that gives them power; they become monsters only because no one stops them. We have made them beasts and mythical gods of evil, but they are just badly behaved men and sometimes women."

The ritual abuse had started in infancy, before she could walk, before she had a sense of boundaries, which made the memories diffi-cult to sort out, "like soup, confusing, enmeshed, hard to know at first what's me, what's not me, what happened to someone else." The hard-est part was the discovery that other children were involved: "It was crushingly unbearable to know that others did not survive. My heart hurt physically in the knowing of that." (Was this how Lucy felt in Prescott, when she told the police she'd seen a baby killed?) Turcotte believes the memory of the deaths of other children — corroborated by other family members — drove her to her life's work. "They [the cult abusers] told me I'd die if I told, I'd die if I remembered, and I finally stopped believing them from a deep inside place. The chapter of torture is closing. The child is being comforted. The monsters have been demystified." She left the stage.

For Turcotte, as for many survivors, the puzzle of the past, once a jum-ble of fragments, has gradually come together. "There are still many black holes," she says, "but I can tell my story, say what happened to me, there's flow. I feel whole. I'll always be multiple, but I'll probably never be split again." She can feel the brain chemistry change, now, when the headache comes that precedes a split, and she can make a choice: to stay calm, to not split, to realize it's just a memory coming up and there's nothing to be afraid of. She is able to breathe deeply and let the memory come — "I might not like what I'm seeing, but I can sit beside it" — just as she learned to sit beside Anibo, to align herself with a split-off part that at first seemed hateful, to use that ferocious energy for the sake of good. "That little two-year-old has been able to grow up. She is me and I am her. That's the wonderful thing about releasing child parts from their frozen state."

Once the core wounds are reached, integration happens naturally. "Nothing can describe the physiological feeling of integration," she says. "It's numinous, like light, a transcendent experience. You lose the feeling of being an alien; you become a human being, like everyone else."

6

Three
Survivors Speak

*When the truth is finally recognized, survivors can
begin their recovery.*

— Judith Herman
Trauma and Recovery

IT'S NEVER TOO LATE TO remember, never too late to heal. Therapy
works — for survivors lucky enough to find therapists who'll remind
them that they're only remembering. The hard part for anyone dealing
with buried trauma is facing the terror that clings to the memories. The
following stories illuminate three different approaches to recovery, as
a trio of survivors — two women and a man, — share strategies
they've developed to make the world a safe place for their emerging
"children."

Much of our new insight into human consciousness arrived via
recent studies of Vietnam veterans, from whom we've learned about
the painful manifestations of post-traumatic stress disorder and the
mind's extraordinary ability to split off from overpowering trauma. A
typical story told by a U.S. Army pilot illuminates how the process
works. The pilot had erased scenes of war and bloodshed in Vietnam
from his memory bank, only to find himself, many years later, back
home in the United States, about to take off in a light plane that hit a
bird. The impact of the bird's body against the windshield triggered a

flashback: he was in a helicopter shot down over Vietnam, an incident he'd "forgotten." The flashback sucked him into a terrifying vortex; he was overwhelmed with fear, as if the war were happening there and then. Fortunately, he managed to bring the plane to a halt. But never, until that day, had he understood he was carrying traumatic memories in his unconscious mind.

It is this natural dissociative response that can lead to multiple personality disorder (MPD), a post-traumatic stress condition usually caused by severe trauma. An American nurse who'd been sent to Vietnam explained why trauma silences the soul: she was in a medical tent in a war zone when a soldier was brought in with a serious head injury. She tried to tend to his wounds but his head came apart in her hands. She went into a deep dissociative state, and acted as if nothing had happened. No one — not the nurse herself or the other medical personnel — spoke about it. They all understood the unspoken rule: "If you talked about it, you would feel it," she said. "And if you allowed yourself to feel it, you could not have continued." So it is for many survivors: if they let themselves feel the pain, they couldn't continue to live.

MPD did not officially exist until 1980, when it suddenly appeared in the *Diagnostic and Statistical Manual*, an essential dictionary for medical and mental health professionals. MPD is often misdiagnosed as schizophrenia, manic depression or borderline personality disorder, and treated with medication that may make the condition worse. There's a great deal of controversy about the prevalence of MPD; some studies show that it occurs in 1 to 4 per cent of the population, but there's scepticism within conservative psychiatric ranks as to whether it even exists. The people you are about to meet were all diagnosed as multiple personalities by reputable therapists associated with mainstream Canadian medical or therapeutic institutions. Although they have not confronted their abusers in court, corroboration comes from other family members who either witnessed the abuse, or were themselves abused, but are not prepared to testify.

Daisy* lives in a modern house in a lush, landscaped Toronto suburb. It is the summer of 1992 and she is elegantly attired in a linen dress, hair pulled into a sleek chignon, skilfully made up; she has the look of a sophisticated Parisienne, though she comes from Polish roots, from a middle-class family in Winnipeg. She is forty-seven years old and has been married for twenty-five years to a corporate executive; she is the mother of two teenagers, was an elementary school teacher and has been told by her psychiatrist that she has MPD.

A teenage son is at home, studying for exams; rock music reverberates through the walls. Daisy leads the way downstairs, through a cool basement recreation room where she conducts art therapy sessions with children, into her private office. Her desk is lined with a collection of stuffed bunny rabbits of all shapes and sizes. Until a few years ago, Daisy knew only that she came from a dysfunctional family in which alcoholism was rampant. "My grandfather, my father and mother, my uncles — all alcoholics," she says. Her parents had a sado-masochistic relationship, though she couldn't have defined it back then. Her father was "a ladies' man," handsome and flirtatious; he'd humiliate his wife at parties, pawing other women in front of her, and at home he'd torment her, telling her she was a stupid bitch, threatening to beat her. She would suffer, be a martyr, then become the persecutor and accuse him of being a lousy rotten no-good failure, though he was a successful businessman.

Daisy was the peacemaker, her older sister the rebellious one. Daisy was Daddy's special girl. He took her on hunting trips and special walks; she didn't remember what happened. In elementary school, she was the sort of child who appeared dazed and distracted, and was admonished by teachers to "wake up and pay attention." If only the teachers had paid attention to Daisy: she was manifesting major symptoms of abuse. "I would find myself at the front of the class, at the blackboard, with the teacher asking me questions, and I didn't know how I got there or what I was supposed to do." She was always apologizing, always forgetting, never knowing what was going on. She failed grade one. She walked in her sleep, had constant nightmares and headaches. Amazingly, she developed a self who was good at school and taught herself to learn.

By the time Daisy reached university, she was taking codeine to dull the pain of constant headaches that interfered with her ability to concentrate; then a doctor put her on tranquillizers, telling her she was under too much stress, without enquiring about its source — not that she could have named it. At twenty-two, she married Ron.* They had two children and moved to Toronto. At thirty, afflicted by debilitating bouts of depression and rage, Daisy went into therapy. Her first therapist, a man, sexually abused her: "He would lie on top of me and feel my body; it was called therapy. It went on for two years, and when I finally realized it was wrong, I thought it was my fault and I was too ashamed to tell anyone."

At thirty-four, addicted to codeine, Daisy was admitted to the Donwood Institute, a Toronto clinic that pioneered the treatment of addictions. She had a rash on her face and itched everywhere, including her vagina. Daisy's body was speaking, but no one knew how to listen. She was labelled a hysteric, she says. When she came out of the Donwood, she accompanied her husband on a trip to New Orleans; her father stayed with the children. In New Orleans, Daisy had a breakdown. She went mute and lost contact with reality. While her husband was sleeping, she shut herself in the bathroom and overdosed on pills. Her husband found her in time and brought her back to Toronto; she was admitted to the Clarke Institute of Psychiatry, where her father visited her and delivered, Daisy recalls, "an Academy Award performance, crying and moaning about his poor darling daughter." Daisy tried to break a window and throw herself out of it. She was put on heavier medication; the drugs masked the pain, she "stabilized," remembered nothing, "got better" and was sent home, heavily drugged. But the volcano was erupting deep in her unconscious. "Looking back, I can see that either I was going to die or I had to remember."

At thirty-five, Daisy developed cancer in her left breast. The breast was removed and she was treated with chemotherapy, successfully. She decided to get serious about counselling, found a non-abusive male therapist and began to talk about incest, without any real memories. Two years later, she wrote to her father and told him he was "a tyrant, a terrible father," and ended her relationship with him. She began to remember more about the hunting trips: her father would take her to visit relatives in the country; he'd get drunk and on the way home at night he'd stop the car by the side of the road to go "hunting" for rabbits. He'd stagger into the woods with a big flashlight and shine the light in the rabbits' eyes, blinding them "so he could bash them over the head and bludgeon them to death. The horror I felt as he snapped the necks of the rabbits was my terror that he'd snap my neck like that too." The rabbits on her desk are a tribute to the rabbits who died.

It was another decade before she grasped the truth. She dreamed of a man coming in a door marked "privates," and her father's hand on the door; she was in the washroom with no clothes on, crying, and he was coming to get her. She had many dreams about snakes, snakes held in front of her face, snakes writhing around her in sticky water. But when she tried to go further, consciously, to reach a memory, she would shut off. "I was afraid that if I got a memory, I'd pass out or die." Then a little girl came to her in a dream and said she wanted to tell her mother she'd been raped by her father.

At forty-five, Daisy went back to the Donwood for a second time, suffering terrible migraines: the memories were coming. Daisy's alters began to emerge and she eventually learned the names of ten different "children" who held separate memories of sexual abuse committed by her grandfather and father, starting when she was two years old and continuing until she was fourteen. The memories did not belong to her, at first. "The dissociation was so complete that the other selves were not part of me. They were very far away in order to protect me from the pain." She believed that she, adult Daisy, had a "memory bank" that was completely separate from the abuse.

The alters terrified her when they "took over," and her central task in therapy was to gain control of her various parts. "When I feel them coming, it's like aliens invading my body. They see through my eyes and talk through my mouth but they're not me." The goal was to establish a "co-operative," in which the parts recognized each other and their unity of purpose. She was learning to discern who was "coming close," but she was still scared when they tried to make her do things. "One self tries to influence me to take codeine, so it's a struggle, a battle." One day she heard a child scream, knew it was her own voice and recognized that the abuse had happened to her. She remembered more about the hunting trips. "One time, I had taken a bag to collect pretty leaves and stones and *thud,* Daddy pushed me down, his gun by my head, and pulled my clothes off." She remembered a knife jammed in her bedroom door, every Saturday night, "so I couldn't open the door to get out." She "saw" her grandfather, down in the basement, drinking: he would call her down and she would have to go. He made her perform oral sex on him starting when she was about four years old, until she was nine or ten.

Daisy wrote to her father and confronted him obliquely, telling him she'd been diagnosed as having a dissociative multiple mind-set disorder, which she said was caused by child sexual abuse. He denied that he'd ever done anything to her. Daisy's mother was dead. "She was very beautiful, like a queen to me as a child, but I was very angry at her because she didn't protect me; she was a neglectful mother, she showed me no affection. She lived with a madman. She was like a ghost in the family."

Ron, Daisy's husband, wrote a paper titled "Partnering an Adult Survivor of Childhood Incest." In it, he described his early mystification at Daisy's behaviour: "Why was she so unable to cope with normal life events such as job stresses, childbirth, or moving to a new city?" He'd tell her to lighten up; she'd rage at being unable to open a jar or get the school lesson plan completed. Her moods were erratic, she was filled with shame or rage for no apparent reason, easily startled if he touched her from behind and cried excessively at movies. She was alternately vivacious and withdrawn; she didn't like sex, didn't want to be touched. He felt she didn't trust him and he was constantly frustrated in his efforts to reach her in an emotional, intimate way. "Always there were nagging questions: Why do I feel closed out? How do I get her to open up to me?" He swung between wondering what was wrong with him and what was wrong with her.

Like many partners of incest survivors, Ron learned "to walk on eggshells" around Daisy, never knowing what would trigger an emotional outburst. "I found myself treating her as if she were a child. At the same time, she exercised extremely tight control over certain elements of our relationship, particularly sexual and child rearing. This put me in a helpless position." Yet he felt totally responsible for looking after the family. "For years, I found myself in battle with an enemy I didn't know, couldn't recognize and couldn't engage."

He described the emergency phase, when Daisy started to remember and was flooded with flashbacks; the family was catapulted into crisis. She cried uncontrollably for long periods of time and was "incapable of even the most routine daily tasks." For Ron, this was "a terrifying time. I found myself helpless and panicking, afraid to let her out of my sight for even fifteen minutes as I feared she might become physically lost while in a dissociated state or even attempt suicide. At the same time it was necessary to cope with two children who also reacted to the dramatic change in their mother, while I continued to work, buy groceries, pay the bills and feed the dog."

Daisy survived the emergency stage, but even as she stabilized, it was hard. "This is my life. I am forty-seven years old and my life has been a horror, a living nightmare, and this is what I have to go through if I want to live — because of what my father and grandfather did to me." Every day was a battle. "Going to bed, a complete change can come over me, a complete possession of my body." Sometimes she heard voices talking in her head, or singing, and didn't know who they were: "It's frightening, it fills me with a horrible dread. I've been able to make a deal with my therapist that they [the alters] don't talk in my head in return for getting to talk to the therapist directly. That's beginning to work." If she did get to sleep, she'd wake up haunted by memories of oral rape, choking on semen. In the morning, she couldn't count on being Daisy, didn't remember things she was supposed to do. Perhaps she'd agreed to meet her husband at the mall for dinner; she wouldn't show up, he'd get angry, but Daisy wasn't aware of the arrangement because Ron had unknowingly set it up with one of her alters. They worked out a system whereby he wrote down major events on a message board in order to inform all of Daisy's parts, but Daisy often seemed "normal," and Ron would forget to write things down.

"It's hard for him," Daisy said. "He treats me as one person but I'm many. I lose things, I lose time, I go in and out of these states. There's one [alter] who's cynical and holds the despair for all the others. Hope is tormenting to the children, because it reminds them of the pain when they hoped Daddy wouldn't hurt them any more." Daisy touched her neck. "I have a pain right now in my throat that's getting worse. The cynic doesn't know how to cry. I still have the fear: I shouldn't be telling all these things; I'm not supposed to tell."

Through it all, Daisy continued to function with heroic determination. She'd taught school for more than a decade and had completed a three-year course at Toronto's Art Therapy Institute; she practised art therapy part-time, participated in weekly group therapy sessions for multiples as well as seeing her individual therapist and taking university courses part-time. She wanted to return to university full-time, but there was a problem among her alters: one of them was afraid of school and sometimes wouldn't go. Daisy had completed two post-graduate courses in the previous year, and received A's, but on one occasion, when she sat down to re-read a paper she'd written, she couldn't understand it. "It was awful. It was as if I'd never seen it before."

Despite the obstacles, Daisy persisted in her recovery, with a passion for life that was astounding. She wanted to write a book, establish a safe house for people with MPD, confront her father in court. In the fall of 1992, she and Ron hired a lawyer and took the first steps in their approach to the criminal justice system. "I want my father to know the silence is broken. I will not keep the secret about what he did to me. People like my father have got to be stopped. This is hope for me, speaking the truth. It hurts, I'm still on pain medication, I still suffer from severe migraines, but I think there's going to be a fusion of a lot of the different selves and some sort of co-existence on a co-operative basis with the rest."

In October 1992, Daisy was told she had a malignant tumour in her throat. A month later she was in hospital with a tracheostomy (a hole through her throat, into her windpipe), ready to undergo radiation treatment as a first non-surgical attempt to kill the cancer. She couldn't talk. She had lost her voice entirely. "We're grappling with the question of to what extent Daisy's finding her voice [about the abuse] contributed to her getting cancer," Ron said. "The enforced oral sex she endured as a child may have damaged her throat. She had so much terror about telling, about what would happen to her if she ever spoke about the abuse, that the internal enforcement of the secret was practically a death sentence."

Once again Daisy overcame the odds. By the spring of 1993, she was making a miraculous recovery. She could speak and she was free of cancer. She'd responded well to radiation treatment, she believed, because she'd consciously fought the disease. During the worst time in hospital, a little boy came to her, Henry — "he's one of my [inner] people" — and "kicked the cancer cells" into submission. Henry had made an important breakthrough: he'd reached the part Daisy called the cynic, the one who couldn't cry. "She's not an easy person to like, she's so completely bitter," Daisy said. "She's always mocking, she pushes you away, she can't trust anyone." The cynic carried the pain of the abuse, and the marvellous development was that the cynic could connect to Henry and perhaps, through him, would release her burden.

But life was not easy. In December 1993, out shopping at the mall, Daisy dissociated, lost time and "came to" after security guards had called the police, who'd called an ambulance that took her to hospital. She had food down the front of her coat and seemed disoriented; a new "alter" had come out and tried to eat, not knowing that Daisy is unable to swallow. (She is fed intravenously.) At the hospital, when she was back in command, Daisy calmly explained that she had MPD, and went home.

The Winnipeg police decided not to pursue Daisy's allegations against her father. She'd made a formal statement, they'd interviewed him, he'd denied her charges and the matter was dropped. The police told Daisy they were "getting too many of these calls" and didn't have the laws to successfully prosecute; without a witness or other victims, they said, Daisy's case would go nowhere. She was left with the impression they simply didn't have the resources to go after "all these old men."

"It hit me," Ron said, "when we talked to the police, and when I visited Daisy in hospital, about the enormous cost to society of child sexual abuse, in medical, legal and social terms, quite apart from all the human suffering. Daisy has already endured so much pain in her life, she's been in and out of hospital, she's had treatments and medication galore, all for something that was done to her when she was a helpless child."

In 1987, Edward* was a senior executive at a major multinational corporation, with dozens of employees reporting to him; at the age of fifty, he was at the peak of his professional career, married, with two children. But behind closed doors, Edward was a tormented man. That was six years ago. In the intervening period, he dedicated himself to recovery. In the fall of 1992, he accepted an early retirement offer from his recession-strapped company, gave up the corporate car and the identity that went with it and wondered what he'd do with the rest of his life. He didn't take long to decide: after an appearance (in disguise) on the Phil Donahue show, talking about being sexually abused as a boy by his mother, he enrolled as a therapist-in-training at the Toronto Institute for Human Relations, a twenty-six-year-old facility housed in a United Church building in downtown Toronto. Within a year, Edward was a man transformed. He had become an activist and was speaking out publicly against child sexual abuse; he had five clients in therapy with him and was apprenticing with a senior therapist who ran a group for male survivors. He had embarked on a new relationship with a woman friend, and was, he said, at the age of fifty-six — for perhaps the first time in his life — a happy man.

In his former incarnation, Edward's corporatism had been a thin veneer concealing private anguish. Deeply ashamed of what he considered his secret perversions, he was plagued by "bizarre sexual fantasies," in his words, that involved masochism, transvestism and gender confusion. It didn't occur to him that these obsessive fantasies could be memories in disguise. He didn't remember that his mother had dressed him up in girls' dresses, or dressed him down in much younger boys' clothing, to make him a sexual toy; he couldn't recall the times she'd prostituted him, selling his sexual services to well-to-do men and women for cash payments; later, he would recover a memory of being sent to a doctor's office and made to crawl on his hands and knees under the desk, to perform oral sex on the doctor. Nor did he remember his mother making him have sex with her when he was a teenager. He'd blocked out the faces of all the perpetrators who filed through his childhood, including Catholic priests and strangers on the street.

"When I got the memories, I couldn't believe it," Edward says. No wonder: he is a gentle, erudite man with a refined and bookish manner. "I had no idea that anything remotely like this had happened to me." The truth was not easy to accept; his many parts glinted like the complex refracted angles of an insect's eye, separating reality into a myriad of pieces, making life bearable for a boy who'd been so exploited so young, by so many people, that he'd become a defenceless target.

Edward's path to healing began with physical symptoms he could not ignore. He'd always suffered from headaches on an erratic basis, but when he hit fifty he was hammered by severe migraine clusters every few weeks; because his job was threatened, he had to seek treatment. Referred to a specialist at Toronto's Sunnybrook Hospital, he was taught self-hypnosis as a stress-reduction technique to control the headaches. One day the doctor mentioned, in passing, that childhood trauma was sometimes found to be the cause of the stress that triggered migraines.

Edward couldn't remember much about his childhood, but he felt it had been unhappy, involving hasty moves when his father, an alcoholic, lost his job, which happened frequently. Theirs was a large Catholic family with several brothers and sisters. The British-born parents were well read, disappointed in life and ill equipped for child rearing or economic survival. A clever boy who underachieved during his teenage years at a Catholic high school in Toronto, Edward was filled with shame and couldn't relate to his peers. "I knew there was something wrong with me, but I didn't know what it was." As Dr. Judith Herman explains: "Traumatized people feel utterly abandoned, utterly alone, cast out of the human and divine systems of care and protection that sustain life. Thereafter a sense of alienation, of disconnection, pervades every relationship....The traumatic event destroys the belief that one can *be oneself* in relation to others."

A buried memory: the prepubescent Edward was picked up by a man, "one of those people who lurk around schoolyards," and sexually abused; filled with guilt, he went to confession at school, and described what had happened. A few days later, Edward was told by a fellow student to go to the chapel, where a priest-in-training dressed in a priest's cassock awaited him. The seminarian was a teacher at the school; he said he'd overheard Edward in confession "and knew what a horrible, filthy boy I was, and he was going to punish me. He made me go into the closet with him and made me fellate him. He made me do it every two or three days for about a month."

Why didn't Edward refuse to go? "Traumatized children are not aware of any freedom not to obey. They don't know they have a choice, because these violations have probably happened before, with people they trusted. It's terrible to feel so lost." After a month of terror, Edward fainted in the closet. The seminarian realized he'd gotten as much out of his victim as he could safely get and said Edward didn't have to come back. But he gave Edward one last task: to approach another boy and tell him that someone wanted to see him in the chapel. "And so each boy was used in the entrapment of the next victim," Edward says.

He dropped out of high school and went to work to help support his family. Two years later, he decided to become a priest and entered a seminary, where he spent six years studying philosophy and theology, had a nervous breakdown and continued with post-graduate work. As he approached formal initiation into the priesthood, he had another breakdown, precipitated by doubts about his religious vocation. "In the Catholic Church, you were taught to consider doubt as coming from the Devil; you're supposed to repress what you feel, because if you 'give in' to your feelings, you'll do bad things, like listen to the Devil or quit the church." He was beginning to see aspects of his religious training as a form of mind control. The church's "tactics of repression, something the church knows a lot about," were losing their grip on him.

He decided to leave the seminary and travelled to western Canada. Working in a small town, he did not remember what he did at night: one of his alters, trained years earlier by his mother to be a prostitute, became involved in the local homosexual sex trade and fell under the control of a pimp. As incredible as it may seem, the Edward who held down a regular day job knew nothing about his nocturnal prostitution or the compulsion to seek out the old familiar pattern of abuse. "I wasn't aware that the [sexual] acts I re-enacted represented submission to the other [mother/abuser]. I found myself doing what my abuser wanted me to do as though it were my own decision, which took some of the terror out of it and gave me the illusion that I had some measure of control."

He endured in a state of servitude for a year, until his health collapsed. Then he returned to Toronto and "re-invented" himself, creating a new persona, wiping out most memories of the past, forging a successful identity. He got married, had two children and battled the troubling sexual fantasies that plagued him by engrossing himself in complex mental tasks. "If I let my mind go idle, the fantasies would come up — the violent things that I now know were done to me as a child." But he didn't seek treatment: "I thought I was so unique no therapist could help me." (That line was repeated, word for word, by

Dr. Richard Berendzen in the fall of 1993. A physicist and former head of the American University in Washington, D.C., Berendzen went public with his own history of incest, perpetrated by his mother, after losing his job and being convicted of making obscene phone calls. Like Edward, Berendzen had not understood that the bizarre thoughts he tried so desperately to repress were memories in disguise. Interviewers expressed disbelief that a man of his intellect hadn't understood the link between childhood abuse and adult behaviour, but Berendzen explained that "when you've been abused, you can't see what's obvious to others.")

Then Edward's migraines got worse, exploding in debilitating clusters; they expressed, and concealed, his rage. The rage was his ally, the force that would drive him forward, to heal. A Sunnybrook doctor referred him to Dr. Lois Plumb, a former chief of psychiatry at Women's College Hospital, who helped him put the pieces of his psychic puzzle together. Dr. Plumb taught Edward that the art of recovery is about developing a strong adult self capable of listening to, and loving, the child parts who'd been violated and abandoned so long ago. Edward learned that he would be able to release their pain, grief and rage only to the extent that he, adult Edward, could give them what they'd never had: compassion, acceptance and the assurance of protection from further abuse. This meant that boundaryless Edward, so practised at pleasing others, had to learn to assert himself, say no and make choices — among the most difficult tasks for those who've survived by pretending there's nothing wrong, and by serving others.

Edward's memory retrieval began with snatches of images, without emotion attached — a disconcerting experience. "At first I saw details of objects that were so clear I knew they were real, like pieces of a snapshot; then I saw more complete scenes. The first time I got a scenario with moving parts, I realized something was happening to somebody 'down there,' and the somebody was me. I had left my body." When he was able to reconnect with himself, he was flooded with memories at all hours of the day and night, at his office, walking down the street, eating dinner in a restaurant. What he uncovered was a lifetime of abuse that started before he could walk and continued into adulthood.

He discovered the power of amnesia. "It's a deliberate act of will, a skill that I acquired in childhood to protect me. It works. The ability to forget is what allows you to go forward and live a life in the real world." He worked hard at going back, tracking split-off parts that gradually revealed themselves as dozens of different personalities with distinct names and characteristics; many of them were girls, and he came to understand his urge to dress up as a girl in adult life (which he did in private, at home). As he delved deeper, he focused more of his energy on healing: through the early 1990s, he saw his psychiatrist every week, and a massage therapist, and attended a twelve-step Adult Children of Alcoholics program that led him to Survivors of Incest Anonymous (SIA), in which he became a mainstay of a local group. The power of the SIA connection— listening and being listened to, without judgement — helped him relate to the human race; he was no longer alone.

"SIA is the place I can go with real people, women and men, and talk about my reality and the terrible things that happened to me and what I'm doing about it, where I can talk about my progress and get a respectful hearing and hear all sorts of other people tell their stories and come out with a sense of being at a gathering of heroes. The brilliance of incest survivors is becoming apparent to me, the way we designed our coping mechanisms, the splitting, the techinques to survive."

Many of the steps toward healing were difficult: he separated from his wife, sold the family house in the suburbs and moved into a down-town apartment. "I had to work alone on my recovery. This is it: I've got to do it *now*. My family thought I was captive to the process, letting it dominate my life. My children sometimes said I'd abandoned them. I said, 'You're right, I never was here for you as much as you need and deserve. If I keep putting this off, I'll never be here for you.' "

Edward was careful about approaching his siblings with his recovered history, but gradually, over time, he was able to speak to most of them; they didn't want to believe him at first, but then some of them began to uncover their own painful memories. His father was dead and he had not confronted his mother, who was in her eighties, though he had stopped communicating with her. "One of the difficulties for men dealing with this issue is that it's hard enough to accept that you were sexually involved with a parent," he says. "It's doubly hard for a male because boys are supposed to be able to fight and defend themselves.

On top of that, to think of accusing your *mother*...." He had great difficulty getting in touch with his rage toward her: in a detached voice, he talks about being forced to have sex with her and coping with *her* rage if he didn't satisfy her.

Edward has a friend, Patrick,* who has had an equally difficult time coming to terms with his feelings toward his own mother. When Patrick was a child, his mother bathed him, played with his genitals and performed fellatio on him. She told him she was like a mother cat licking her kittens. Patrick's season of hell, as a drug-addicted teenager roaming Vancouver's Skid Row, ended with a religious conversion, but he was plagued by feelings of rage against women and fantasies of having sex with children through his twenties and thirties. Now a church minister, married and divorced, the father of two children, he dealt with these issues in counselling and leads a therapy group for abused men. He's convinced that much of the violent pornography and sado-masochistic sex that pass for erotica are repackaged child abuse scenarios. Victims can get stuck in it, he says, as passive addicts or active perpetrators.

As Edward and Patrick recovered, it occurred to them that women were exposing the horrors by telling their stories publicly, but that men, for the most part, had been silent — until recently. At self-help groups, they witnessed the flood of men coming forward, talking about what had been done to them as children, and heard many female perpetrators being identified by both male and female victims. Fundamental assumptions about child sexual abuse — whom it happens to, who does it, under what circumstances — were being challenged in makeshift meeting rooms where for the first time in history, survivors were crawling out of hiding to share their stories.

Edward got his chance to speak out on a wider scale. In March 1991, I had interviewed him for an article that appeared in the *Toronto Star*. A year later, a producer from the Phil Donahue show called the *Star* from New York; she'd done a computer search of newspaper databases for information about the newfound phenomenon of males sexually abused by their mothers, and she had found Edward's name.

A month later, travelling to New York to appear on the Donahue show, Edward felt emotionally paralysed. He *couldn't tell.* In the hotel room the night before the taping, he fell into a state of disbelief — an amnesia hangover in which he didn't believe himself — and heard voices saying it hadn't happened. *It couldn't have happened! Mothers don't rape their sons! Boys are invulnerable!* He became extremely agitated. "It was the old fear that someone would appear and say I'd made it up." Recovered memories have a strange propensity for seeming surreal and unreal at the same time, he said. "It's ironic that people worry about false allegations, when most survivors are completely unable to speak about the abuse because they can't believe it themselves."

While he was in the make-up room before the show, Edward's mood changed again: he was raring to go, surprised to realize how much he wanted to speak out, how strongly he resented having to disguise his appearance. The make-up woman fitted him with a fake beard and asked him to take off his glasses but he kept them on; he wanted to see the audience response to his words. Then he recoiled yet again, minutes before the show began, convinced his mother would call Phil Donahue and say, "Don't believe a word he says." He understood in a flash why people deprived of their history lose their identity; he needed to reclaim his past in order to recover.

Edward appeared on stage with three other men who'd been sexually abused by their mothers. Donahue seemed truly shocked by their stories. One man, Ariel, exuded so much anger at his mother, who'd used him, he said, "like a human dildo," that he dominated the show. Edward was relatively subdued, but afterward he was elated, and a little scared, too, that maybe he'd said too much.

Back at home, he started writing, recovering more memories; inundated with insights, he connected the popularity of horror stories and vampire movies with peoples' need to touch buried trauma. He explored his own ambivalence about being a man. And in the fall of 1993, resuming his studies at the Toronto Institute for Human Relations, he was full of optimism. "There is no one path to recovery," he says. "That's not to say there aren't universal truths in all this. Through reconstructing my story and listening to other people, I've gained immense respect for what heroes we were as children. We had no resources and we faced life-threatening situations with no support and found incredible ways to survive. As adults we may never again need to rise to the levels of heroism we rose to daily as children — but we can do it if we have to; that courage is not lost to us. That bravery is going to change the world. That's why it's so important to go back and find these heroic children and integrate them with our adult selves, absorb their courage and go out and make the world a safe place for everyone."

Amy Laird* is a more typical survivor, if there is such a person: unlike Edward, she did not moonlight as a prostitute; unlike Daisy, she did not develop a chemical dependency or obviously disturbed behaviour patterns. Amy was a nurse, a quiet, hard-working woman who remembered nothing unusual about her childhood until she was thirty-eight years old. She grew up in a small community in Ontario, in a respectable, religious, Anglo-Canadian family. Janice Laird,* Amy's mother, stayed at home to raise the four children, three girls and one boy; their father, Bob Laird,* was an avid Bible-reader who often stood in as minister when the regular pastor couldn't make it to their rural Anglican church. There was no alcoholism, no obvious sign that this was not a normal family.

As a child, Amy thought her parents were perfect, as abused children often do. Alice Miller observed, in twenty years of working with clients, "the way they denied the traumas of their childhood, idealized their parents and resisted the truth with all their might. Gradually, it became clear to me that genuine liberation was possible only for those who could bring themselves to experience their childhood pain."

Amy resisted the truth with all her might; she had to, to survive. She was a quiet, serious child, with a few odd quirks. She "went mute" for six weeks in kindergarten and was plagued by nightmares. She learned to calm herself by imagining God was watching over her, protecting her. She prayed to God as a mother and father. "I felt God raised me," she says. When she graduated from high school, Amy wanted to become a minister, but the Anglican Church didn't ordain women then, so she went into nursing, "because that's what girls did." It was as if her life started at nursing school; her childhood was a black hole, but she didn't think there was anything abnormal about that, at the time.

Amy worked as a nurse in the 1970s and was then hired by a campus religious service that required her to travel around the province, dealing with students at various universities. Her private life was almost non-existent; in her early twenties she'd been engaged to an abusive man, and now she avoided men. She worked sixty to eighty hours a week and justified her workaholism by saying how dedicated she was to her job: "I was totally absorbed in what I did, and I just didn't have time for relationships."

In her late twenties, clues to the abuse began to emerge, though Amy denied them at every step. Weighed down by unexplainable anguish, she sought the spiritual support of her chaplain-adviser. When he wondered about the source of her problems, she was vague. "The pain of my childhood" was all she could muster. He asked if she'd been abused as a child. "No," she responded, "my mother would beat me if I said that." She couldn't hear herself; like most abused children, she was unable to identify abuse. Not long afterward, she had a nightmare about being beaten as a child and gradually realized she had been physically abused by her mother. But her father was a sweet old man, she believed, "who wouldn't hurt a fly." She felt protective about him; he'd had a nervous breakdown, her parents had split up and he was living on his own.

But Amy felt the need to separate from her family in a symbolic way. At thirty-four, she changed her last name, an act that, to her surprise, precipitated a profound sense of loss, followed by months of grieving. "Then I had my first flashback, and I told a friend...." Amy stops talking and closes her eyes. She can't speak for a few minutes; she shudders. "It's like I'm in it, in the downstairs bathroom — we got an upstairs bathroom when I was twelve, so it must have been before I was twelve — and I had the sensation of coming back in through the bathroom window, slamming back into my body. I was bleeding [from the vagina], I was about eight, I was saying, 'He put his penis in me, he put his penis in me.' " She sits quietly for a few moments, to calm herself. The friend she'd revealed the flashback to hadn't known what to say, so hadn't said anything. The non-reaction had silenced Amy. If her friend couldn't hear her, who would?

By Christmas 1987, Amy was deeply depressed; her doctor wanted to put her on antidepressants but Amy instinctively knew not to suppress her feelings chemically. At work, she was leading seminars and group discussions on the topic of child abuse; she was reading in the field, gravitating to books and articles about sexual abuse — groping through the fog of dissociation, still emotionally detached but grappling for an intellectual framework with which to understand her history.

In the spring of 1988, Amy quit her job and was accepted into post-graduate school. There, in the fall of 1990, she sought the spiritual counselling of Helen Bronson*, a minister who asked her, after a few sessions: "Were you sexually abused by your father?" Amy's denial was adamant. "Bob's a lovely, dear man," she said. "He'd never do anything like that." In January 1991, she was referred to therapist Lisa Walter, but the therapy sessions didn't lead anywhere. Amy would arrive for appointments and clam up. "You've got a *Don't Tell* message," Walter said. "If we can figure out where that *Don't Tell* comes from, we might get somewhere." Amy didn't know what she was so afraid of, "but the closer I got [to the truth] the more terrified I was. It was so strange, so knowing and unknowing at the same time." She would stare at the floor and not speak; Walter would ask, "I wonder if you dissociate when you dive into the floor?" Amy would get angry. After five months in therapy with Walter, Amy was furious. "I felt Lisa wasn't getting to it, wasn't taking me seriously." Amy decided she needed a new therapist, but while she searched for one, she continued to see Walter, and one day, "I let it rip, I told Lisa exactly what I really thought about how the therapy wasn't working and what she wasn't doing right; she listened and she didn't get mad. That was a breakthrough for me. That was the first time in my life I'd ever been honest and said how I felt; I was heard, and it was okay. She didn't die."

After the next session, Amy went home, lay down on her bed and felt pressure in her vagina and cervix: "I felt a finger pushing around inside and I said, *Who's doing this?* A voice said, *Don't tell, don't tell.* I asked: *Who are you?* A child broke into tears: *It's my daddy.*" At the next session, Walter again asked Amy if she thought she dissociated, "and when she said the word *dissociated,* I knew that was the key." Amy went home, lay on her bed and the flashback continued: "I saw the child was outside her body, seated on top of her own chest while she was sexually abused."

In the fall of 1991, after the initial burst of memories, which were often devoid of emotion, the "feeling flashes" began, accompanied by a lot of body pain, "sometimes like a knife stabbing my vagina." Amy was on medication for arthritis and some days had to wrap her forearms in elasticized athletic tape. "The pain in my arms feels like a crushing in the bone," she said. "My father used to pin me down with his weight on my arms. I've got a lot of memory that's stored in body pain."

Amy lowered her eyes and fingered two tiny cloth dolls she had placed on the table. Her hands were trembling. "I think we've got little people here," she said. Something about her was changing — a subtle shift in her face, her manner of speaking, the expression in her eyes. Her adult attitude gave way to a look of intense vulnerability. "They want to come out," she said. "Is that all right?" She was switching into one of her split-off parts. She began to speak in a child's voice, using child-like phrases and intonation: "I was seven, my big sister was at swimming lessons, my mother had taken the baby out and I came home from violin lessons. The violin was too big for me and I put it behind the door and it fell down. I picked it up and it fell down again and my father got mad at me because I made a noise outside his room. He beat me with a stick and then he grabbed me and held me down on his bed and then, and then, he put his penis in me. It hurt.... I rolled off the bed and got away. I went up to the attic and scrunched up and rocked myself. That was in grade two. Every Saturday when I came home from my music lesson, he raped me, sometimes in my vagina, sometimes in my back end. Every Friday I would get a terrible headache.... It's very sad, but we don't live there any more. Now we live with big Amy. She takes care of us."

She lowered her head and shut her eyes and then she was big Amy again. "That's how I survived," she said. "I dissociated. My kids have the memories, not me. They were created to contain memory, and they do. That's where I see God's grace, that I didn't get crushed. When the pain was too great I'd leave my body, I'd be gone, then I'd come slamming back into my body when it was over."

Lisa Walter, Amy's therapist, wrote a post-graduate thesis on incest survivors, "Women Remembering Incest: A Phenomenological Account," based on interviews with women who had no conscious knowledge of childhood abuse until they were adults. "We don't understand very well the mechanisms that allow people to carry repressed memories," she says, "and we have to be careful when we talk about memory. People think it's like a movie that runs in your head, but it's not like that for everyone. Memories can come as feelings, in fragments, physical sensations, pictures or slices of pictures." And they can be hidden within a complex multiplicity of arrangements that Walter regards as coping mechanisms. She rejects the "dissociative disorder" label and instead describes multiplicity as "a spontaneous way our minds grow to cope with an intolerable reality, a way to store unspeakable information until it can be spoken and believed." For survivors to safely "come to know," she says, "they need an infrastructure on which to hang their memories. Otherwise, it's chaos and they're revictimized."

The ultimate goal for many recovering incest survivors is to organize a formal confrontation with the perpetrator and non-offending family members present. The survivor prepares a statement about the abuse and delivers it; she is usually supported by her therapist; the aim is to break the silence, tell the secret, be heard by the family and experience the offender taking responsibility for the harm caused and apologizing for the damage done. Needless to say, the longed-for outcome rarely occurs. Abusers who take responsibility, incest families who listen — these are oxymorons, things that don't belong together.

During my hundreds of hours of interviews with survivors, one theme emerged: the yearning of many not for revenge but for understanding. It seems incredible that after being so horribly used and abused, they just wanted to be heard, believed and loved. They are trying to undo what has been done. As Dr. Judith Herman puts it, "A secure sense of connection with caring people is the foundation of personality development. When this connection is shattered, the traumatized person loses her basic sense of self." Amy was determined to recover her self, and wanted to confront her father. Deep down, she may have been hoping for a magical transformation of her family.

Lisa Walter warned her: confrontations should be approached with extreme caution. Survivors can be retraumatized if they're not ready to face the shock of the family's collective denial. Amy decided to confront her father by letter. With Lisa Walter's support, she wrote to him and sent copies, with covering letters, to his priest, to her brother and one sister, to her chaplains and to Lisa Walter. This is a portion of the letter she sent, at the end of March 1992.

Dear Bob,

...In my late thirties I have been thinking about who I am as a person, and what kind of person I want to be. I realized that something seemed to be holding me back.... It was as if I had some really painful secret hidden deep inside. I wasn't exactly sure what it was but I could feel the pain of it. There was a lot of shame attached to the secret. It kept me from really believing in myself. It gave me a lot of fears and made me think the world is an unsafe and terrifying place. I decided to get some help. We began looking at the shame, pain and fear I feel as an adult. I began talking to the counsellor about what my childhood was like, to see where the pain and fear began. I started having memories, nightmares and flashbacks.... There have been many many memories and they still continue, covering a seventeen-year period.

She described being "a young child in the downstairs bathroom, bleeding and in a stunned state repeating over and over, *he put his penis in me.*" She recalled the last time he threatened her, the day after her grade-twelve prom, when he barged into her bedroom "and I didn't have anything on. You had a wild look in your eyes. I told you to get out and never come into my room again."

Some of the memories were deeply hidden because they were so painful. Some I had always remembered but didn't think about much. They were too hard. Finally I could no longer pretend not to know what the secret was. In order to let my feelings of shame, and pain, and fear change I had to admit what the secret is. Dad, I need to let you know what I've always known in my body but kept buried deep inside me. Dad, I still know you raped me repeatedly from the time I was a baby until I was seventeen. I need you to know I still know. I'm not asking you to do anything or say anything, I just need to let you know I still know.

Bob received the letter on a Friday and by Saturday he'd called his priest and Amy's siblings. He told Amy's sister Sarah* that the letter was "mumbo jumbo." He told Amy's brother Tom,* a police officer, that Amy had "gone crazy." Tom called Amy and said that from what he'd learned in police training, Amy was "a textbook incest case." He believed her, but "now that you've upset Dad so much, what are you going to do to help him?" Sarah screamed at Amy over the phone and said Amy had wrecked her weekend. "It was hard," Amy said. "Nobody hears you. 'Excuse me! I said I'd been raped for seventeen years by my father. Hello!' "

Bob's priest phoned Helen Bronson, Amy's minister, and said that Amy had always been unstable. "Bob's a nice old man," the priest told Bronson. "I've had a cup of coffee with him many times over the years and he's not capable of doing anything like this." Bronson told the priest that she'd known Amy for a long time, had provided her with spiritual counselling and believed her.

The lack of support for the victim — typical of an incestuous family — came as a shock to Amy. No matter how well prepared, survivors are devastated, in adulthood, to encounter the same cold hard denial that trapped them in childhood. But this time, Amy was supported by a therapist and two chaplains and was able to look after "the kids" and acknowledge their pain. She realized that even if she were the pope, her family wouldn't believe her. (Amy has memories of her siblings being sexually assaulted by Bob but hasn't told them. "When and if they're ready to remember, they'll need to uncover their memories at their own pace," she says. One of her sisters, who's been diagnosed as both manic-depressive and schizophrenic, is particularly vulnerable. She's been on psychiatric medication since she was twelve, and has had numerous hospitalizations and shock treatments.)

Amy wasn't satisfied by the outcome. "Sending the letter wasn't enough," she said. "I want some accountability. It's unfair that he's walking around as if nothing happened and I'm going through hell." She had been informed by Lisa Walter that she met all the diagnostic criteria for atypical multiplicity; she was high-functioning, not disordered and not violent; she didn't lose consciousness for long periods of time or find unfamiliar objects or clothing in her room. But as she let out her "trauma parts" in therapy, she sometimes became confused in reality. Her adult self was bombarded with information from the past, and she had to exert enormous energy to keep her grip on the present. Was the classroom in which she found herself in graduate school, nursing school or grade two? Internal parts struggled for control: required to deliver a lecture as part of her university course, she searched for her authentic adult voice, torn between feeling she would be punished for speaking at all (as some of her younger parts felt) and being convinced she should deliver one of the impromptu fundamentalist speeches that had earned her so much praise ten years earlier, in a former job.

Initially terrified by the diagnosis of MPD, Amy gradually gained insight into the internal organization of her multiplicity and learned to draw maps depicting layers and clusters of newly emerging "kids." In 1992, she referred to eighteen "internal children." Within a year, she'd identified sixty. (This number is not unusual; Edward, for instance, identified hundreds of "parts.") Some were labelled "caretakers," others "executive kids" or "memory kids." She listened to them talk in her head: "They're so real to me that when I wake up in the morning I expect to see their little bodies in the bed." One of the new groups was "the firstborn," clustered around Amy's original self. "The firstborn feel they're entitled to be loved and cared for," she said. One of the most active parts was Miranda, an eight-year-old executive kid: "She's what the literature [on MPD] calls the internal self-helper. She's the one who knows everything about everybody; she has information I still don't have." Sometimes Miranda phoned Bronson at night to reveal more memories; Bronson had learned to report back to Amy to make sure she had the latest news from Miranda. If Bronson felt stuck with Amy, she'd call on Miranda, who always seemed to know what to do next.

For a while, the expansion was outward as Amy discovered a swirling array of "parts" — as many as four splits for each traumatic event. But by the end of 1993, Bronson was seeing a remarkable integration of Amy's many selves. Amy had also joined a support group for multiples, most of whom were ritual abuse survivors. Through it all, she worked hard at her studies and at a part-time job in her professional field. Her energy and ability to manage her life through this war zone of pain were astounding.

In March 1993, Amy sought a personal confrontation with her father. Helen Bronson spoke to Bob's priest and Bob agreed to come to Toronto, accompanied by the priest; but a few days before the scheduled meeting he begged off sick. Amy decided to approach the criminal justice system. "The kids really want to say what they could never say." A lawyer advised her that she wouldn't get anywhere: Bob was an old man, and she had no witnesses and no support from her family, except for a cousin.

Amy was undeterred. A women's shelter near the town where she grew up, where her parents still lived, reassured her that local police had expertise in dealing with child sexual abuse. She took the plunge and made the call. The small-town police officer she spoke to surprised her with his sensitivity; he suggested she come to see him, to make a statement.

On May 10, 1993, Helen Bronson drove Amy to her hometown. When she walked into the police station, Amy dissociated so severely that she became almost catatonic; Bronson had to call on Meribeth, a seventeen-year-old self "who initiated the project," as Amy put it, to "come out" and take charge. The police officer was supportive but warned Amy/Meribeth that "nothing might come of it. Your father's an old man and the Crown prosecutor may think there's no point pursuing it."

Afterward, Bronson drove Amy past her childhood home, where her mother still lives; Amy saw two evergreens that had been small when she was a child and were still small in the kids' world. The evergreens had shot up above the roof and crowded against the house, covering the windows with darkness. "It was really powerful for the kids to see how everything had grown and changed," Amy said. "They realized that time had passed."

Back at home, Amy was relieved. "This is the thing we were told all our life we couldn't do, and we did it: we told. But it's not something you can be happy about. If they don't arrest him, it's the end of the story." On July 9, 1993, the police officer called to say the Crown attorney had reviewed her statement and the investigation would proceed. In mid-August, the police arranged to interview Amy's mother and siblings, who subsequently denied any knowledge of abuse. In September, Amy was informed that charges would not be laid. A few weeks later, Sarah called Amy: "Mom said you won." Amy was baffled. Sarah added: "Mom said the police believed you, so you won." Sarah revealed that she believed Amy too, but she hadn't been able to tell the police.

The courage of Daisy, Edward and Amy is typical of many survivors. If you met them on the street, or at your workplace, or at a party, you would never guess what they'd endured. There may be hundreds of thousands of people among us who have experienced a piece of these horrors, children who are suffering today — children we know, in our neighborhoods, in our families. A minority will grow up to perpetuate the cycle of violence; that's easy to understand. Why is it that many more will, like Daisy, Edward and Amy, emerge as heroes? Their struggle toward the truth exemplifies the mystery of the human spirit.

7

Incest Survivors
Go to Court

*Everyone has the right to tell the truth about her life.
Although most survivors have been taught to keep
their abuse a secret, this silence has been in the best
interests only of the abusers, not the survivors.*

— Ellen Bass and Laura Davis
The Courage to Heal

IN JUNE 1990, Jill McNall, then thirty-one, and Julie McNall, twenty-seven, embarked on a journey that changed their lives. They made an appointment to see Mary Hall, the senior Crown attorney for Metro East, based in the Toronto suburb of Scarborough, and began the process of bringing their father to trial, charged with sexually assaulting three of his daughters and one of their friends. The decision to pursue legal action had come slowly, over many years, after much agonizing; what tipped the scales was their fear that Donald McNall was still doing to other children what he'd done to them. He was a predatory man who'd had numerous extramarital flings with adult women, hiding his taste for sexual violence under a cloak of respectability. He had started abusing the girls when they were five years old — Jill, Julie, their sister, Joy, and Julie's best friend, Constance — sexually assaulting them into their teenage years. (Another McNall sister, the eldest, declined to participate in the case; she lives outside Canada, and her sisters wish to respect her privacy and not discuss her situation. Their only brother, Stuart, died in his teens.)

Entering the criminal justice system was a frightening experience for the women. When his victims were small, Donald McNall threatened to kill them if they ever told what he was doing to them, and they still saw themselves, unconsciously, as powerless children up against a giant monster. When he was arrested in September 1990, they were terrified by the knowledge that they'd started the process and didn't know how it would end. Infuriated by his daughters' "vengeful act," as he saw it, outraged by their attempt to "destroy" him, Donald McNall called his wife and issued a warning: "Tell them not to do this." Mrs. McNall was shocked; though she knew her daughters had been sexually assaulted by their father, she hadn't known of their intention to go to the police, who advised the McNall sisters not to inform their mother in case she let him know. (Jill views her mother as a victim too, is very protective of her and does not want her blamed for what their father did.)

Three days after Donald McNall's arrest, Jill and Julie, accompanied by Jeff David, Jill's live-in partner, went to the Humane Society to adopt a dog. They walked into a huge warehouse full of homeless animals. Barking and howling, the dogs ran to the front of their cages. Stunned by their desperate clamour, Jill broke down and wept uncontrollably, for the first and last time in this entire process; it was the only time in their five-year relationship that Jeff had seen Jill cry. "She normally doesn't allow herself to get upset," he says. "She doesn't like to lose control." But she lost it with the dogs; she was sobbing, totally distraught, and Jeff and Julie had to take her home.

But not without a fierce-looking German shepherd whose presence gave the sisters some sense of security against the threat of their father's rage. "I was afraid if he went over the edge and couldn't face what was coming — his *reputation* meant so much to him — he wouldn't just kill himself, he'd kill us too," Jill said.

Within weeks, their older sister, Joy, who'd been away on a European vacation, returned to Toronto and joined the case. Not wanting to ruin her long-planned trip, Jill and Julie hadn't told her about their intentions before she departed. But Joy had a similar assessment of the threat posed by their father; after she gave her statement to the police, she showed a picture of Donald McNall to her colleagues at the library where she worked and said: "If this man comes in here looking for me, he's dangerous. Dial 911."

People who knew Donald McNall casually couldn't understand how he generated such fear. He seemed like a charming guy — a smalltown boy from Blyth, a village in southwestern Ontario that's now home to a summer theatre festival; he had grown up to be a successful salesman who eventually had his own tire-service business; he had a special interest in aviation, a pilot's licence and a glib public persona that concealed private demons. "He'd be a raving lunatic, the phone would ring and he'd pick it up in perfect control: 'Hello, how are you?'" Jill says. She'd seen him in rages where she thought he was capable of murder, but he could turn it off in a flash for someone he wanted to impress.

Jill fingers the silver dolphin ring on the little finger of her left hand. She looks like an Irish sprite: red-haired, slender, wary, with a steely spirit, high-speed energy and quick articulation. "I refuse to be a victim," she says firmly. "I *was* a victim, I *was* victimized, but I refuse to allow him to destroy my life or take credit for who I am." Her identity was forged in a horrific childhood acted out under bright lights, in pretty dresses. Jill and Julie were successful child models; they had an agent, belonged to ACTRA (the Association of Canadian Television and Radio Artists) and had professional "comp" sheets that highlighted their photogenic versatility. Among their clippings are faded ads of the smiling McNall sisters selling Christie's cookies, raspberry jam and catalogue clothes, with never a hair or an emotion out of place. "We specialized in pretending to be happy," Julie says. "Like, I'm six years old, I was sexually abused last night and here I am smiling at the cameras this morning."

In public, the family was on show; Donald McNall played the role of the proud father surrounded by his bright, attractive children, "and we all carried out the charade," Jill says. But in the privacy of their home, there was no protection. The abuse could happen in the daytime, on weekends, anywhere — in the bathroom, the basement, at the cottage, in the boathouse. By the age of six or seven, Jill was being raped on a regular basis by her father, although she doesn't remember exactly when penetration began. "We couldn't define it as rape, we didn't have words for body parts, no one had ever explained sex to us, we didn't live on a farm and see animals, we just didn't know what he was doing." Jill's response to the abuse was to try to be perfect. If she made a tiny mistake, she was devastated.

At home, the only time the family relaxed was when Donald McNall was away on business; when he returned, it began all over again. His grip over the prison of his family was so tight that his captives rarely discussed among themselves the torture that was their common bond. The children had nightmares about their teeth falling out, and later made the connection in therapy that "your teeth fall out when you're five, and that's when he started on all of us," Jill says. They wore clothes to bed and rolled themselves in blankets, but nothing stopped him. "Nobody had any power except him. When he came home from trips he'd take my mother into the bedroom and lock the door and I'd think, *Is he doing to her what he does to me?*" The children saw their mother as another child, helpless, like them. At the legal clinic where she works, Jill often deals with abused women who are so totally beaten and controlled by their husbands that they can barely speak. Yet people always ask them, "Why didn't you leave?" not understanding that battered people — male or female — usually lose their autonomy and self-esteem, and end up submitting to the will of their abuser. In 1991, University of Cincinnati psychologist Edna Rawlings reported her research into nine "hostage" groups: concentration camp survivors, cult members, battered women, prisoners of war, civilians in Chinese Communist prisons, procured prostitutes, incest victims and physically and emotionally abused children. "Bonding to the abuser occurred in all nine hostage groups," Rawlings stated.

Once, when Jill was fifteen and her father was on a rampage, she and her mother escaped from the house. There was no place to go, no women's shelter, so they sat in a hospital cafeteria and made tentative plans to leave permanently. Mrs. McNall seemed to catch a glimmer of hope, but then they returned home and she collapsed under the weight of her fear of her husband. "She thought we couldn't survive on our own, even though she had a good job," Jill says. (Mrs. McNall was, and still is, a teacher in the post-secondary education system.)

Jill survived by maintaining a sense of inner resistance, character-istic of prisoners of war. Her greatest fear in going to court and telling the secret was that "people would see me only as his victim, not as myself. Becoming my own person was the most important thing in my life." In childhood she had dissociated by "compartmentalizing." She never "forgot" the abuse, but was able to place the trauma in "separate boxes" so no one would know what was happening at home. Like a proud warrior, she was armoured and defiant. "Instead of separating myself into different personalities, the way some people do, I separat-ed reality into different pieces."

Julie was more open, more overtly hurt. At the age of eleven, she disclosed to her mother that she was being sexually abused by her father. "You have to understand your father's sick," Mrs. McNall said. "Don't worry, I'll put a stop to it." She spoke to her husband and he subsequently attacked Julie, threatened to kill her if she told anyone else and choked her until she was unconscious; she thought she was going to die.

Julie and her mother saw a counsellor; Julie mentioned incest, but the counsellor didn't say, This should be looked into, or Call the police. Why not? "That was the seventies," Jill shrugs. "Nobody did anything about sexual abuse."

If Jill was the good girl, the disciplined intellectual who became a community legal worker, Julie was the wild one, the rebel. "I'm not as polite as Jill," says Julie, who grew up to become a bartender and restaurant manager. Like her sisters, Julie always knew she'd been abused, but her sense of childhood was "pretty foggy," though she remembered New Year's Eve when she was fourteen. She wanted to go to a party with friends, but her father trapped her in the house and threw her mother against the wall, and when her grandmother tried to call the police he tore the telephone out of the wall. In the chaos that ensued, Julie escaped; she didn't go home for a month. When Julie was fifteen, her father caught her smoking a cigarette and screamed at her, "Only sluts smoke." He hit her across the face so hard that the ciga-rette stuck to her cheek. When her brother, Stuart, was a teenager, Julie saw her father throw him down the basement stairs. Before she was born, her mother had come home from the movies — pregnant with Stuart — and Donald McNall had kicked her in the stomach: "My grandmother told me about that. It was so twisted and sick and screwed up in our family, you can't even describe it. Then he'd have business people over to the house, or he'd take us all out to dinner and show us off. I always knew I hated my father."

At eighteen, Jill made her escape: with a grade-thirteen average of 85 per cent, she was selected for a student exchange program in Mexico for a year. While she was there, Stuart, who was fourteen months younger, was killed in a car accident. He had been Julie's protector and his death was a shattering blow to her; the last child at home, she had a hideous year and dropped out of school. Her life stabilized when Jill returned and the two sisters found an apartment in Toronto. They set up a little family unit, with Jill working her way through university, studying sociology, having refused financial support from her father. Julie worked at part-time jobs and went back to school.

Like Jill, Julie refuses to label herself in association with the abuse. "I knew from the age of five that he was to blame for what he was doing to me, and that I had nothing to be ashamed of," she says. She doesn't like the word "survivor" or the term "healing process," doesn't talk about the "inner child," and says the only reason she went into therapy at nineteen was "because I was capable of murder." She'd wanted to hire a biker gang to deal with her father; Jill had dissuaded her.

In 1982, Jill and Julie bought a small, two-storey house near the Danforth; their mother gave them the down payment. Jill lived in the upstairs apartment and Julie lived downstairs with her boyfriend. Mrs. McNall had separated from her husband but then resumed her relationship with him, much to her daughters' distress. Jeff, who moved in with Jill in 1989, was aware that she didn't like her father, but didn't know why. One night she told him she had something important to say. But she couldn't get the words out, and had to call Julie to come upstairs and say it: *"We were sexually abused as children by our father."* Once Jeff knew, Jill was able to talk to him about the abuse. She wanted to do something about it, and he encouraged her, but she didn't know what she could do.

From Jeff's perspective, the major catalyst was Constance, Julie's childhood friend. As a little girl, Constance had to go to the McNall house every day after school, supposedly to be taken care of until her own parents got home from work. Constance had been abused between the ages of five and thirteen by Donald McNall; she entered therapy long before the sisters did and was the first to confront the damage they'd all tried to bury. "It was like they all brought something essential to the process," Jeff says. "With Constance, it was the emotion. She got in touch with her feelings, which seemed to trigger Jill and Julie. Jill was the rationalist; she provided the light of reason and figured out how to do it. Julie had the anger; she was the drive, the engine. Joy gave them hope, they saw how much Joy grew in the process; she came out of herself and she blossomed."

Joy has the McNall red hair and gift of the gab; she talks even faster than Jill, and never about her father, if she can help it. Married for fourteen years, she has no plans to have children. (None of the McNall sisters has children.) Joy avoids personally revealing conversation, but Constance can draw her out. Constance talked about Donald McNall, how as a child she hated the smell of rye on his breath; her husband no longer drinks rye. Talk of the smell of the man reminded Joy of the scent of Donald McNall's aftershave, which had triggered her severe perfume allergies. (Hypersensitivity to smells, foods, sounds or gestures suggestive of the perpetrator is a common symptomatic response to abuse.) One day a stranger came into the library where Joy works and, momentarily engulfed in the smell of his cologne, which reminded her of her father, she nearly passed out.

Constance understands, in a very different context, the victim's susceptibility to flashbacks. The birth of her first child was a traumatic event in a way she hadn't anticipated. "When the baby was born, I tore, I felt the burning pain and it brought it all back, the way I felt when he raped me. It hurt walking; the redness, the soreness — it must have been so uncomfortable for us, being so little, walking around with torn vaginas. It made me so angry, to have the happiest day of my life, the birth of my child, marred by memories of being raped by Donald McNall."

Constance had three children in rapid succession, and went into therapy after her first child turned five, the age Constance was when McNall started on her: "That's when it really hit. My rage came out around protecting my children and I began to see what he had done to me. I didn't know it but I dissociate all the time; it's scary, my body's there, but I'm off in my mind somewhere else; it makes me feel like a zombie. I'm just learning to catch myself when I come out of it. I dissociated when he did it to me, and that's why it's so hard for me to be present for sex with my husband."

By the late 1980s, the McNall sisters and Constance had started to see items in the media about sexual abuse. The floodgates were opening. In 1987, Sylvia Fraser's autobiography, *My Father's House: A Memoir of Incest and of Healing*, was published; it became an international bestseller and was translated into seven languages. A well-known Canadian novelist, Fraser revealed that in her mid-forties, shortly after her father's death, she'd suddenly remembered having been raped as a child by her father. Also in 1987, the National Film Board of Canada released *To a Safer Place*, Shirley Turcotte's documentary film about her incestuous childhood. The following year, *The Courage to Heal: A Guide for Women Survivors of Child Sexual Abuse*, by Ellen Bass and Laura Davis, appeared on bestseller lists and stayed there for two years, selling almost one million copies to date. During that period, the two most powerful women in American television, Oprah Winfrey and Roseanne Arnold, "came out" as survivors of childhood sexual abuse. (Roseanne's father denies her allegations.) In Canada, the inquiry into allegations of physical and sexual abuse of boys at Mount Cashel began in 1989, and consciousness in this country was transformed.

The McNall sisters and Constance rode the crest of the wave into court. They wanted to protect other children and "make him face up to what he did to us," Jill says. They were afraid of the ostracism that often comes with telling family secrets, but felt that even if all their relatives rejected them, they had each other. They were lucky in that sense; most incest survivors are forced to act alone, and are therefore more likely to be disbelieved.

There are two paths victims can take in pursuing legal redress. In the criminal justice system, the police investigate, the state prosecutes and victims are merely witnesses in the state's case against the accused. In the civil system, the focus is on fair compensation for the plaintiff, or injured party, who goes to a lawyer and files a claim against the person alleged to have done the damage. It's like being in a car accident and suing the person who smashed your car; the jury in a civil suit can award you damages, but they can't send the defendant to jail. Only the criminal system can sentence offenders. On the criminal side, the accused chooses whether to be tried before judge alone or judge and jury; in civil cases, the plaintiff makes that choice.

In criminal cases where the victim suffers financial loss through burglary or fraud, judges may order the offender to pay financial compensation or make restitution to the victim. But when victims suffer a violation of bodily integrity, such as sexual assault, financial compensation comes only from the civil system, where juries can set the amount of damages. On the criminal side, juries have no say in sentencing; if they find the accused guilty, the judge then determines the punishment.

In 1992, the civil system produced two major precedents that recognized victims' pain and suffering in significant monetary terms. First came a $375,000 award in April, from a British Columbia Supreme Court jury to Cynthia Shelford, an incest survivor who'd been sexually assaulted by her father between the ages of seven and fifteen. Leonard Roy Klassen, her father, had been convicted four years earlier in criminal court and sentenced by a judge to a paltry ninety days, to be served on weekends. Outraged, Shelford initiated a civil suit in which the jury evidently shared her view. Shelford's lawyer, Jack Cram, says he thinks the award was so high because it came from a jury, not a judge; judges, in his view, are somewhat out of date regarding society's response to sexual abuse.

In December 1992, $500,000 in damages was awarded to an Ontario woman whose father had pleaded guilty to incest charges in criminal court two years earlier. Sentenced to five and a half years in prison, he was already out of jail when the civil suit was resolved. He'd sexually abused his daughter for twelve years, starting when she was five years old; between the ages of twelve and seventeen, she was subjected to fellatio and intercourse at least every other day. However, she may not collect any money since her father transferred his assets — including a house and a business — to a girlfriend and other relatives.

The strangest incongruency between the two systems is that a perpetrator can be acquitted in a criminal court and held liable in a civil suit. That's because the criminal test is more stringent, requiring the Crown to prove guilt "beyond a reasonable doubt," whereas the civil test of liability is "a balance of probabilities" — the plaintiff only has to prove that it's more likely the alleged event happened than that it didn't.

For the McNall sisters in 1990, however, the civil system would have presented a roadblock: there was a statute of limitations that required lawsuits in Ontario relating to sexual assault to be initiated within four years of the offence. (As we've seen, as a result of the 1992 Miersma decision from the Supreme Court of Canada, the statute of limitations for sexual assault begins when victims become aware of the impact of the abuse and are able to act on their knowledge.) There is no such statute of limitations for serious charges in the criminal system, which was, in any event, the McNalls' first choice.

Their first step was to find people with expertise in child sexual abuse to investigate and prosecute the case. Since she worked in a legal clinic, Jill was in a position to make the necessary inquiries, and recommends that survivors contemplating legal action do as much research as possible in order to avoid revictimization. "You *have* to try and find a police officer and a Crown attorney who understand this issue," she says. "It's really important to get the support."

Such basic steps as writing a victim-impact statement are extremely difficult for survivors; in going to court, the McNall sisters and Constance had to acknowledge the suffering in explicit terms. "How do you define the impact of something that has totally twisted and poisoned your entire life and how you relate to human beings?" Constance says. She didn't know where to begin her victim-impact statement. "Trust? I could never trust anybody." She couldn't let her children out of her sight, apart from going to school, and couldn't use babysitters. Her son asked if he could play Nintendo at his friend's house and she wouldn't let him go, because the father was at home that day. "It's sick, I feel sick, I am sick. I lament the child I would have been. I have no memories of childhood that abuse isn't part of. If I was raped today, I would suffer but it wouldn't affect the foundation of my entire life."

Being asked to write a victim-impact statement almost offended Jill; she hated having to show her wounds — especially when it was so hard to acknowledge them herself. "That was the hardest part for me," Jill says, "writing down what I'd never told anybody." She had steadfastly refused to display her pain, not wanting to give her father the satisfaction of knowing he'd hurt her. She hadn't sought therapy until she embarked on the legal process, because she wasn't ready to admit the damage done, even though she was reminded of it by the most insignificant details: she couldn't look at the cover of a Canadian Tire catalogue that showed a picture of a little girl with her father in his basement workshop, because that's where a lot of the abuse had happened.

Constance understood; she too confused innocent events with remembered horror. When her husband romped with the children, she had to leave the room because it reminded her of Donald McNall. One day her husband was upstairs and Constance heard their daughter call out, "No, Daddy, that hurts." Constance couldn't stop herself: heart pounding, she raced upstairs in a panic. "I felt so bad — he saw the look on my face. He was combing her hair." How could she explain the ever-present suspicion and sense of doom that pervaded her life? How can anyone adequately describe a childhood shattered by sexual violation?

The trial began on June 7, 1991, in Scarborough, before His Honour Judge Harvey Salem. The clerk of the court read the charges against Donald McNall: lengthy descriptions of activities in which he "unlaw-fully did have sexual intercourse" with three daughters and one neigh-bourhood girl. McNall pleaded guilty — not surprisingly, given the number of victims. His plea meant the only evidence presented ver-bally to the judge would be a reading of the facts, agreed upon before-hand by the accused and the prosecution.

Donald McNall elected to be tried by a judge without the necessi-ty of a preliminary hearing. The reading of the facts was put over until August 14, 1991, but did not take place, due to various delays, until October 16, when Crown prosecutor Mary Hall set out the family details: the accused had been married to his wife for forty years; they had four girls and a boy, the latter killed in a car accident in 1977. Three McNall sisters were seated in court that day — Joy, thirty-seven; Jill, thirty-two; Julie, twenty-eight — and Constance, also twenty-eight.

In 1959, when Joy was five years old, Donald McNall had embarked on a reign of terror that lasted nineteen years, ending when his youngest child was fifteen years old. The assaults ranged from dig-ital penetration to enforced fellatio to vaginal rape; penetration was initiated with each girl between the ages of five and seven.

Donald McNall was a typical perpetrator, in terms of denial. He'd pleaded guilty and agreed to the facts of the case, but he persisted in "not remembering" what he'd done, and had his lawyer, Kerry Evans, dispute some of the victims' claims: "My client's best recollection is that with respect to intercourse with Constance, that did not happen until she was...nine or ten years of age, not at age five" — as if the sexual assault of a nine-year-old were acceptable. "With respect to frequency, he [McNall] indicates that it happened often, but he has no regular idea of how often.... There were comments about being dragged into a back bedroom, but there wasn't any dragging or anything. He used his force as a father, I guess.... I don't know if that makes it any better or not, but certainly he does not say there was any physical assault." His client, Evans would reiterate, was a successful businessman and a solid family man.

From evidence presented by Evans, however, it was clear that Donald McNall had carried the cycle of incest from one generation to the next. He was living proof of what monsters victims could become. Dr. Robert Coulthard, a psychiatrist who'd been treating McNall since his arrest, testified as a witness for the defence. Coulthard said McNall's mother was extremely promiscuous. She'd exposed her son to her numerous affairs with relatives and with boyfriends of her daughters. At the age of ten, Donald had had sexual intercourse with a cousin who was two years older. "And in addition, later on, sexual involvement at the instigation of the mother, but he [was] completely willing," Coulthard said.

Defence counsel Kerry Evans underlined the point: "He had sexual intercourse with his own mother?" Coulthard confirmed it and added that "there was a lot of other incestual activity in that grandfathers may have been involved with the accused's mother, and that uncles may have been involved too...."

When Mary Hall cross-examined Coulthard, she confronted the issue of Donald McNall's continued denial. For Hall, it is as important as it is difficult to get rapists and pedophiles to admit they've caused serious harm. On the one hand, McNall had pleaded guilty; on the other hand, he was telling his psychiatrist that he didn't remember what he'd done, and what he did remember wasn't so bad. (Treatment for sex offenders is often a dismal failure precisely for this reason: if they believe they've done nothing wrong, they can't be treated.)

"So McNall still has not totally acknowledged to you what he has done?" Hall said. She wouldn't let Coulthard — or McNall — off the hook: "It's not just normal lack of memory when someone abuses four young girls for nineteen years and says he doesn't remember." Coulthard explained his analysis of McNall's denial; there were two processes at work, one in which the accused was partly dissociated, suppressing his memories of the sexual assaults; the second in which he was conscious of his deeds but unable to face what he'd done. How, Hall wanted to know, could Coulthard treat a patient who'd committed incest and denied he'd had intercourse with his daughters? She quoted from a pre-sentence report by another professional: "He states that at the time of the assaults he did not believe he was hurting the girls. However, the victims report that he threatened them against disclosing the assaults, and the acts became progressively violent as the girls tried to resist his attacks. It seems that he was not willing to empathize with the victims' pain."

Hall wanted to know what stage McNall was at now. Did he accept that he'd hurt the girls? Had he read their victim-impact statements? "I haven't gone over that with him," Coulthard said. Hall was amazed. "How on earth do you treat someone if you don't go over with him the hurt his behaviour has caused?" Coulthard admitted he wasn't treating McNall for his violent sexual behaviour, but for his depression — an admission that gave Hall an opening to point out that McNall was depressed not because he'd damaged his daughters and their friend but because he faced the prospect of going to jail. She quoted from a report by another psychiatrist who had assessed McNall: "He does recall that the youngest daughter Julie and a friend would jump on him at times, and that there may have been some kind of mutual sexual stimulation which occurred in a light-hearted way."

Mutual sexual stimulation: the phrase made the McNall sisters gag, suffused as it was with the pathology of perpetrators. If there is a core to evil, this is it: the bland self-centredness of abusers who, in their obsession, obliterate the humanity of their victims. McNall's utter lack of empathy is characteristic of psychopaths — and to see him revealed in such a cold, clear light in a court of law was, for the McNall sisters and Constance, at once nauseating and liberating. Through it all, for the first time in their lives, the four women had a powerful voice: prosecutor Mary Hall.

The Scarborough courthouse is located in a bleak strip mall. Down long corridors lined with wooden benches, an astounding diversity of people mill about before disappearing into hushed courtrooms, from which they emerge in varying states of elation or distress. This is a world of sharp contradictions, where the rule of law — with its imperfections and biases, its traditional concern for the rights of the accused and its failure to acknowledge the rights of victims — collides head-on with the messy stuff of human tragedy. Everyone is caught up in the clamour, the drama, and the mind-numbing boredom as the wheels of justice grind forward; the air crackles with a particular intensity that is not to be found in any other institution; you can see it in the faces, hear it in the voices. There is nothing like a requirement to appear in a court of law to focus the mind.

In Mary Hall's windowless office, framed academic documents rest on the back of the sofa; she hasn't had time to hang them up. She is seated behind a desk littered with Easter bunnies and paraphernalia for making Easter baskets for the two little girls in her life. At the age of forty, as the senior Crown attorney for Metro East, in charge of twenty assistant Crowns, she has a superior track record with a specialty in prosecuting sexual assault cases. This is one of the toughest areas of law in which to get convictions, because the crime usually occurs with only two people present, the victim and the offender; because defence lawyers are allowed to mount wide-ranging attacks on victims; because sexual assault has not been treated as a serious crime and victims have not been believed.

Hall started as an assistant Crown attorney in 1979 at Toronto's City Hall courts, and was only the third female Crown hired in the downtown office. "The inclination in those days," she says, "was to assign the prosecution of sexual assault cases to women." She didn't object; she found the work challenging and developed her expertise as the Ministry of the Attorney-General's appointee to the Metro Special Committee on Child Abuse, and to the Task Force on Public Violence against Women and Children, which in 1984 became the Metro Action Committee on Public Violence against Women and Children (METRAC). METRAC developed a unique database containing a thousand sexual assault sentencing decisions, collected across Canada from 1980 on; its analysis, which proves useful to Hall, documents some alarming facts:

• Judges often blame victims for "allowing" abuse to occur, and minimize the long-term harm done to them. In case after case, judges justify lenient sentences by saying that "no violence was used." [Asked if her father became more violent over the years, Julie McNall said: "He was never not violent. Every act of sexual abuse is an act of violence."]

• Most judges fail to identify breach of trust in sexual assault cases. An important legal concept, breach of trust is a standard aggravating factor and reason for stiffer sentences for crimes involving property. For example: if a head cashier was convicted of stealing money from her boss, a judge would determine the crime was particularly heinous because the head cashier was in a position of trust and responsibility. Yet judges often ignore breach of trust in child sexual abuse cases, even though most victims are sexually assaulted by trusted authority figures.

• White male judges give lighter sentences to white, male, middle-class offenders. Significantly, judges mete out much stiffer sentences to female abusers.

• Many judges do not consider sexual assault a serious matter, in criminal terms, but juries in civil suits, where complainants seek damages for pain and suffering, are responding to the plight of victims.

The criminal justice system has an inherent, structural blind spot concerning victims because the system was designed with only two parties in mind: the state and the accused. The victim has no right to counsel, no right to legal aid and no right to address the court. The Canadian Charter of Rights and Freedoms, the highest law in the land, governs criminal procedures; its focus is on granting rights to, and protecting, people charged with criminal offences. There are no such protections for victims. One of the areas of gravest concern involves disclosure: while the Crown is required to fully disclose to the accused all information pertaining to the victim, the accused has no such obligation to the Crown. In practice, victims are often treated as if they are the accused. The defence lawyer can gain full access to victims' medical and psychiatric records, while the Crown has no similar access to the accused's records.

In *Regina versus O'Connor* in the British Columbia Supreme Court in 1992, Bishop Hubert Patrick O'Connor was charged with sexually assaulting four aboriginal women when they were students at the residential school where he was the principal in the 1960s. The judge threw the case out of court because Crown prosecutor Wendy Harvey, a specialist in sexual assault cases, did not make the victims' entire psychiatric files available to the defence, which won a stay of proceedings. Harvey, a thirteen-year veteran in the Ministry of the Attorney-General, was subsequently pilloried by media and legal pundits, investigated by the Law Society and targeted by death threats — all because she tried to protect victims from defence demands for sweeping disclosure of private records that she believes contravenes basic human rights. "We have to redesign the justice system," Harvey said, "to accommodate the needs of users, apart from the accused." The Women's Legal Education and Action Fund agreed, and applied in June 1993 to intervene before the British Columbia Court of Appeal, arguing that the law should not require disclosure of irrelevant information about victims.

Yet Mary Hall is optimistic that the system is changing: more victims are coming forward at an earlier age, because of education programs in schools and protocols that require teachers, doctors and social workers to report suspicion of abuse; more charges are being laid; police and Crowns are prosecuting more effectively and judges are being educated; there are more convictions now than a decade ago and sentences are getting longer.

One of the most significant advances, in Hall's view, is the development of the victim-witness program, and one of the most critical players in the McNall case was Susan Physick, their victim-witness coordinator. A former nurse married to an Anglican minister, Physick worked with battered women until one night, on a call that kept her out until 3:00 a.m., taking a woman who'd been beaten by her husband to a shelter, Physick decided she needed more training. In 1988, she enrolled in Advocate Counselling for Assaulted Women and Children, a two-year diploma course at Toronto's George Brown College. Her first work placement put her on the sexual assault team at Women's College Hospital in Toronto; she counselled women with rape trauma syndrome and accompanied them to court, where she saw that victims were not only ignored by the criminal justice system but revictimized by it.

Physick wanted to do frontline court work and on August 1, 1990, became the victim-witness coordinator in Mary Hall's office. At first she couldn't sleep at night, she was so overwhelmed by the caseload, half of which involves women, victims of wife assault; of the other half, 80 per cent are sexually assaulted children under the age of sixteen. She is tired of people making excuses for abusers: "They'll say he raped his daughter because he got drunk, or because he lost his job, or his wife wouldn't have sex with him. Excuse me, but lots of people get drunk, lose jobs, have spouses who won't sleep with them, and they don't rape their kids."

Perpetrators usually act like martyrs, in her experience, displaying a *How could she do this to me?* attitude, like Donald McNall. In court, "these guys often try to make the judge feel sorry for them." And often succeed, partly because, in Physick's experience, "you see an ageing offender who looks sick and weak, and a mature adult charging him, and you can no longer see the power imbalance that existed when the abuse occurred."

Despite the horror she deals with daily, she loves the work: "It's a privilege to walk with people through their pain and grief, to share that experience and help them move to the other side. It's not so much what you say, it's your presence, being a witness to what they're going through, allowing them to express their feelings, supporting their struggle to reclaim their lives." She expresses great admiration for the McNall sisters and Constance: "They named the crime and took back control over their lives. Telling the secret is so important; as long as the secret is kept, the offender is protected."

The court proceedings in the McNall case dragged on. Joy kept a list of court dates, with reasons for delays: "May 3, 1991, all geared up to go, court cancelled at the last minute, defence psychiatric report not ready, devastating letdown. June 7, he pleaded guilty. August 14, court cancelled, defence lawyer's wife sick. August 21, all geared up but it was just a set-date. October 16, proceedings started, psychiatrist had to go to another trial. November 8, psychiatrist completed his testimony; submissions re sentencing. December 3, snowstorm, sentencing put over until January 9, 1992."

For victims, *every* delay is agonizing. "It's like a knife stuck in your heart," says Jeff David, who accompanied Jill to most court dates. "Your life is on hold," Jill says, "you're counting down the days to the next court appearance, you're stressed out, you're terrified of the offender in ways that might seem irrational, but he's out on bail and you've experienced his rage." Yet the delays were unexpectedly therapeutic. Constance hadn't laid eyes on Donald McNall for ten years, and was terrified of having to confront him. "In counselling, I saw him as a demon, a beastly thing," she said, "and there he was in court, a pathetic human being who did those awful things to helpless little children."

It helped, Jill said, having three people on their side: the Crown attorney, the police officer and the victim-witness coordinator. Mrs. McNall didn't come to court; she'd been married to Donald McNall since 1952, had separated from him in 1985 but continued to see him. "She wasn't able to confront the issues," Jill said. She wasn't the only one. During the trial, Brian McNall, Donald's younger brother, admitted that Julie had told him, when she was twelve, that she was being sexually abused by her father. Mary Hall asked Brian why he hadn't done anything to help his niece. Brian said he couldn't believe there was "such a horrendous problem going on in a family where you love everybody, and if you don't acknowledge it you think it's going to go away…."

Joseph Schill, a friend of Donald McNall's since 1974, when they got their pilot's licences, testified: "I consider Mr. McNall my nearest and dearest friend. He's a buddy." Schill said he often visited the McNall home and saw them as "always happy, jovial. The family always sat down to dinner together and ate, and discussed current affairs, and whatever." In 1978, he admitted, Jill told him that Donald McNall had sexually abused his daughters. Did Schill ask his good buddy what was going on? "No, I never discussed it with Mr. McNall. Until this time, he never knew that I knew it." He attempted to justify his inaction by saying he'd respected Jill's privacy. After he testified, Schill approached her outside the courtroom; she turned and walked away.

As Donald McNall's trial approached its conclusion in November 1991, seven months after its scheduled start date, his lawyer, Kerry

Evans, delivered submissions to Judge Harvey Salem relating to sentencing. Evans extolled his client's virtues: "You have a man that has absolutely no criminal record.... He is a man that has existed in the business world, and in the family world, that has looked after his familial responsibilities." Evans acknowledged that McNall had "perpetrated acts that have damaged his own children," but in a strange twist of logic he attempted to minimize the accused's crimes by noting that Mrs. McNall was "supportive" of her husband. "They live together, he has been with this woman, he has resided with her all summer," Evans said. "He is not an individual that has to be locked away for twenty years or fifteen years or eight years, to be hidden in a cage somewhere because he is going to reach out and grab some small child. He has been involved in his community, he has talked in schools.... This is a very proud man.... There is nothing before you that shows this man is a danger to any young children."

In her final submissions on sentencing, Mary Hall asked for a penitentiary term of six to eight years. "Mr. Evans says by way of mitigation that Mr. McNall is a victim himself of sexual abuse.... Well, I'd ask you to look at that. Mr. McNall has fathered five children...he has had a long and successful career, he has a good friend, he has a close relationship with his brother.... I would ask you to compare the long and full life Mr. McNall has had with what is indicated in the future for his daughters. His three daughters do not have children, they are of an age to have children...and they are not likely to have children as a result of this abuse. Mr. Evans says that this is an illness that Mr. McNall suffers from. In my submission...there is no mental illness here. What this man did is legally wrong, it's misconduct, it's not an illness."

They had to wait until the new year to find out Donald McNall's fate. "The roughest day was the day the judge delivered his sentence," says Susan Physick. "It was a shattering experience. We were in a state of shock." On January 9, 1992, the first item of court business was the matter of the publication ban, which had been instituted, as is common practice, to protect the privacy of the victims. Mary Hall told Judge Salem that the McNall sisters and Constance, "for the sake of other victims out there, wish [Donald McNall's] name published so that if what they believe is true, that other women have been victimized, they may have some sort of satisfaction in reading in the newspaper today that at least some form of penalty has been imposed on him for the many, many years of abuse…. So I would ask you to rescind that order [banning the publication of names]." This was an extraordinary request on the part of victims, and a decision they had not taken lightly.

Kerry Evans argued to retain the publication ban, raising the spectre of Joseph Fredericks, a convicted pedophile who was released from jail in 1988, raped and murdered eleven-year-old Christopher Stephenson and after a much-publicized trial was subsequently killed by another inmate at Kingston Penitentiary. Evans expressed his concern for Donald McNall's safety should his name be published, but Mary Hall countered that the victims were concerned about the safety of other children. "They have reason to believe that there have been other women or children who have been the victims of Mr. McNall." She added that Jill was prepared to explain to the court why she wanted the publication ban rescinded. This was a heart-stopping moment for Jill, as it would be the only opportunity for any of them to speak during the entire court process — but Judge Salem flatly refused to hear from her.

Mary Hall persisted: the publication ban was "the right of the complainants," to protect *their* privacy, not the accused's, "and they now wish to give up that right for another — in my submission — good and proper reason." But Judge Salem refused their request: "I don't think that it's in the best interests of the victims in a situation where they are so emotionally involved…. The order stands."

At that point, Jill McNall got angry; to be silenced by a judge who refused to hear her reasons, whose action protected her father, was intolerable. But it was going to get worse. Donald McNall stood up to make a brief statement. (Defence lawyers usually advise offenders to apologize and show remorse, in order to win sympathy from the judge.) "I'd just like to say that I sincerely regret all the things that happened those years ago and I wish there was some way to take it back, but there isn't." Donald McNall's voice was flat; he betrayed no emotion. "I just want the court to know that I really regret what happened, and the damage I did to other people's lives." *All the things that happened.* The victims heard the verbal blur, and their anger mounted.

Judge Salem summed up the facts: "The accused is a sixty-year-old man, with no previous criminal record...." He mentioned the nineteen years of abuse, the severity of the trauma suffered by the victims, and sentenced Donald McNall to two years less a day, plus a term of probation of three years.

"Two years less a day," said Susan Physick. "Mary Hall was in shock." The victims were stunned. Donald McNall would be eligible for parole after serving one-third of his sentence; he could be out in eight months. "We all went back to Mary's office and looked at each other and the emotions set in — the anger, the frustration," Physick said. "They had done everything right, and he got two years less a day for nineteen years of abuse. Is that justice?"

The McNall sisters were not silenced this time. DAD'S SENTENCE A BITTER VICTORY FOR SEXUALLY ABUSED DAUGHTERS, said the front-page headline in the *Toronto Star* the following day. "Unidentified incest victims" were everywhere in the media, photographed in shadows, faces obliterated by blobs. "Tonight on *CityPulse*," said Gord Martineau, Citytv anchor, "incest victims speak out." Jill, viewed from the back of her head, said: "He'll be out in eight months, after abusing four of us for nineteen years." On CFTO's *World Beat News*, "Outraged incest victims" were the lead item, with Mary Hall quoted as saying the sentence was "woefully inadequate." Jill, Joy and Constance appeared in disguise on Dini Petty's CTV talk show in a lineup that included glitz novelist Judith Krantz and the question *Will women ever get to play hockey in the NHL?* On they came, outfitted in huge wigs and fancy face masks. Jeff David recoiled when he saw their costumes, but Dini Petty was empathetic and made her point: her guests had been ordered to comply with a publication ban and not reveal their identity, she said; what would the penalty be if they whipped off their masks and wigs? "Six months in jail or a $1,000 fine," Jill said, to groans from the studio audience. Dini asked if they could sue for damages. Constance said she and Julie were considering it. Off camera, they expressed sarcastic appreciation for Judge Salem; in the long run, he had done them a big favour. By imposing a minimal sentence and continuing the publication ban, he had handed them a media platform.

The Crown initiated an appeal of Judge Salem's sentence and of the publication ban. In support of that effort, Joy wrote a letter to Mary Hall: "It is my understanding that the ban is put in place to protect his victims. I am 37 years old, and a functioning adult.... I have already suffered as a result of the abuse; I shouldn't be forced into silence.... We also want his name published, as anonymity prevents other people from knowing the nature of the charges [against him]. I know that a condition of probation is no contact with children under 16 without an adult present. There are two problems with this. 1. Probation is only for three years. 2. It is a well known fact that pedophiles often continue their crimes — even after treatment. Parents should be warned...." Publication bans, she concluded, made "criminals feel secure in the knowledge that their names will not be published."

In Jill's letter to Mary Hall, she wrote that "Judge Salem has perpetuated the notion of shame and guilt for incest and sexual abuse victims. We were prepared to speak out about our experiences to try to assist other victims and to inform the public.... For far too long, incest has been a shameful secret, which no one would talk about and which victims were afraid to admit.... Judge Salem is perpetuating the secret and sending the message that we as victims are not able to decide for ourselves what is in our best interest."

These letters were included as Exhibits E and F in the Ontario Court of Appeal hearing five months later, in June 1992, along with an affidavit from Dr. Elaine Borins, a psychiatrist who specializes in treating victims of child sexual assault. Dr. Borins noted that the McNall sisters "are competent to make informed decisions that have long range importance," and that victims who choose to disclose their identities receive therapeutic benefits: "There is a cathartic effect to uncovering the secret and disavowing the shame.... The ability to reach out to other victims, both of the same abuser and other abusers, can also be important to the process of recovery." (This affidavit was part of the submission made to the Court of Appeal by Elizabeth McIntyre, the lawyer hired by the McNall sisters and Constance in a successful bid to oppose Judge Salem's publication ban.)

On Monday, June 8, at Toronto's historic Osgoode Hall, Crown attorney Eric Siebenmorgen addressed the Court of Appeal, represented by three grey-haired, white male judges; Jill, Joy and Constance observed the proceedings without much hope, given their experience with Judge Salem. In an eloquent presentation, Siebenmorgen attempted to convey the massive extent of Donald McNall's abuse: "For each of the three daughters, ten years of abuse were suffered," he said. "For the neighbourhood friend who was raped, there were eight years of ongoing abuse." He added it up, deliberately: "Ten plus ten plus ten plus eight, that's thirty-eight years of people's lives, being sexually assaulted." Siebenmorgen compared the case to others: "It is the Crown's submission that from the standpoint of the *duration* of abuse and the *number* of victims, this case is virtually *unprecedented* in its gravity. It is submitted that the victim impact in this case is, in a word, *staggering*. The degree of human suffering represented by these four counts is, in my submission, incalculable."

It didn't take the judges long to decide. They withdrew briefly and returned with their decision; two years to the month after Jill and Julie first met Mary Hall, it was all over. The Ontario Court of Appeal quadrupled Donald McNall's sentence to eight years and did not apply a publication ban. Afterward, Siebenmorgen commented on the importance of the McNall case: "For the first time that I know of, victims of childhood sexual abuse started out, in court, wanting privacy, wanting to remain hidden, as it were, and then changed their minds during the trial process. They realized they had nothing to be ashamed of, and wanted their own names used because they wanted their abuser identified, in order to protect other children. By rejecting the publication ban, and increasing the sentence from two years less a day to eight years, the Appeal Court sent a very strong message to the trial judge that he was very wrong in his handling of the case. It is very unusual for the court to *quadruple* sentence on appeal." Even so, Donald McNall will be eligible for parole after serving one-third of his sentence, and is likely to be released early in 1995.

No longer forced to be photographed in the shadows, Jill and Joy faced the cameras with dignity. For the first time, the two sisters were identified by their real names; Donald McNall's picture was published in the *Globe and Mail*. The McNall sisters now know of six more women who say they were sexually assaulted as children by Donald McNall, though they are not prepared to go to the police. For Jill, the media onslaught this time was at once liberating and a little scary. When she heard the first radio broadcast that said his name and her name, she quaked and thought, *Oh boy, this is it, the secret is out.*

Some of her friends made no mention of her media presence,

others called or wrote to say, "Good for you." Jill appreciated the latter response: "It's nice to know people are supportive and don't think differently about you." Months later, as the court case receded, she realized she'd been in a fog for a long time. "The stress of the trial had more impact than we anticipated. Now we can get on with our lives." Constance agreed. "We succeeded where he failed. He was hurt as a child, those deep wounds were put into him, he got infected and he infected us; we have the wounds but we are healing. We broke the cycle. He has no control over our lives any more."

"The justice system lags behind the community in recognizing the severity of the harm caused by sexual assault," says Judge Lauren Marshall, the senior administrative judge for Metro Toronto North Court. She is also the co-chair of a judicial education committee that organizes seminars on issues relating to sexual assault, to teach awareness about power differentials, to give judges a greater understanding of male-female, adult-child power dynamics as they're expressed in cases before the court.

"We send bank robbers who've caused no physical harm to the pen because they've committed a criminal act and have got to be deterred," she says, "but with rapists and pedophiles we say, 'They need treatment,' as if they haven't committed a serious crime, and give them these 'two years less a day' sentences so they don't have to go the pen." ("The pen" refers to federal institutions such as Kingston Penitentiary or Warkworth, where criminals serve two years or more.)

Judicial leniency in relation to rape and child sexual abuse is due to the fact, Marshall says, that "we've *refused* to recognize the harm done by sexual assault." In her view, it is now "common knowledge" that the psychological trauma of sexual assault can be worse than physical injury. But many judges "still sentence low on the basis of no obvious physical damage." They need to discuss these issues, Marshall says, because many of the symptoms of sexual abuse are used against victims to discredit them. It's difficult to grasp, without special training, that not only children but adult survivors testifying in court about horrendous abuse can still be emotionally attached to the perpetrator. The trauma bond has a tight grip: "I've seen that bond to the abuser, over and over again. Children, no matter what their age, don't want to destroy their family."

Most perpetrators refuse to acknowledge their crimes. "Your typical offender is in gross denial, even after conviction." It isn't uncommon for abusers who've pleaded guilty to refuse treatment "on the grounds they didn't really do anything to hurt the child; that's a common denial reaction. Down deep, these people don't think they've done anything wrong, because they only consider their own needs; they have no empathy for anybody else and they blame the child: *Well, she sat on my lap. Well, he kept coming after me for attention.* Pedophiles are not concerned about trauma to children; if they had cared, they wouldn't have done it."

The dilemma, for a judge, is that there is no ideal solution. Most mothers or non-offending caregivers know at some level that the abuse occurred, in Marshall's experience, but won't acknowledge it. "So the victim has been doubly abandoned. It's very frustrating, as a judge: we're dealing with the end result of social problems we can't change from where we sit."

Yet Marshall is optimistic. Most judges are caring and conscientious, in her experience, and they're willing to learn. In fact, they are in urgent need of support; the number of reported sexual offences across Canada has increased more than 200 per cent during the past decade, from 15,701 in 1977 to 35,835 in 1988, the most recent year for which national statistics are available. The majority of victims are children and teenagers. Marshall believes that "skyrocketing disclosure rates" are a phenomenon of our times: "This an epidemic, all right, but it's not new, in my opinion, it's always been there, we're just seeing it, children are reporting it and they're being believed." At the end of the day, however, judges face the ultimate decision: "If there's any doubt in your mind, you cannot convict. It's better that the odd guilty person get off than that innocent people be convicted." In Scotland, she adds, "they have three verdicts: guilty, not guilty and not proven." In some cases, she'd like to have the third option.

After Donald McNall went to jail, Julie and Constance initiated a civil lawsuit against him. He made an out-of-court cash settlement, which they are prohibited from discussing. Jill and Joy didn't participate: "We have such revulsion at the thought of engaging with him in any way," Jill said, "that the money's not worth it." In October 1993, she and Joy received a financial award from the Criminal Injuries Compensation Board, to help pay for their therapy bills and legal fees.

(Hearings in sexual assault or incest cases are usually held *in camera* with a publication ban on the decision and the award to protect the victims' privacy.) Jill subsequently wrote to the board, encouraging it to sue Donald McNall to cover its expenditures on their behalf.

Jill is ever more determined to speak out publicly, to help other sexual abuse survivors. She participated in a Global TV panel aired after the screening of an Oprah Winfrey–hosted special on child sexual abuse; she appeared in a video for the Institute for the Prevention of Child Abuse, and in a TVOntario broadcast — live and interactive — for high school students; and in the spring of 1993 she addressed a group of ninety Ontario Crown attorneys.

Looking back, she feels the court case marked a turning point in their lives. Society, through the criminal justice system, in the person of the investigating police officer, the Crown attorney and the victim-witness coordinator, supported them. The abuser was held accountable and he was punished.

"The process was long and difficult," Jill says, "but it made us stronger. We took back control of our lives, and we did everything in our power to stop him from hurting another child." However, she has a word of caution: "Going through the system won't suddenly solve everything or make the pain go away. But it was worth it, for me — even though it's still the *criminal* justice system, not the victim justice system." Yet the achievement of the McNall sisters and Constance is the ultimate goal for many survivors. They had the advantage of power in numbers, and together, as adults, they did what they couldn't do as children: they confronted the monster. They bear the scars, but now they can go on with the rest of their lives.

8

Conclusion

In every eye there is a spot that is incapable of sight.
The optic disc exists as a black hole right next to the
central point of clearest vision. Yet anyone who has
not learned the trick of finding it would swear there
is no such void.

— Dr. Roland Summit
in *Lasting Effects of Child Sexual Abuse*

THIS BOOK WAS precipitated by a telephone call from a man who said he was the father of two boys who'd been sexually abused by John Gallienne. Donald Swainson, a history professor at Queen's University, reached me in the newsroom of the *Toronto Star* in the summer of 1991, and asked me to come to Kingston to meet with some of the parents of John Gallienne's victims. I'd never heard of Gallienne, who was already incarcerated, and I was not aware of how pedophiles operate. "We thought it would be over when Gallienne went to jail," Swainson said. "Nothing's over." Indeed, the impact of child sexual abuse never ends.

"Why are you writing this book?" It was eighteen months later, I was deep into the research for *Our Little Secret*, and Ned and Daphne Franks had finally agreed to meet me. The question was Daphne's, spoken while she poured tea into tiny cups at a Chinese restaurant in downtown Toronto. Ned was seated beside her, crying openly, unabashedly; they were both still devastated by their son Tim's suicide in 1989. Together, they precipitated the collapse of Gallienne's intricately constructed house of cards. In confronting Gallienne's crimes, the Franks faced their own limitations as parents. No family is perfect; we are all vulnerable. That is why I wrote this book.

Journalists are usually able to observe other people's tragedies from a distance, without feeling personally threatened; in this case, I realized it could have happened to me — I could have been one of these parents. They were all so different from each other, as individuals, and so much the same, in their pain. Like me, they had not known enough about the way child abusers operate.

I had not understood that abusers often romance and seduce their victims before closing the trap. That adults can basically do anything they want to a child. That children hardly ever disclose right away, and when they do, non-offending adults usually instantly deny the allegations and align themselves with abusers. I had not understood that the sexual touching of a child by an adult is psychologically destructive because it's an invasion of personal boundaries that can lead to the obliteration of the child's ego, the erasure of identity, the end of autonomy.

Most victims do not become abusers, but without early intervention, a small percentage of abused children will grow up to repeat the cycle of sexual violation. Donald McNall was an incest victim turned perpetrator, who targeted his daughters and neighbourhood children. Sammy, a Prescott boy, was sexually abused since infancy, and on the brink of becoming a sex offender, doing to others what had been done to him. He couldn't see that he was exploiting other children *because* he'd been exploited as a child.

We have to stop this vicious cycle; the repercussions are too costly, in human and societal terms. Andrew Swainson isn't a criminal, he's a kid driven crazy by childhood exploitation; Edward didn't choose to be a prostitute, he was simply repeating childhood conditioning; Daisy became addicted to codeine because she was an incest survivor trying to deal with the pain of buried memories. And so it goes: so many people trapped in the prison of childhood sexual abuse, struggling toward the truth. They need to be heard. And their perpetrators have to be held accountable.

Ending the epidemic of child sexual abuse requires systemic changes to our police forces, courts, hospitals and schools — changes that are well under way. On March 1, 1993, at Toronto's Old City Hall, another small step was taken: a specially renovated courtroom was dedicated to cases involving children, with four specially trained Crown attorneys assigned to handle the prosecutions. "We feel this is going to allow children to give better evidence," says Judge Claude Paris, of the Ontario Court's Provincial Division. Paris helped develop the concept, which provides children with extra sensitive microphones, screens to shield them from the alleged abuser and an attached playroom in which they can relax before coming into court. "If they're intimidated to the point where they're in shock and they can't talk, then I don't think justice is being done," Paris says.

Nor is justice being served when offenders receive minimal sentences. In the spring of 1993, social worker Pam Gummer had only to look out her office window to see the Prescott perpetrators clustered around the town clock, returning to their old haunts after being in jail for as little as six months. "If we believe in the principle of deterrence, the courts have got to hand down more serious sentences," she says. "In the United States, the sexual abuse of children is being treated as a major crime and offenders are getting twenty years to life."

In Canada, the mood is becoming less tolerant. Local groups are publicizing and protesting the presence of convicted child abusers in their communities. And in May 1993, the federal government released a draft bill to keep violent criminals in jail indefinitely; the initiative arose partly as a response to the abduction, rape and murder of eleven-year-old Christopher Stephenson by Joseph Fredericks, a convicted pedophile who was out on parole. Under the old law, the "dangerous offender" designation could be made only at the time of sentencing; under the new proposal, convicted offenders could be denied parole and held indefinitely, allowing the Crown to take into account new information made available since the conviction. However, in November 1994, the liberal government announced it had abandoned, as unconstitutional, any effort to create such a law.

We still, as a society, don't know what to do with child abusers. We still, collectively, haven't accepted the enormity of the harm they cause. There is no cure. This is a power dysfunction manifested as a sexual dysfunction, perpetrated by damaged people who manipulate and control non-offending adults in order to have access to children. We must stop making excuses for their criminal behaviour.

We can go a long way as individuals to protect children, and to help victims disclose, by paying attention. Survivors often disclose to friends or siblings, whose reactions are crucial; we must respond seriously, ask the victim how she or he feels about what happened, if they've sought help, if they've considered going to the police.

To be good parents, good teachers, good friends to children, we must respect their feelings and honour their autonomy. If children say they don't want to go somewhere with someone, find out why; if they become withdrawn or aggressive, try to communicate. If we blame the child for everything that goes wrong, the child won't open up. We need to align ourselves with our children. It is our responsibility as parents to reach out to them; if we can't, we need professional help.

Children should not be forced to show affection to people they don't like. If a child is told to "kiss Uncle John, don't hurt his feelings, don't make him feel bad," the child's instincts are negated and the child is set up for an abusive adult who touches the child sexually and says, "Don't make me feel bad." Children need to be told that they have choices, that they can say no to things they don't want to do and to people they don't want to be with.

"I couldn't say no; it was more important to please the abuser than to please myself," says Oprah Winfrey, underlining the distortion caused by child sexual abuse. But it's not just survivors who have to learn to say no, it's all of us. We have harboured the perpetrators, and we have to draw the line. The sexual abuse of children is a crime; *we will not tolerate it.*

Finally, we have to look within, at the roles in our families. Too often, women are expected to take care of everyone's emotional needs, but it's not humanly possible; women who try to do so inevitably fail, and then are blamed when things go wrong. Women aren't perfect nurturers; children need male attention too. Intimacy is based on mutual respect and caring. We all, men *and* women, need to learn to listen to each other and to our children; to *hear* each other is the beginning of intimacy. And the end of abuse.

Where to Find Help

Sexual abuse prevention education programs teach children to "tell a trusted adult, and keep telling until you are believed." The same persistence may be necessary for an individual seeking help or information — it may involve contacting several different sources before reaching the desired service.

Disclosure is often a painful and frightening effort for a child. The supportive reaction of the adult receiving the information is of critical importance. The most reassuring stance is to listen, to accept the information as being factual, and to let the child know that you will help. It is equally important that the child is not pressed for details at the time of disclosure as this is an area that is best left to investigating agencies.

Resources are available at national, provincial and local levels. Scattered across the country, a variety of groups and organizations provide important "grassroots" services to their communities. Some groups operate in relative isolation and listings are not always readily available. Support services to victims and their families might be found locally through children's mental health services, associations for community living, public libraries or education facilities. Significant efforts are underway to develop national information networks that will facilitate awareness of and access to available resources.

The introductory pages of your telephone directory provide the first line of enquiry, listing, where available, your local:
- child protection agency (children's aid society/family and children's services)
- police
- sexual assault/rape crisis/distress centre
- helpline

Each province and territory has legislation which outlines the legal duty to report suspected child abuse. The provincial/territorial department or ministry in charge of child welfare can provide information on these laws as well as on child abuse in general and resources within the community. The ministries are listed below under the relevant province or territory.

The following is a selection of government and non-government organizations currently active in the field of family violence. While not all-inclusive, the list identifies agencies that can facilitate access to information and support services in Canada.

NATIONAL

National Clearinghouse on Family Violence
Health Canada
Finance Building, Tunney's Pasture
Ottawa, ON, K1A 1B5 1-800-267-1291 (613) 957-2938 Fax: (613) 957-4247
The Clearinghouse is an information resource centre on family violence prevention for all Canadians. It maintains a collection of fact sheets, articles, reports, and kits of information on family violence, including listings of certain types of community services across Canada.

Canadian Council on Social Development
Family Violence Program
P.O. Box 3505, Station C, 55 Parkdale
Ottawa, ON, K1Y 4G1 (613) 728-1865 Fax: (613) 728-9387
CCSD is a national, voluntary organization working to promote progressive social policies and programs in Canada. Its family violence newsletter, Vis-à-vis, is available free of charge.

Canadian Resource Centre on Children and Youth
Child Welfare League of Canada
180 Argyle Avenue, #316
Ottawa, ON, K2P 1B7 (613) 788-5102 Fax: (613) 788-5075
Research and issues affecting Canadian children, youth and their families are the focus of this resource centre's extensive collection of documents, including directories of treatment programs and community service organizations.

Institute for the Prevention of Child Abuse
25 Spadina Road
Toronto, ON, M5R 2S9 (416) 921-3151 Fax: (416) 921-4997
IPCA originated as a provincially funded charitable organization working for the prevention of child abuse through research, professional training, public education and consultation. Now, as a privately funded, nationally focused organization, IPCA is taking a leading role in the development of national information networks. The Institute offers a broad child abuse training curriculum, organizes regional and national conferences, and distributes public education and prevention materials.

National Victims Resource Centre
Justice Canada
222 Queen Street
Ottawa, ON, K1P 5V9 1-800-267-0454 or (613) 957-9608 Fax: (613) 941-2269
The NVRC is a component of the Access to Justice and Law Information Programs Section with the Department of Justice Canada. It disseminates information and provides referrals for organizations and individuals who are interested in the criminal justice system as it relates to victims of crime.

RESOURCES FOR ABORIGINAL PEOPLES
Assembly of First Nations
55 Murray Street, 5th Floor
Ottawa, ON, K1N 5M3 (613) 241-6789 Fax: (613) 241-5808

National Association of Friendship Centres
396 Cooper Street, Suite 204
Ottawa, ON, K2P 2H7 (613) 563-4844 Fax: (613) 594-3428

Native Council of Canada
384 Bank Street, 2nd Floor
Ottawa, ON, K2P 1Y4 (613) 238-3511 Fax: (613) 230-6273

REGIONAL
Alberta
Alberta Family & Social Services
Children's Advocate
10405 Jasper Avenue, #660
Edmonton, AB, T5J 3N4 (403) 427-8934 Fax: (403) 427-5509

Office for the Prevention of Family Violence
Seventh Street Plaza, 11th Floor
10030 - 107 Street
Edmonton, AB, T5J 3E4 (403) 422-5916 Fax: (403) 427-2039

Society for the Prevention of Child Abuse
740 - 4th Avenue South, Office #216
Lethbridge, AB, T1J 0N8 (403) 320-9040 Fax: (403) 327-9112

British Columbia
Ministry of Social Services
Family & Children's Services
Parliament Buildings
Victoria, BC, V8V 1X4 (604) 387-7060 Fax: 604-356-7862

British Columbia Institute on Family Violence
290 - 601 West Cordova Street
Vancouver, BC, V6B 1G1 (604) 669-7055 Fax: (604) 669-7054

Society for Children and Youth of B.C.
3644 Slocan Street
Vancouver, BC, V5M 3E8 (604) 433-4180 Fax: (604) 433-9611

Victims Information Line
202 - 3102 Main Street
Vancouver, BC, V5T 3G7 (604) 875-6431 Fax: (604) 660-9415, 1-800-563-0808

Manitoba
Manitoba Family Services
Child & Family Services
114 Garry Street, 2nd Floor
Winnipeg, MB, R3C 1G1 (204) 945-6964 Fax: (204) 945-6717

New Brunswick

Department of Health & Community Services
Family & Community Social Services Division
P.O. Box 5100
Fredericton, NB, E3B 5G8 (506) 453-2181 Fax: (506) 453-5243

Newfoundland

Department of Social Services
Director of Child Welfare
Confederation Building
P.O. Box 8700, St. John's, NF, A1B 4J6 (709) 729-2666 Fax: (709) 729-0583

Community Services Council
Working Group on Child Sexual Abuse
Virginia Park Plaza, Suite 101, 2nd Floor
Newfoundland Drive, St. John's, NF, A1A 3E9 (709) 753-9860 Fax: (709) 753-6112

Northwest Territories

Department of Social Services
Family & Children's Services
Family Violence Prevention Programs
500, 4920 52nd Street
Yellowknife, NT, X1A 3T1 (403) 920-8920 Fax: (403) 873-0317

Arctic Public Legal Education and Information Society
4916 - 47 Street
P.O. Box 2706
Yellowknife, NT, X1A 2R1 (403) 920-2360 Fax: (403) 873-5320

Nova Scotia

Department of Community Services
Family & Children's Services
P.O. Box 696, Halifax, NS, B3J 2T7 (902) 424-4279 Fax: (902) 424-0502

Nova Scotia Family Violence Initiative
Resource Centre
at above address. (902) 424-2345 Fax: (902) 424-0502

Ontario

Ministry of Community and Social Services
Operational Coordination Branch
Hepburn Block, 80 Grosvenor Street, 7th Floor
Toronto, ON, M7A 1E9 (416) 327-4724 Fax: (416) 325-5500

Institute for the Prevention of Child Abuse
[see under National] (416) 921-3151 Fax: (416) 921-4997

Ontario Association of Children's Aid Societies
75 Front Street East, Suite 203
Toronto, ON, M5E 1V9 (416) 366-8115 Fax: (416) 366-8317

Ontario Prevention Clearinghouse
415 Yonge Street, Suite 1200
Toronto, ON, M5B 2E7 (416) 408-2121 Fax: (416) 408-2122

Prince Edward Island

    Department of Health & Social Services
    Child & Family Services Division
    P.O. Box 2000, Charlottetown, PE, C1A 7N8 (902) 368-4940 Fax: (902) 368-4969

    Catholic Family Services Bureau
    P.O. Box 698, 129 Pownal Street
    Charlottetown, PE, C1A 7L3 (902) 894-8591

    Prince County Family Services Bureau
    P.O. Box 1648
    Summerside, PE, C1N 2V5 (902) 436-9171

Québec

    Ministère de la Santé et des services sociaux
    Directeur général
    1075, chemin Ste-Foy, 4e étage
    Québec, PQ, G1S 2M1 (418) 646-3251 Fax: (418) 644-2009

    Fédération des CLSC du Québec
    5455, rue Chauveau
    Montréal, PQ, H1N 1G8 (514) 255-2365 Fax: (514) 255-1443

    Ville Marie Child & Youth Protection Centre
    2155 Guy Street, Suite 1010
    Montreal, PQ, H3Z 2R9 (514) 989-1885 Fax: (514) 939-3609

Saskatchewan

    Saskatchewan Health
    Child & Youth Services, Mental Health Services Branch
    3475 Albert Street
    Regina, SK, S4S 6X6 (306) 787-3298 Fax: (306) 787-2502

    Partnership Committee on Family Violence
    Department of Social Services
    1920 Broad Street
    Regina, SK, S4P 3V6 (306) 787-3835

Yukon

    Yukon Health and Social Services
    Family and Children's Services
    P.O. Box 2703
    Whitehorse, YT, Y1A 2C6 (403) 667-3002 Fax: (403) 668-4613

Selected Sources
and Suggested Reading

Bass, Ellen and Laura Davis. *The Courage to Heal: A Guide for Women Survivors of Child Sexual Abuse*. New York: Harper & Row, 1988.

Bessner, Ronda. *Report on Child Witnesses*. Toronto: Ontario Law Reform Commission, 1991.

Blume, E. Sue. *Secret Survivors: Uncovering Incest and Its Aftereffects in Women*. New York: John Wiley & Sons, 1990.

Burgess, Ann Wolbert, ed. *Child Pornography and Sex Rings*. New York: Lexington Books, 1988.

Butler, Sandra. *Conspiracy of Silence: The Trauma of Incest*. Volcano, Calif.: Volcano Press, 1985.

Campagna, Daniel and Donald Poffenberger. *The Sexual Trafficking in Children: An Investigation of the Child Sex Trade*. Dover, Mass.: Auburn House, 1988.

Danica, Elly. *Don't: A Woman's Word*. Charlottetown: Gynergy Books, 1988.

Fraser, Sylvia. *My Father's House: A Memoir of Incest and of Healing*. Toronto: Doubleday, 1987.

———. *The Book of Strange: A Journey*. Toronto: Doubleday, 1992.

Herman, Judith Lewis. *Trauma and Recovery*. New York: Basic Books/HarperCollins, 1992.

Hyde, Christopher. *Abuse of Trust: The Career of Dr. James Tyhurst*. Vancouver: Douglas & McIntyre, 1991.

Jackson, Ed and Stan Persky, ed. *Flaunting It! A Decade of Gay*

Journalism from The Body Politic. Toronto: Pink Triangle Press, 1982.

Kendall, Christopher N., "'Real Dominant, Real Run!': Gay Male Pornography and the Pursuit of Masculinity." In *Speech, Equality and Harm*. New York: Farrar, Straus and Giroux, 1994.

Lew, Mike. *Victims No Longer: Men Recovering from Incest and Other Sexual Child Abuse*. New York: HarperCollins, 1988.

Marshall, Dr. W. L. and Sylvia Barrett. *Criminal Neglect: Why Sex Offenders Go Free*. Toronto: Doubleday, 1990.

Masson, Jeffrey Moussaieff. *The Assault on Truth: Freud's Suppression of the Seduction Theory*. New York: Farrar, Straus and Giroux, 1984.

Miller, Alice. *For Your Own Good: Hidden Cruelty in Child-Rearing and the Roots of Violence*. New York: Farrar, Straus and Giroux, 1983.

——. *Thou Shalt Not Be Aware: Society's Betrayal of the Child*. New York: Penguin/Meridian, 1984.

——. *Pictures of a Childhood*. New York: Farrar, Straus and Giroux, 1986.

——. *Breaking Down the Wall of Silence*. New York: Penguin/ Meridian, 1991.

Minister of Justice and Attorney-General of Canada, Government of Canada. *Sexual Assault Legislation in Canada: An Evaluation*. Ottawa: Government of Canada, 1991.

——. *Studies on the Sexual Abuse of Children in Canada*. Ottawa: Government of Canada, 1992.

Rivera, Margot. *Multiple Personality: An Outcome of Child Abuse*. Toronto: Education/Dissociation, 1991

——. *Multiple Personality: A Training Model*. Toronto: Education/ Dissociation, 1992.

Stoltenberg, John. *Refusing to Be a Man: Essays on Sex and Justice*. New York: Penguin/Meridian, 1990.

Summit, Roland. "The Child Sexual Abuse Accommodation Syndrome." *Child Abuse & Neglect*, Vol.7, 1983.

Terr, Lenore. *Too Scared to Cry: Psychic Trauma in Childhood*. New York: Basic Books/HarperCollins, 1990.

Vachss, Alice. *Sex Crimes: Ten Years on the Front Lines Prosecuting Rapists and Their Collaborators*. New York: Random House, 1993.

Acknowledgements

Thanks to John Honderich, editor-in-chief of the *Toronto Star*, which has led the media in turning the spotlight on child sexual abuse; to Doug Pepper, executive editor of Random House, for his early belief in this project; to David Kent, president and publisher of Random House, for his dedication to this issue; to my agent, Helen Heller, for coming up with the title *Our Little Secret*; to my editor Catherine Yolles at Random House, who pushed me to clarify and condense, and pulled the manuscript together with great care. Thanks for insight and inspiration to Dr. Marcellina Mian, Detective Wendy Leaver, Jill McNall, Andrew and Marika Swainson, Holly Mitchell and Jon Barna, Sylvia Fraser, Shirley Turcotte, Harvey and Mary Armstrong, Vicki Kelman, Catherine Stewart, Krishna Lalla, Dr. Lois Plumb, Susan* and Steven Johnson*, Kate* and James Burton*, Amy Laird* and Edward*. As always, much gratitude to my partner, Lankai Lamptey, to Nadine for her friendship, creativity and courage, and to my daughter, Emily, for her keen legal insights, compassion and commitment to justice.

Finally, I want to pay tribute to those brave feminists who, in the 1970s, established the first shelters for battered women and began to expose the brutal secrets of our society. It was Ned Franks who said it: "This is the great gift of the women's movement to us all," that we are now confronting the source of the sexual violence that permeates our culture.

Index

An asterisk indicates a pseudonym.

Dick Loek

Judy Steed is a feature writer for the *Toronto Star*. She has written extensively on the subject of child abuse for the *Star*, is the recipient of four National Newspaper Award citations and is the author of the number one national bestseller *Ed Broadbent: The Pursuit of Power*. She lives in Toronto.